Why Does Popcorn Pop?

and 201 other fascinating facts about food

by Don Voorhees

BARNES
& NOBLE
BOOKS
NEW YORK

Fine Communications
322 Eighth Avenue
New York, NY 10001

Why Does Popcorn Pop?
LC Control Number 2001090909
ISBN 1-56731-490-2

Manufactured in the United States of America

MJF Books is a trademark of Fine Creative Media, Inc.

QM   12   11   10   9   8

To Eric and Dana,
chocolate milk, pizza,
and ice cream.

Contents

ʏ

Surf and Turf

Why should you eat oysters in months with an R?

This bit of silliness began with a fussy English parson named William Butler. He proclaimed, in 1599, that it was "unseasonable and unwholesome" to eat oysters in a month lacking an *r*. Butler, of course, was referring to the flat European oysters, which brood their eggs inside the shell during the summer months. The baby oysters inside the parent's shell taste somewhat sandy and unpleasant. American oysters also spawn during the *r*-less months (May–August) but their young brood outside the shell, so this old adage doesn't apply here! During this time, the parents are full of sperm and eggs. Some gourmets, however, consider this to be a delicacy. After their early summer spawning, oysters are leaner and rather less tasty, but are definitely still edible and enjoyable.

Of the more than four hundred oyster varieties found around the globe, only three are widely popular—the small European flat oyster (*Ostrea edulis*), the larger American oyster (*Crossostrea virginica*) of the East and Gulf coasts, and the huge Japanese variety now found in France and along the Pacific coast of the United

States. Oysters flourish in bays, estuaries, and lagoons, and at one time were almost boundless in supply.

In fact, at various times throughout history, oysters were all the rage. The Romans were the first to engage in oyster-mania, collecting them from all corners of their far-flung empire. With the fall of the Roman empire, oysters fell out of favor until the Renaissance, after which oyster frenzy peaked between the late seventeenth and nineteenth centuries. In America and England, vendors plied passersby with plentiful and cheap oysters. People ate dozens of them in one sitting. Since oysters stayed fresh for months in cold storage, they were shipped all around the country. Even Abe Lincoln, in Illinois, couldn't resist them. But alas, all good things must come to an end.

By the turn of the century oyster supplies were nearly depleted. Overharvesting and a natural disease have steadily lowered their numbers. Today, wild oysters are increasingly rare, and farm oysters rule.

You may have heard of the oyster's powers as an aphrodisiac. Oysters are packed with zinc, which the male body needs to maintain normal testoterone levels. The great lover Casanova ate fifty oysters every evening.

Why aren't scallops sold in the shell?

Scallops (*Placopecten megellanicus*) have beautiful shells; however, we never see them sold in their decorative little houses. Unlike other bivalves, such as mussels and clams, scallops never completely close their shells, and are thus prone to spoilage. (Tightly closed shells are a sign of fresh, live clams.) Scallops are shucked as soon as they are harvested. Their shells are removed, as well as their guts. All that is left is the large abductor muscle that the scallop uses to rapidly open and close its shells to swim through the water.

The two most popular kinds of scallops are sea scallops and bay scallops.

Sea scallops are harvested from the North Atlantic throughout the year. Their muscles range in size from one to two and a half inches in diameter.

Bay scallops are caught in the waters between Massachusetts and Long Island, primarily around Nantucket Island. They are smaller and more expensive than sea scallops, but are definitely worth the extra money. Expect to pay up to twelve dollars per pound for real bay scallops.

It has been rumored for years that meat is stamped from the wings of the skate (*Raja*) and sold as scallops. This, however, is not the case. Skate meat does not look like scallop muscles, and the additional processing involved would offset any profit to be made by selling bogus scallops. If you think the scallops you are buying aren't the real article, they are probably calico scallops, which are a smaller, inferior quality scallop. Another sneaky practice that sometimes occurs in the scallop business involves soaking the scallops in phosphates before sale. This causes them to absorb water and increase in size and weight. Caveat emptor!

What popular expensive seafood was once the food of the poor?

You guessed it—lobster! The American lobster (*Hamarus americanus*), which is found from southern Labrador to Cape Hatteras, is considered by most to be the best tasting of the lobsters, and a culinary delight.

During the 1700s and early 1800s, however, the American lobster was so plentiful in the waters off New England that one could walk down the beach and pick them up. There were so many, in fact, that they were used as fertilizer and food for the poor!

Why is Maine lobster so highly prized? Simple: The colder the water, the better tasting the lobster, and the waters off of Maine are frigid. These waters are ideal for lobster growth. Given enough time, the American lobster can grow as big as three feet long and weigh some forty-four pounds!

Female lobsters taste better than the males and have more tender meat. How can you tell the sex of a lobster? Flip it over and look at the place where the head meets the body. You will see two little spiny appendages. If they are soft to the touch, you have a female; if they feel hard, you've got a male.

Other areas of the world have their own version of the lobster. A similar European lobster—the Norway lobster—is quite popular. The spiny lobster, which lacks the delicious claws of the American lobster, is found in the waters off of Florida, California, Australia, New Zealand, and South Africa. They do not compare in taste, however, to the robust Maine lobster.

What is the most popular shellfish?

While lobster may be our favorite shellfish, the more affordable shrimp is the most popular. In fact, shrimp is the most popular fresh or frozen seafood, period.

Shrimp is the common name for any of two thousand species of crustaceans belonging to the order *Decapoda*—the same order that contains crabs and lobsters. Like crabs and lobsters, shrimp have ten legs. Shrimp species can range in size from a quarter inch to eight inches. The larger ones are commonly known as prawns.

Americans have always loved shrimp, but before the age of refrigeration, only those living along the coastlines enjoyed it. In 1917, shrimp boats began using refrigeration. Frozen shrimp first appeared in the 1950s, and now almost all the shrimp sold has been frozen prior to sale. Today, with our modern shipping technologies, people can enjoy shrimp no matter where they live.

In the United States, shrimp are harvested by the Southern states along the Gulf of Mexico. Half of that catch is taken by Louisiana's shrimp fleet. Americans eat over 800 million pounds of shrimp a year. Of that total, about 600 million pounds is imported, much of it from farms in China, Ecuador, and Taiwan. While all domestic shrimp is caught, most imported shrimp is grown on farms.

What is mako?

There are some three hundred species of shark swimming around in the world's oceans. Most of the shark we consume in the United States comes from the waters off the Southeastern coast. Mako (*Isurus oxyrhychus*) is considered the best-tasting of the common shark species. Many restaurants and supermarkets sell any number of shark species under the name mako, including blacktip, bull, dusky, hammerhead, lemon, silky, and tiger. Thus, your "mako" can look and taste somewhat different each time you buy it. There is actually nothing wrong with the other species—it's just nice to know what you are actually paying for.

What is scrod?

Somehow, the name doesn't conjure up a pleasant image! What do you think of when you think of scrod? Whatever it is, it's probably wrong. There is no such thing as a scrod fish. The word "scrod" is a generic term used to describe different kinds of small cod, haddock, or Alaskan pollock (all members of the *Gadidae* family), depending on where you live. The Alaskan pollock is the most abundant seafood in American waters. It totals one third of our annual fish catch. Regardless of what you call it, Americans eat more cod (*Gadus morhua*) than any other finfish.

What is "seafood" salad?

We've all seen it. Some of you have probably even eaten it. But what is it? It looks kind of like crab or lobster salad. It is neither of these, you can be sure! It's actually ground up, rinsed, and molded Alaska pollock, or surimi, as it's called in the industry. It is an amazing seafood—it has almost no actual flavor of its own and is so gelatinous that it can be molded into almost any shape. Manufacturers simply add whatever natural flavorings they desire and can create a host of seafood lookalike products. People seem to like the stuff: it sells quite well!

What is Mississippi's largest industry?

You might think it would be the petroleum industry or cotton, but it's actually the catfish business. Catfish (*Ictalurus punctatus*) is really catching on nationwide. Just twenty years ago, the annual catfish catch was about five thousand tons, most of which came from large rivers or lakes. Today the catfish industry has mushroomed into a 150,000-ton-a-year business in Mississippi, thanks largely to catfish farming. Virtually all the catfish you find in supermarkets today has been commercially farmed.

What is lox?

Lox, a Jewish favorite, is smoked salmon (*Oncorhynchus* or *Salmo*) that has been soaked in brine containing sugar. It is somewhat saltier than Scotch and Nova Scotia smoked salmons, which are considered to be the best.

The word "lox" derives from the Norwegian *gravlax*, which means "buried salmon." The Norwegians used to bury their salmon catch under the stones along the beach. This helped preserve the fish by naturally salting it and keeping it chilled.

What are the different types of tuna?

Tuna has been a prized source of food since the time of the ancient Greeks. Today, canned tuna is the most popular seafood in America, far out in front of runners-up shrimp and cod. Tuna inhabit the upper layers of open waters in the Atlantic, Pacific, and Indian oceans. Swimming at speeds of up to forty-five mph, tuna are long-distance travelers. They follow the warm water currents, since they cannot tolerate temperature changes of more than ten or fifteen degrees.

There are basically four types of fish you are likely to encounter in a can of tuna:

Albacore (*Thunnus alalunga*) are the only white meat tuna. They are steely blue, with a silver band along the belly, and weigh between ten and sixty pounds. Albacore are found off the coast of southern California and northern Mexico. In late summer, they migrate to the coast of Washington and Oregon.

Bluefin (*Thunnus thynnus*) are the monster tuna of the Atlantic, weighing up to a thousand pounds. They are considered a great sport fish. In the Pacific, however, they are much more modest in size (around eighty pounds) and are caught primarily by commercial fishermen. Deep blue and green in color, Pacific bluefin are found in the waters from Alaska to southern California. They are canned as chunk light tuna.

Skipjack (*Katsuwonus pelamis*) are the smallest of the tuna. They are dark metallic blue on top, with dark stripes along the bottom, and are found from the Gulf of California to northern Chile. Skipjack are canned as chunk light tuna.

Yellowfin (*Thunnus albacores*) are the most popular species for canned chunk light tuna. They share the same waters as the skipjack and weigh anywhere from 5 to 150 pounds.

Albacore are sold as "solid white" tuna. The can contains large pieces of albacore, cut by special machines to fit into the round cans. Solid white (or fancy) tuna has an excellent mild flavor and is creamy white in color.

Chunk light tuna is canned as small, bite-sized pieces of bluefin, skipjack, and yellowfin. It has a darker meat than albacore and a stronger flavor.

Albacore and chunk light tuna have similar nutritional values. Both are excellent sources of protein, vitamins, and minerals. Americans eat about three pounds (2.4 billion cans) of tuna per year, most, as you would assume, in the form of tuna salad or tuna sandwiches.

How are tuna caught and processed?

Catching tuna is a long, dangerous job. Crews live on board tuna boats for months at a time and endure extremely harsh weather conditions.

In the traditional method of spotting tuna, the lookout man climbs the rigging to the crow's nest at the top of the ship's masthead. From this vantage point he can survey the waters for miles around for schools of tuna. The tuna boats also rely on measurements of water-current temperatures and weather reports to locate tuna. Some use helicopters to scout the waters.

As soon as the fish are found, the nets are deployed and tons of fish are hauled aboard. Once in the ship's hold, they are fresh frozen and taken directly to canneries, which are located near seaports (San Pedro, California, is the largest tuna port in the United States) so the fish can be quickly processed. A cannery is basically a huge kitchen for cooking tons of fish. As soon as the tuna arrive, they are inspected, cleaned, sorted, and steam-cooked. It takes two and a half hours to cook a ten-pound tuna, while a hundred-pound fish takes up to ten hours to steam. After cooking, the tuna are cooled, skinned, and boned. The best meat goes into cans for human consumption; the dark meat is used for cat food. Vegetable oil and broth, or water and broth, is added to the cans before they are sealed and pressure cooked for sterilization.

The broth is added to keep the fish moist and to enhance its flavor. Tuna packed in oil and broth is high in polyunsaturates. Tuna in water and broth is lower in fat.

Why are dolphin sometimes caught with tuna?

Many consumers and animal rights groups have voiced concern over the number of dolphin that are inadvertently killed by commercial tuna fishing. (No one seems worried about the poor tuna, however!) To realize why dolphin are caught with tuna, it is important to understand the close association between these two species.

In the Eastern Tropical Pacific, a coastal zone that runs from southern California to Chile, dolphin naturally swim above schools of yellowfin tuna. For some unknown reason, this is the only area in the world where dolphin swim with tuna, and only with the yellowfin. Scientists believe that tuna and dolphin mutually benefit from this natural association. The tuna's sharp eyesight complements the dolphin's keen hearing, creating a natural alliance between the two. Since dolphin swim near the surface, fishermen find it easier to locate the tuna by finding the dolphin.

The most common technique of catching tuna is purse seining. The net is set around the tuna and the bottom is pulled together, like a purse drawstring, to trap the fish. When dolphin are swimming above the tuna, they are inadvertently caught with the fish. Purse seining is an acceptable way of catching tuna as long as the net is not set on dolphin.

In April 1990, the major American tuna canners, StarKist and Bumble Bee among them, instituted a "dolphin safe" policy. This policy states that companies will not buy any tuna caught in association with dolphin in the Eastern Tropical Pacific, or any tuna caught by gill or drift nets. These nylon nets are virtually undetectable in the water and can stretch some forty miles in length. They are totally indiscriminate in what they catch. It is common for dolphin, sea turtles, seals, whales, and even birds to be killed by them.

Saying that you will not buy tuna from such sources is all well and good, but how does one ensure that tuna labeled as "dolphin safe" really is? For tuna that has been caught in the Eastern Tropical Pacific to be labeled "dolphin safe," it must be certified as such by U.S. government observers aboard U.S. flag tuna fishing boats. These observers are trained and directed by the National Marine Fisheries Service, a branch of the U.S. Department of Commerce. Thirty percent of foreign flag tuna fishing boats in the Eastern Tropical Pacific also have observers aboard, who report to the Inter-American Tropical Tuna Commission, a group funded by the U.S. government.

To meet the guidelines for "dolphin safe" tuna, fishing boats can use other methods of locating the tuna, aside from following the dolphin. Such methods include looking for stirrings at the surface of the water, sea birds, or floating objects, or using electronic tracking devices. With these methods, tuna can be caught in the Eastern Tropical Pacific (the world's second most productive tuna fishery) with little harm to dolphin and a clear conscience for those of us who enjoy tuna salad for lunch.

What fish's name means "leaper"?

The fish famous for its leaping ability is the salmon. The ancient Romans called it *salmo*, or "leaper." The salmon has been a staple of man's diet since before Roman times, though. As long as ten thousand years ago, an unknown caveman took the time to carve a salmon's picture on a reindeer bone. Back then, man probably caught salmon the way bears do today—by grabbing them as they fight upstream to spawn.

At present, some 30 percent of salmon are raised on fish farms, mostly in the Pacific Northwest. The other 70 percent are harvested by giant fishing boats with nets as the fish return home to spawn. Federal agencies and private concerns operate hatcheries that release salmon into hundreds of rivers to keep the fish from becoming depleted and to introduce it into new areas. Salmon are most abundant in the Columbia River, between Washington and Oregon, and the Yukon River in Alaska. No freshwater salmon are ever found south of the forty-fifth parallel in the north Pacific.

Pacific salmon (*Oncorhynchus*) are the most abundant. There are seven different species:

Sockeye (*O. nerka*), also known as red salmon, are one of the two major sources of canned salmon. They are blue and silver, weighing about seven pounds. The sockeye's flesh is the darkest of all the salmon species, a true salmon red color, firm and rich in oil. Sockeye live four to six years. Their first year is always spent in a snow-fed lake before they go to sea.

Pink salmon (*O. gorbusha*) are the other major canned salmon. They are the most plentiful and the smallest of the salmon, at about four and a half pounds. These fish have the shortest salmon lifespan (about two years). Their flesh is pink and they are low in oil. Pink salmon are nicknamed "Humpie" because the males develop a hump on their backs during spawning season.

Chum salmon (*O. keta*) are also called keta. The third most canned species of salmon, they are pink-fleshed and low in oil. Chum weigh around ten pounds at the end of their three-year life cycle.

Silver salmon (*O. kisutch*), also known as coho, are prized as fresh or frozen fish. Coho have a three-year life cycle and reach about eight to ten pounds.

Chinook (*O. tschawytscha*) are also known as king salmon. They are the largest of all the salmon, averaging around twenty-five pounds (some can reach 125 pounds), but are also the fewest in number. Their flesh color ranges from deep red to white. Chinook are very rich in oil and live from four to six years. They are considered the best of salmons and are usually the most expensive.

Steelhead (*O. mykiss*) were classified as seagoing trout until 1989, when they were reclassified as salmon. They are silvery in color with a reddish band down either side. Steelhead are unique among Pacific salmon in that they can live to spawn many times.

Cherry salmon (*O. masou*) are a Japanese species. They are reddish in color and weigh around nine pounds.

Atlantic salmon (*Salmo salar*) are cousins of the Pacific salmon. While outnumbered by the various Pacific species, Atlantic salmon are also important commercial fish. Like the steelhead, they do not die after spawning and can spawn for many seasons. Being an endangered species, Atlantic salmon are commercially farmed for sale, mostly in Maine. These fish are rich and fatty, with a pinkish orange color.

All salmon eggs are spawned in stony riverbed nests in the fall, where they are protected over the winter. By late spring they hatch into hundreds of millions of "fingerlings" (baby salmon). As finger-sized smolts, they descend the rivers and live in the coastal ocean waters until they are ready to head for the open sea to fatten up. At maturity, they return to their former nest to spawn and die. The round trip will take them thousands of miles and bring them back to the exact stream of their birth.

The Japanese lead the world in salmon consumption. They eat three hundred thousand tons a year, one third of the world's annual catch, much of it raw. It is not advisable to eat salmon that has not been cooked or frozen, though, as it can carry a parasite that can cause digestive problems. If kept on ice, the fish has a shelf life of three weeks. Don't be afraid of salmon, though. It is a wonderful source of high quality protein that contains all the essential amino acids. Unlike protein from some other animal sources, such as beef and eggs, salmon is low in cholesterol, saturated fat, and calories. Its oils are also rich in omega-3 fatty acids, which are believed to lower cholesterol and reduce the risk of heart disease. Salmon is also a natural source of vitamin D. The nutritional value of the different salmon species is about the same. The main variation is in the amount of oil in the different fish—ranging from the lean chum to the oil-rich chinook.

What is the world's favorite meat?

The modern chicken (*Gallus gallus*) was domesticated some four thousand years ago from the red jungle fowl of Southeast Asia. By 1500 B.C., the chicken had arrived in Europe. Today, it may be the most common bird in the world. The United States broiler industry alone raises 5.9 billion chickens a year! It is this enormous overproduction that keeps the price of chicken so low.

Broilers (or fryers) are seven-week-old chickens weighing between two and three and a half pounds. Roasters are eight- or nine-week-old hens weighing three and a half to six pounds, with enough fat to brown well when roasted.

The leading broiler states are Arkansas, Georgia, Alabama, North Carolina, Tennessee, Mississippi, Texas, and Maryland. Five companies dominate the industry. They are, in order of size, Tyson Foods (Holly Farms), ConAgra, Gold Kist, Perdue Farms, and Pilgrim's Pride. Tyson is more than twice as big any of the rest. Each American eats an average of twenty-four broilers annually. Chicken and pork are the world's largest sources of meat.

What is the origin of Peking duck?

Ducks (members of the *Anatidae* family) have always been plentiful in the wild and thus were domesticated rather late in history. The Chinese have always loved duck and domesticated the mallard (*Anas platyrhynchos*), while the Europeans didn't domesticate it until the 1600s. Wild duck tends to taste gamy, and if a particular bird has eaten a diet of fish, its taste can be decidedly fishy. Low-water wild ducks, such as mallards, which feed in nearby grain fields, have a much improved taste. Mallards are ancestors of today's domesticated duck.

The return of the Crusaders during the Middle Ages spurred the consumption of duck in Europe. By stuffing wild ducks with oranges or lemons brought back from the Middle East, the unpleasant fishy taste was much reduced.

The most popular duck is the Peking or Long Island duck, which is descended from a flock of Chinese ducks brought to the United States in 1873. It is usually eaten at an age of around ten months and a weight of four to seven pounds. The meat tends to be whiter and juicier than that of a wild duck. It is from this white variety that the Chinese make their famous Peking duck.

The introduction of Peking ducks occurred when a Yankee trader, James Palmer, purchased a small flock of white ducks from a British sailor stationed in Peking. He arrived in New York on March 13, 1873, with one drake (male) and three ducks (females). He began to breed them in Manhattan, and then Connecticut and eastern Long Island. Before long, there were over 125 duck farms on Long Island. Today, Long Island is still a big duck producer. In fact, New York State is second only to Indiana in duck production, and just ahead of North Carolina.

Do turkey hens taste better than toms?

Many people prefer turkey (*Meleagris gallopavo*) hens to toms. They think the hen is a better tasting bird. There is, however, no difference in taste or quality between a hen and a tom. Toms are just a little bigger than hens.

Most turkeys, hens and toms, are sold to market as young birds, around fourteen to twenty-two weeks old.

Why do turkeys have dark meat in their legs?

In the avian world, muscles that do a lot of work are darker than inactive muscles. Active muscles store a lot of oxygen, imparting a dark color. Domestic turkeys don't fly around very much, but their legs get a pretty good workout. Hence, the well-rested breast meat is white, while the well-exercised legs are dark.

Most people prefer white meat, so turkeys are bred to have big breasts. In fact, turkeys today have breasts so large that they interfere with the bird's reproduction. Apparently the turkeys cannot get close enough to copulate and must be artificially inseminated. Does PETA (People for the Ethical Treatment of Animals) know about this?

Why do we pull a turkey's wishbone apart?

This silly practice probably dates back to the fifth century B.C. The Etruscans had sacred chickens they used to interpret omens based on the bird's pecking of corn grains placed in a Ouija-boardlike circle of letters. When the birds died, their clavicle bone was dried and rubbed to make a wish. The Romans later picked up on this custom. If one "wishbone" was good, two would be better, so the Romans began breaking them, hoping to get the larger piece with the "head" on it. They took this custom with them when they conquered Britain. It is now the larger turkey that we more commonly use for wishbones.

How do self-basting turkeys work?

Many cooks, especially inexperienced ones, believe it is hard to cook a moist turkey, and therefore buy self-basting birds. How does the bird baste itself? Simple. Vegetable oils, water, salt, emulsifiers, and artificial flavors and colors are injected under the skin. When you cook the turkey, this mixture melts and moistens the bird, altering its flavor somewhat. Many manufacturers inject the mixture into their turkeys to compensate for an inferior bird.

Basting a turkey yourself is easy. A good quality bird generally will be moist and juicy all on its own. One simple way to baste your own bird is to butter or oil a piece of aluminum foil and wrap it over the top of the turkey. By roasting at 350° F and removing the foil one hour before the bird is done, you should have excellent results.

What is a capon?

A capon is a cock castrated while young. But why did they start castrating cocks in the first place?

The Romans created the first capons, but not because they felt these birds were superior. Roman law limited the number of cocks and hens that could be eaten, lest the citizens should overindulge. Not to restrict their feasting because of some silly law, the Romans sidestepped it on a technicality. By castrating the cock and creating the capon, which was neither a cock nor a hen, they could continue in their chicken gluttony.

The act of castration causes a hormonal change to occur in the bird. This results in the development of fatty layers within its muscles and a marbling unique to the capon. Capons today are full breasted, meaty, and tender, weighing between four and seven pounds, with succulent meat.

What are Rock Cornish game hens and squab?

Rock Cornish game hens are the result of an American cross of the Cornish game hen and the Plymouth White Rock hen. These miniature chickens are ready for eating at the tender age of five or six weeks old.

Another small bird we like to eat is squab. They are young pigeons (Columbidae family) bred especially for human consumption. The most popular commercial variety is the white king, which are killed just before they are old enough to leave the nest.

What is a hot dog?

Do you know what is really in your favorite brand of hot dogs? There are all kinds of rumors about what actually goes into hot dogs. Thankfully, the hot dog industry is strictly controlled in the United States.

All manufacturers must list their hot dog ingredients on the label. Ingredients are listed in descending order, according to the amount of their content in the product. Thus, the first listed ingredient is present in a higher amount than the second. The words "beef," "pork," "chicken," "turkey," etc. can only be used if these meats come from the muscle tissue of the animal. If you see the words "meat by-products" or "variety meats," the hot dog contains various parts of beef, veal, lamb, pork, or even goat, such as snouts, stomachs, tripe, hearts, tongues, lips, spleens, fatty tissue, and so forth.

Originally, frankfurters contained only beef and pork. Now they can legally contain ground-up sheep or goat, and up to 15 percent chicken. They may contain up to 30 percent fat, 2.5 percent carbohydrate fillers, and 10 percent added water. All in all, most hot dogs are about 55 percent water.

A premium brand, like Oscar Mayer, contains the following ingredients:

Meat: Only selected cuts of beef and pork, including the round, chuck, and flank of beef, and the side and shoulder of pork, are used.

Water: Used because it facilitates mixing and even distribution of ingredients.

Salt: The ingredient that gives sausage its name. The word "sausage" comes from the Latin *salsus*, meaning salted or preserved. The salt not only adds flavor, but also acts as a binder and helps maintain freshness.

Flavorings: Sugars and spices are used as seasonings. Hot dogs contain about 4 percent sweetener and 1 percent flavoring. Corn syrup and dextrose are the common sweeteners. Nutmeg, mace, cardamom, allspice, and other spices are used.

Cure: Sodium ascorbate is used to retain freshness and to prevent the meat from fading when exposed to light. Sodium nitrate or nitrite give the hot dog its characteristic color, flavor, and texture. It has been added to sausages since ancient times.

Hot dogs are made by grinding meat with water, seasonings, sweeteners, salt, preservatives, and binders. This mixture is then forced into casings of either cellulose or the intestines of cows, sheep, or pigs. They are then cooked and most have their casings removed prior to packaging.

Regardless of what is in hot dogs, we Americans love them. They are one of our favorite sources of meat, and we eat over 8.5 billion of them every year! That's about sixty-five a year per person!

Why is a frankfurter called a hot dog?

You may have guessed this one already: Because it resembles a dachshund. Around the turn of the century, a concessionaire at New York's Polo Grounds named Harry Stevens had his vendors yell out, "Get your red-hot dachshund sausages!" The famous sports cartoonist T. A. Dorgan liked this expression and took to calling them hot dogs. In 1900, as a joke, he drew a frankfurter shaped like a dachshund inside a bun. A new expression was born!

Today, the words "hot dog," "frankfurter," and "weiner" are synonymous. The name "frankfurter" derives from a coarsely ground, highly seasoned sausage that was popular in Frankfurt. The word "weiner" has its origins in a less seasoned, finer-ground sausage common in Vienna.

A Bavarian—Antoine Feuchtwanger—brought the frank idea to America in the 1880s, selling them in St. Louis. They were sold hot, without buns, and were hard to handle. So Feuchtwanger's brother-in-law, a baker, created an elongated bun to hold the hot franks.

Today, neither Vienna nor Frankfurt wants to take credit for the hot dog. Apparently, they consider their own local cuisines to be above association with this American classic!

What's America's favorite cold cut?

Bologna is America's number-one cold cut. We eat nearly 800 million pounds of the stuff every year—about seventy slices per person per year!

Sausages of one type or another have been around since at least 900 B.C. They are even mentioned in Homer's *Odyssey*. Many sausages are named for the early city-states that they originated in. Bologna is named for Bologna, Italy; salami for the ancient city of Salamis on the island Cyprus; and Thuringer Cervelat (summer sausage) for the Thuringer region of Germany. Braunschweiger, the smoked liver sausage, was developed during the Middle Ages in Braunschweiger (Brunswick), Germany. More recently, Lebanon bologna was first created by German immigrants in Lebanon, Pennsylvania.

Most people don't realize that packaged cold cuts, of which Oscar Mayer is the leading producer, are fresher than meats sliced at the deli counter. Cold cuts are vacuum-packaged in airtight containers within seconds of being sliced at the plant. Therefore, they do not dry out or spoil quickly. They are sliced in chilled rooms to reduce bacteria. To avoid the transfer of bacteria or flavors, as can happen to deli-sliced cold cuts, only one meat is sliced by the same blade.

People often wonder what's in the average cold cut. A product like cooked ham, for example, is 95 percent meat, 3 percent salt, 1 percent sweetener, and 1 percent flavoring and cure. Not that bad.

Is there any corn in corned beef?

There is no corn in corned beef, nor is the beef obtained from corn-fed steer. This kind of meat gets its name from the Old English word for a kernel or grain of salt—"corn." Corned beef is brisket or plate beef that has been pickled. Pickling spices, garlic, and sugar are all added to the brine.

What makes one cut of beef better than another?

Beef generally comes from steers (castrated male cattle). Cows fatten too slowly to be a commercially viable source of beef. The most common beef cattle in the United States are shorthorn, Angus, or Hereford, all breeds of the species *Bos taurus*. Today's domesticated species are believed to be descendants of the now extinct wild auroch (*Bos primigenius*) of Eurasia and North Africa.

The choicest cuts of beef come from the rib, short loin, or sirloin on the upper half of the steer. They include filet mignon, porterhouse, T-bone, sirloin, rib roast, and tenderloin. These are all best cooked by dry heat.

The chuck (shoulder area) and all of the lower half of the steer yield the leaner, less tender cuts of meat. Most of these need slow, moist cooking, except for the ground meats.

The USDA grades beef by the following categories: prime, choice, good, standard, and commercial. Prime is the best, but rarely appears in markets. Most prime meat is sold directly to restaurants and butcher shops. The best grade found in supermarkets is usually Choice. Good beef is used in institutionalized food, Standard and Commercial in everything else.

The main difference between grades is marbling, the thin veins of fat that crisscross a piece of meat. Tougher meats have less marbling. The choice cuts of meat are from the muscles of the animal that do little work, like the muscles of the upper back. Cuts from the hard-working leg muscles have very little marbling and are thus tough.

Grain-fed cattle are more tender than grass-fed. Some grass-fed animals are grain finished, or fed grains before slaughter. Beef cattle are slaughtered when they reach a weight of one thousand to twelve hundred pounds and are about a year old. Another way to tenderize beef before butchering is to allow the meat to remain on the carcass for two to six weeks after slaughter. This allows enzymes to begin breaking down (tenderizing) the meat. Aged meat is more expensive and is usually not found in supermarkets.

We Americans each eat about sixty-five pounds of beef a year, which is a lot, but is down considerably from the ninety-five pounds a year we ate in 1980, due to the recent trend toward healthier eating.

How did porterhouse steak get its name?

Porterhouse steak is a cut of beef loin adjacent to the sirloin, which is more succulent, but has a lot more waste. In England, no distinction is made between sirloin and porterhouse. It was an American named Martin Morrison who gave porterhouse steak its name in 1814. He ran a New York City tavern called Martin Morrison's Porterhouse, which specialized in this particular cut of meat. A porterhouse was a tavern that served dark beer and ale, or porter, so named because it was a favorite drink of porters and laborers. Ironically, these blue-collar workers could seldom afford to eat the steak that bore their name!

Where is the hamburger from?

Yes, the hamburger really **does** have its roots in Hamburg, Germany. People there ate steak tartar (shredded raw meat), which was popular in the neighboring Baltic states. German immigrants brought the beef patty to America, where it was introduced to the public at the Louisiana Purchase Exposition in St. Louis in 1904. We Americans added the now mandatory bun. Since the 1920s, hamburgers have been America's favorite form of meat.

What is the best meat for hamburgers?

Hamburgers are America's favorite meat, followed by chicken, steak, and hot dogs. There are several types of meat suitable for making hamburger patties, but which one is right for you?

Ground beef (hamburger meat) may contain up to 30 percent fat, but only fat attached to the beef can be used—no added fat is allowed.

Ground chuck (lean ground beef) is the best all-around choice for burgers. It has a perfect fat content (about 15 percent), just enough to make a nice, juicy burger, with excellent flavor at a moderate price.

Ground round (extra lean ground beef) is leaner than chuck (15 percent or less fat) and will produce a dry burger if cooked beyond medium rare. It is also more expensive, although it is a good choice for those who care more about calories than taste. A quarter pound of ground round has about 220 calories.

What is "natural" veal?

A lot has been said lately about the terrible conditions under which veal calves are raised. "Natural" veal, however, is produced under somewhat better conditions. Instead of being raised in a tiny box, separated from its mother, the calf has free access to the barn and grazing areas.

The veal business is a by-product of the dairy industry. Dairy cows will not produce milk unless they give birth once a year. Therefore, many calves are born for no other reason than to keep the cows' milk flowing. Male calves serve no useful purpose. They will never produce milk, and basically just take up space. Thus, we have a veal industry.

Some calves are slaughtered within a week of birth, weighing between eighty and one hundred pounds. Some are milk fed for eight to ten weeks before slaughter. They must be below 225 pounds to be called veal. Since these calves don't get to exercise their muscles, milk-fed meat is grayish pink when raw, and almost white when cooked. There isn't as much true milk-fed veal in the United States (most calves are fed fortified soybean milk) as there is in Europe. Because of a scarcity of pastureland, European farmers will often slaughter young milk-fed beef animals for veal. Consequently, veal is more abundant in Europe than in the States.

Calves used for natural veal are usually allowed to live a little longer, feed on grass, and exercise their muscles, with the result that the meat is rosy pink when raw and pink when cooked.

Veal cutlets are boneless cuts taken from the rump or round. The best cutlet is scaloppine, which is cut across the grain of a top round muscle. The lower quality veal cutlets have a small piece of bone and are crosscuts of the hind leg.

How bad is bacon for you?

People have been curing pork sides for over twenty-five hundred years. Salting and smoking meat has been a popular way of preserving fresh cuts since ancient times. Although the curing process has changed in recent times, bacon continues to be a favorite. English and American breakfasts are not complete without bacon and eggs. In Ireland, people like their bacon boiled with cabbage. The Germans prefer using bacon as a base for stews. In fact, *backen* is German for the wild pigs that once inhabited Bavaria.

The best meat comes from the center portion of the bacon side because of its desirable fat-to-lean ratio. Meat taken from the flank end has more fat. Bacon cut from the shoulder end has a higher lean percentage, which causes it to be tough and cook unevenly.

Bacon today is about 10 percent leaner than it was ten years ago, due to the breeding of hogs with leaner pork. After cooking, bacon is lower in calories than you might think. Two slices of cooked bacon contain four grams of protein and only eighty calories; however, three quarters of the calories come from fat. In fact, in a bacon-and-egg breakfast, the two slices of bacon have fewer calories and about the same fat content as one boiled or poached egg. In a BLT sandwich, there is as much sodium in the two slices of bread as there is in the two slices of bacon. Cooked bacon contains 93 percent meat, 4 percent salt, 2 percent sugar, and 1 percent sodium phosphate.

All in all, bacon isn't as bad for you as you may have thought. But bacon, like all of the best things in life, is best enjoyed in moderation.

What's special about Virginia hams?

Hams are cured meats made from fresh pork hind legs. Hams are cured in two ways, either in a dry salt mixture or in a flavored brine solution (a mixture of salt, sugar, and saltpeter). After curing, hams can be smoked or air-dried. They are smoked with hickory wood or mahagony sawdust in the United States. The two most popular kinds of ham in America are canned and country.

Canned hams are soaked in and injected with brine, and are usually smoked. They are then partially or fully cooked. Most hams come fully cooked. If it is not labelled "fully cooked," assume that it must be cooked before eating.

Country hams are legs that are salted for about four weeks, washed, coated with peppercorns, chilled for about two weeks, smoked for about ten days, and then aged for up to one year. The most famous country hams are Virginia hams, especially those that come from the town of Smithfield.

Since 1639, the Smithfield area has been exporting hams to other parts of America. Smithfield hams come from hogs that have been fed peanuts in addition to their normal corn feed. In 1926, the Virginia General Assembly passed a law stating that genuine Smithfield hams are those from peanut-fed hogs raised in the peanut belt of Virginia or North Carolina and cured, treated, smoked, and processed in Smithfield, Virginia.

The taste of canned hams can't approach that of country hams. However, country hams are a little more complicated to prepare. They generally must be soaked in several changes of water for twelve to twenty-four hours before cooking.

Pigs were first introduced to America when the explorer Hernando de Soto brought them to Florida in 1525. The pigs of this time were lard pigs, produced from a medieval cross between the European pig and the Chinese pig. Lard pigs remained the sole variety until the mid-nineteenth century, when the meat pig was bred. As the demand for lard in such things as margarine and shortening decreased, leaner meat became more and more popular.

Meat pigs are usually slaughtered when they weigh about 220 pounds and are five or six months old. About 44 percent of the carcass is ham and loin. Today Iowa, Illinois, and Missouri raise the most hogs.

Spam. What is it? Who eats it?

Apparently some 60 million Americans eat Spam on a regular basis. Where do these "Spamophiles" live, you may ask?

The number one Spam-consuming state is Hawaii, with over 4.3 million cans of the stuff sold annually. (Spam and pineapple ... perfect together!) That's more than four cans of Spam per Hawaiian each year. The other heavy Spam-consuming states are Alaska, Arkansas, Texas, and Alabama. Each year Americans spend $175 million on Spam. Outside the United States, the United

Kingdom and South Korea are the next largest Spam eaters. For some reason, Spam is considered a delicacy in South Korea and is one of its leading American imports. Business executives in Seoul often prefer exchanging cans of Spam as gifts over the more traditional wine or chocolates.

So what is in Spam that makes it so popular around the world? Spam is a very simple product. It was first introduced in 1937 by the Hormel Food Company as a chopped pork shoulder and spiced ham mixture. Spam is 100 percent pork and ham, with no cereal fillers or meat by-products. The only other ingredients are salt, water, sugar, sodium nitrate (a preservative), and spices. These ingredients are blended together, canned, sealed, and cooked. That's it. Five billion such cans have been sold thus far.

So why is Spam so universally popular? World War II has a lot to do with it. Millions of people were exposed to Spam during the war, when the U.S. government sent tons of it to Europe to feed our troops and our Russian and European allies. Nikita Krushchev is quoted as saying, "Without Spam, we wouldn't have been able to feed our army." The U.S. military still buys about 2.7 million pounds of Spam a year for the troops' dining pleasure.

One last Spam question: What's the only hamburger that actually has ham in it? Answer: A Spamburger! Hormel is currently running an advertising campaign featuring Spamburgers—a big slice of fried Spam on a hard roll. Apparently the Spamburger has caught on. Since the campaign began, sales of Spam are way up. Watch out, McDonald's!

How is lamb different from mutton?

You have probably never eaten mutton if you are an average American. Although lamb and mutton come from sheep, the difference is in the age of the meat.

Baby lamb are milk fed and slaughtered at the young age of three to five weeks. Like the lambs' age, the pale meat is very tender, with a delicate flavor. It is hard to find and very expensive.

Spring lamb is also milk fed but is allowed to live to the age of six months. Spring lamb is available at any time of year, but in days gone by this was not the case. Lambs used to be born in September or October. Thus, they were ready for slaughter right around Easter and were an eagerly awaited treat. Spring lamb is white with a delicate flavor.

Lamb is butchered at between six and nine months and has been weaned and grass fed. It is more flavorful than spring lamb.

Yearling lamb is any lamb between twelve and twenty-four months of age. It has a strong flavor, like mutton.

Mutton is any "lamb" over twenty-four months old. We don't eat much mutton in the United States, but it is an English favorite. The British eat ten times the amount of lamb and mutton that we do.

Much of the lamb sold in the United States is grown in New Zealand and Australia. All imported lamb is shipped frozen. Foreign lamb has a stronger flavor than domestic lamb, due to feeding differences. Also, the flesh of the imported lamb is reddish, while the American lamb tends to be more white.

What is the origin of the barbecue?

You would think that barbecuing wouldn't have to be "discovered," but before the early Spanish explorers landed on Haiti, the practice of barbecuing was unknown in the Old World. The word "barbecue" comes from the Spanish *barbacoa*, meaning "frame of sticks." The Spanish used this word to describe the Haitian Indians' method of grilling and smoking their meat outdoors on wooden racks over open fires. Settlers of the Spanish Southwest took up barbecuing on ranches in Texas, New Mexico, Arizona, and California. It was the Spaniards who introduced the zesty sauces of tomato and chili pepper to barbecuing that are prevalent today.

Apples and Oranges

What is the difference between fruits and vegetables?

The answer depends on whether you ask a botanist or a culinary expert. Technically, a fruit is the mature, sexually produced seed-bearing ovary of a flowering plant. Vegetables come from the vegetative or nonsexual parts of the plant (leaves, roots, stems). So fruits include apples, oranges, nuts, and such seed-bearing "vegetables" as peas, beans, squash, eggplant, and tomatoes. The tomato is actually a berry.

The various types of vegetables include roots (carrots and radishes), leaves (lettuce and spinach), flower buds (broccoli and cauliflower), and stems (rhubarb).

In the culinary world, tomatoes are considered a vegetable and rhubarb is considered a fruit. Nuts fall into a separate category. In culinary terms, a fruit is described as the edible, fleshy part of a perennial plant associated with its flower, which tastes good due to its astringency, acid content, and sugars.

Why are fruits and vegetables often waxed before sale?

What could be more tempting than a nice shiny red apple? They are irresistible—just ask Adam! Most shiny fruits and vegetables in the market look that way, as you probably know, because they are coated with a thin layer of wax.

While waxing fruit makes it look pretty, it has practical benefits as well. The Chinese dipped food into beeswax or paraffin to preserve it some two thousand years ago. Today, waxes are most commonly used on thin-skinned produce to cut down on dehydration. Citrus fruits are thick-skinned, but rather porous, so they are also coated with wax. Melons get waxed as a barrier to bacteria and fungi.

Modern produce is "waxed" with various coatings, including vegetable, petroleum, beeswax, or shellac-based waxes or resins.

What favorite American fruit is a member of the rose family?

Nothing is more American than apple pie. Right? Maybe, but the apple itself is a native of Central Asia and did not appear in the United States until the seventeenth century.

The apple tree (*Malus pumila*) is actually a member of the rose family. Did you ever notice how similar rose hips and leaves are to apples and their leaves? An apple is a kind of fruit called a pome, as are pears and quinces. Pomes have a fleshy outer layer and an inner core with five seeds and parchmentlike walls. The rose family (*Rosaceae*) also includes such important fruits as the strawberry, blackberry, raspberry, and peach.

Apples thrive in a cool, humid climate and are the most popular fruits in temperate climates, ahead of other favorites such as oranges and bananas.

Why is the Red Delicious such a popular apple?

Go into virtually any supermarket in the country and there it is— the Red Delicious. How did this one apple get to be king of the heap?

The crisper an apple is at picking, the longer it can be stored in a warehouse before sale. Red Delicious apples picked in the fall in Washington State can still be sold in June, anywhere in the world. They are stored at temperatures near freezing, in a low-oxygen atmosphere. Before cold storage, there were many varieties of apples sold throughout the summer and autumn, depending on their time of ripening. Today, those that store the best and look good (Red and Golden Delicious) are the ones grown and sold coast to coast. Depending on where you live and the time of year, you can also find Granny Smiths, McIntoshes, Jonathans, and Romes, but not much else. Only about twenty varieties are commercially grown.

This is a shame, because there are thousands of varieties of apples. In fact, every apple seed is genetically different from the rest in any given apple. Therefore, apples do not reproduce true to form. For this reason, apple trees are not propagated from seeds, but from cuttings that are taken from a desirable tree and grafted onto roots or trunks. This makes the breeding of new apple varieties difficult. New varieties are usually the result of happy accidents found in an orchard. This was the case with some of the most successful American varieties.

The Baldwin was found in Massachusetts in 1740; the McIntosh was discovered by John McIntosh in Ontario, Canada, in 1870; and the Delicious was discovered as a seedling growing in Iowa in 1895. Granny Smiths, a relatively new variety in U.S. markets, come from New Zealand.

Nearly half of the 10 billion pounds of American apples grown annually come from Washington State. New York, Michigan, California, Pennsylvania, and Virginia are also big apple-growing states. You may think that we Americans are big apple eaters, but not really. Actually, the Dutch are the apple-eating champs. While we eat eighteen pounds per person per year, the Dutch wolf down one hundred pounds per person a year.

Was there a real Johnny Appleseed?

So many of our American folk heroes are either mythical or greatly embellished. Neither is the case with Johnny Appleseed. He was a real-life, walking, talking, apple-planting legend.

The first apple seeds probably came to North America with the Pilgrims in 1620. As Americans moved west, so did the apple. People commonly planted apple trees along the trails that they traveled so that later travelers could have a snack along the way. One great planter of apple seeds was John Chapman (1774–1845) also known as Johnny Appleseed.

Chapman was a preacher and a nurseryman. He collected apple seeds at western Pennsylvania cider presses and planted thousands of acres of orchards throughout the Ohio Valley. He gradually moved farther and farther west, traveling on foot and by canoe, until he reached Fort Wayne, Indiana, where he died in 1845.

Not all of the lore surrounding Johnny is true, however. Contrary to popular belief, he was neither poor nor a hermit. In fact, at the time of his death, he had acquired over 1,200 acres of land. It is also highly doubtful that he went around in his bare feet, especially in winter, as he could easily afford shoes. But it is said that he actually did wear a saucepan for a hat!

What produce company owns one of the Hawaiian Islands?

This one ought to be easy, if you think about it! In a rather unique situation, the Dole Food Company owns the sixth-largest Hawaiian Island—Lanai. Dole purchased it for $1.1 million in 1922 as a pineapple plantation.

The man who made pineapples a major success in Hawaii was James Drummond Dole. He came to Hawaii in 1899, the cousin of the Hawaiian Republic patriarch Judge Sanford B. Dole. Pineapples grew well in the Hawaiian climate, but fresh pineapples could not withstand the long sea voyage to the States. In order to become commercially viable, they had to be canned. Once a cannery was built, the pineapple business boomed, and the island of Lanai was turned into a huge plantation.

Lanai was totally undeveloped at the time. Dole had to build a harbor and roads, tap underground water, and erect houses, schools, and a hospital for the workers. Today the company has a world-class resort on the island.

Hawaii now produces 75 percent of the world's pineapple supply, 95 percent of which is canned.

Why do so many Colonial homes have pineapple symbols near the entrance?

If you live on the East Coast you may have noticed that many Colonial homes have carved or painted pineapples by their front door or gate. During Colonial times the pineapple was used as a symbol of hospitality.

The pineapple (*Ananus comosus*) is native to the tropical regions of the Americas. Columbus found pineapples growing on Guadaloupe and brought them back to Europe in 1493. It was the Spanish who gave them the rather odd name "pineapple." To them it somewhat resembled a pine cone, and was known as Pine of the Indies. The English added the word "apple" because it was so sweet.

The Spaniards also learned that the local Caribs used the pineapple as a sign of hospitality. If the Spaniards approached a village and found a pineapple placed near the entrance, they knew they were welcome. (Presumably, if there was no pineapple they still entered the village and took what they wanted anyway.) The Spanish brought this custom back to Europe, where as a highly prized rare fruit, the pineapple also became a symbol of the social elite. The welcoming custom soon spread to America.

Pineapples should be picked ripe, as they don't mature after harvesting. A pineapple is ripe if its bottom smells sweet and its leaves pull off easily.

What kind of fruit is a banana?

The banana (*Musa sapientia*) was considered an exotic fruit when first brought to the America's in 1820; however, it has been widely cultivated since before recorded time.

Native to Southeast Asia, bananas are one of the most prolific food plants today. They were brought to Africa by the Arabs in the seventh century. The Spanish introduced them to the New World in 1516.

Many people consider bananas to be the perfect food. Contained in their own yellow wrappers, bananas contain 20 percent assimilable sugars and are high in vitamins A, B, C, and B2. They also contain calcium, iron, phosphorus, and potassium.

Its extensive cultivation in Central America has helped the banana become one of America's favorite and least expensive fruits. Unlike other popular fruits, which are often consumed as juice, as jellies, or in baked goods, bananas are almost always eaten raw.

A banana tree (actually a gigantic herb) grows to about twenty feet and produces one large bunch of up to three hundred bananas. After the harvest, the tree is cut down. Another tree will grow from its roots and bear fruit in a year's time.

The main variety of banana sold in America is the Cavendish. It replaced the Gros Michel, which was wiped out by the fungal Panama disease in 1962. The Europeans eat a variety called the Canary Island banana, which is somewhat smaller and sweeter than the Cavendish.

Regardless of the variety, the bananas we eat today are seedless, sterile clones of bananas that grew in the wild and were domesticated hundreds of years ago. For this reason, bananas are not grown from seed, but are propagated from replanting sprouts from mature plants.

Bananas should not be refrigerated, but should be kept cool. Those black spots indicate ripeness, not decay.

Strangely enough, the banana is botanically classified as a berry!

What is the origin of the term "banana republic"?

The exotic banana was first introduced to the United States in 1870 by the Boston Fruit Company, one of five banana growers who later joined together to form United Fruit in 1899. The owner of another one of United Fruit's member companies was a man named Sam "the Banana Man" Zemurry. He was instrumental in the overthrow of the Honduran government, which had laws unfavorable to the banana growers.

United Fruit was no less ruthless than Sam the Banana Man. In 1954, it too aided in the overthrow of a government to benefit the company. A Guatemalan leftist leader had thoughts of nationalizing United Fruit. Bad idea! The power of the banana growers was stronger than that of the government. Through overthrows like these, and bribing national leaders, the banana growers controlled who governed the countries they did business in. Hence the term "banana republic."

What are boysenberries?

Boysenberries seem to be more popular on the West Coast than on the East Coast. Most Easterners have never seen or tasted a boysenberry.

The boysenberry is not a naturally occurring plant species, but is a hybrid created by a man named Rudolph Boysen. It was developed by crossing the blackberry, red raspberry, and logan-berry. (The loganberry was created accidentally in 1881, when a Judge Logan crossed a blackberry with a raspberry.)

The new boysenberry plants were propagated by Walter and Cordelia Knott, of Knott's Berry Farm fame, during the 1930s.

How are California oranges different from Florida oranges?

If you have ever had the pleasure of eating a Florida orange picked right off the tree, then you know the incomparable taste of truly fresh oranges. Florida oranges don't look as appetizing when picked as their California cousins, though. Both states grow the same species of orange—*Citrus sinensis*. The differences between the two is a result of climate, not botany.

Oranges are one of the most abundant tree fruits in the world. The United States produces one third of the world's total.

Florida oranges never get that perfect bright orange coloration that the California oranges do. Often they are still quite green at maturity. This has nothing to do with the quality of the orange, however. California oranges look like we expect oranges to look because the California nights get much cooler than those in Florida. Oranges are a winter or early spring crop, and need a little nip in the night air to develop full coloration. They do not ripen once they are picked as lemons do.

Because we Americans insist that produce look a certain way, Florida growers either color their oranges or sell them for juice. Florida oranges are plumper, juicier, and thinner-skinned than California oranges due to the moist subtropical climate and are thus better suited for juice making. The drier, thicker-skinned California fruits are generally sold as eating oranges. Since there is a much greater demand for juice oranges, Florida's production far exceeds that of California. Oranges are also grown commercially in Texas and Arizona.

There are three main types of American-grown oranges: seedy, such as Parson Brown; nearly seedless, such as Valencia; and seedless, such as navel. (Navel oranges are the result of a mutant tree found in Brazil in the early 1800s.) Valencia and Washington navel are the most important commercially.

Who is the Bartlett pear named after?

The pear (*Pyrus communis*), which is native to China or Western Asia, has been cultivated for about four thousand years. Today there are over five thousand varieties, but one accounts for 75 percent of all American production—the Bartlett.

It is an English pear (the Williams *Bon Christien*) that was introduced to America by Enoch Bartlett of Dorchester, Massachusetts. The ripened Bartlett, unlike other pear varieties, is yellow, with a granule-free pulp. It is primarily grown in Washington and Oregon.

What fruit's original name meant "testicle"?

Avocados (*Persea americana*), members of the laurel family, are native to Central America, where the local populations have enjoyed them for centuries. Their name is a derivation of the Aztec word for testicle—*ahuacatl*—which they somewhat resemble. The Spaniards twisted this word into *aguacate*, and we know it today as "avocado," certainly a more appetizing name than the original! It was only after the turn of the century, when they were planted commercially in California and Florida, that avocados started to gain acceptance in the United States.

The avocado intimidates some shoppers because they aren't sure how to tell if one is ripe. One thing that is confusing is that there is more than one type of avocado. There are actually three kinds—the small, thin-skinned Mexican variety; the larger, bumpy Guatelmalan variety; and the larger, leathery West Indian varieties. An avocado should yield when lightly squeezed. It should not be hard, nor should it be soft, as avocados bruise easily. Bruises affect the quality of the flesh.

Most people buy avocados just before they are fully ripe, because the fruit has a relatively short shelf life at maturity. Avocados remain hard while on the tree and ripen only after picking. Once picked, the best quality fruit will ripen in five to seven days.

If you have a hard, unripe avocado, you can speed the ripening process along by putting it in a brown paper bag or wrapping it in foil. This will concentrate the carbon dioxide released by the fruit and hasten ripening. Or if you're in a real rush, you can microwave an avocado for two minutes on medium (50 percent), then turn over and microwave for another minute.

How do American grapes differ from European grapes?

Ninety percent of cultivated grapes are from the five thousand varieties of *Vitis vinifera*, the Old World grape that was originally from Anatolia. American grapes come from many wild species of *Vitis*. They differ from European grapes in odor and in flavor, and by the fact that their skin slips easily from the fruit pulp. California grows 80 percent of America's table grapes. New York, Pennsylvania, Washington, Michigan, and Arizona also are commercial growers. Italy and France lead in worldwide production, supplying 16 percent and 13 percent of the world's grape supply respectively. The United States grows only 8 percent of the world total.

What about seedless grapes?

How are seedless grapes grown? Actually, seedless grapes are propagated by cutting seedless vines and grafting to new root stock. How did seedless grapes come about, you may ask? It is believed that the original seedless grape was discovered thousands of years ago in present-day Afghanistan or Iran. It was probably the result of a natural genetic mutation in which the seed's hard covering failed to develop. Today, one of the most popular types of seedless grape is the green Thompson, from which about 90 percent of all raisins are made.

What is the difference between black and golden raisins?

As you probably know, raisins come from sun-dried grapes. Right? Not always.

When grapes reach a sugar content of 22 percent, they are picked by hand and laid out on paper trays between the rows of vines to dry in the sun for three to five weeks. The paper trays are then rolled and placed under the vines for one to three weeks. The resultant raisins are sent to packing plants, washed, sorted, sized, and packaged.

California produces over half of the world's raisins, almost all of them from Thompson seedless grapes. Golden raisins, like black raisins, come from Thompson seedless. These grapes, however, are not sun-dried—they are shipped to a processing plant right after picking. There, the grapes are dipped in hot water and treated with sulfur dioxide to retain their color. Then they are dried in large dehydrators. Due to this processing, they are much moister than ordinary raisins.

Why is the grapefruit named after grapes?

If there is one fruit that tastes nothing like a grape, it is a grapefruit (*Citrus paradisi*)! The grapefruit was not named for the way that it tastes, but for the way it grows in bunches.

Before the middle of the nineteenth century, there was no such thing as a grapefruit. What we know as a grapefruit today is probably a descendant of another fruit, the pummelo (*Citrus maxima*), which was introduced to the West Indies from its native Southeast Asia in the seventeenth century. No one knows if it is a pummelo mutation or an orange-pummelo hybrid.

Since the beginning of this century, the best grapefruits have been grown in Florida.

What's the difference between jams, jellies, and preserves?

Jams, jellies, and preserves have been made around the world for centuries. Internationally, they are known as jams, extra jams, preserves, conserves, etc. While formulations may vary, in general, these products are still made from the age-old formula of one cup of fruit to one cup of sugar. United States law requires jams and jellies to be forty-five parts fruit juice (or solids) for every fifty-five parts sugar. Jellies and preserves also must meet the U.S. Food and Drug Administration's Standards of Identity, which specify the ingredient content of these products.

Some common terms for various fruit products are listed below:

Preserves are usually made from whole fruits or large chunks of fruit, so that the fruit is "preserved" in shape.

Jams are made from smaller pieces of fruit or crushed fruit, from which the seeds can either be removed or remain.

Jellies are made from strained, pure fruit juice. Jelly is transparent and will retain its shape when out of the container. The word "jelly" comes from the French *gelee*, meaning "to congeal."

Marmalades are jellies that contain small bits of fruit, usually citrus. "Marmalade," which originally meant "quince jam," is the French version of the Portuguese word for quince.

Fruit butters contain a high proportion of fruit, which is simmered to obtain desired flavor.

Did you ever eat a "real" cantaloupe?

Unless you have traveled to Europe, it is doubtful that you have ever eaten a real cantaloupe. What we call a cantaloupe in the United States is actually the netted melon (*Cucumis melo reticulatus*). The true cantaloupe (*Cucumis melo cantalupensis*) is strictly a European fruit.

The true cantaloupe, like the netted melon, is a muskmelon. It was developed during the Renaissance on land owned by a Pope near his villa of Cantalupo. The European cantaloupe is football-shaped, with coarse, deeply grooved skin and scribblelike markings. The flesh is dark orange and very sweet and juicy.

By comparison, our familiar "cantaloupe" is smaller and rounded with a corklike netting on the surface (hence the name netted melon) and a light green skin beneath.

While we often eat cantaloupe for breakfast, Europeans usually eat their cantaloupe as a dessert.

To tell if a muskmelon is ripe, look at the stem. If there is a
crack all the way around where the stem meets the crown, the
melon has been fully vine-ripened.

What is a nectarine?

A nectarine is really a smooth-skinned variety of peach. They are
both of the same species—*Prunus persica*—so named because of
its Persian origins.

The nectarine is one of the most curious oddities of the fruit
world. It is a natural mutation of the peach. Occasionally in
peach orchards, a tree will grow that produces nectarines. A nectarine tree can grow from a peach pit. Conversely, a peach tree
can grow from a nectarine pit. Peach trees can produce nectarines through bud mutations and nectarine trees can similarly
produce peaches. Both trees can also produce individual fruits
that are part peach and part nectarine. Thankfully, you are not
likely to see such a weird mutation in the supermarket produce
section.

What fruit is named for a bird's egg?

It is fuzzy, brown, and associated with New Zealand. Yes, it is
the kiwi. The green-fleshed kiwi (*Actinidia chinensis*) is actually
a berry. While it is widely grown in New Zealand, the kiwi is a
native of China and is also known as the Chinese gooseberry. Several generations ago, the vinelike kiwi plant was brought to New
Zealand, where it prospered. The New Zealanders renamed it kiwi
because of its resemblance to the egg of their national bird—the
kiwi. While the kiwi is also cultivated in Australia, Hawaii, and
California, New Zealand supplies the bulk of kiwis for the U.S.
market. California kiwis are available from November through
May, while New Zealand kiwis dominate the market the rest of
the year.

What flowers are edible?

You are probably aware of two flowers that we commonly eat—broccoli and cauliflower. You may not realize, however, that several common garden flowers are also edible, and some are considered gourmet items.

Chrysanthemum: The Japanese and Chinese often use chrysanthemums in cooking. In Japan, where it is the national flower, chrysanthemum fritters are a specialty. In the West, the flower petals are sometimes used to decorate salads.

Daisy: Daisy (Compositae family) flowers used to be candied and eaten in Old England. Today, the buds are sometimes eaten in salads.

Dandelion: When fried in butter, dandelion (*Taraxacum officinale*) flower buds are said to taste like mushrooms.

Jasmine: A genus in the olive family, jasmine (*Jasminum*) has showy flowers and is used in oriental cooking. Its petals are also used to add a delicate aroma to some teas.

Lavender: A member of the mint family, lavender (*Lavandula*) has purple flower spikes. The best known, English lavender, imparts a bitter flavor to jellies, marinades, punches, and stews.

Marigold: The common golden pot marigold (*Calendula officinalis*) has deep yellow or orange flowers that have several culinary uses. In England, a crusty egg custard called marigold pie is made with its petals. The Dutch use it in meat and eel soup. Marigold's yellow coloring is used to color soups, stews, custards, and margarine, at a price well below saffron's. It is known as poor man's saffron.

Nasturtium: These brightly-colored, aromatic flowers were once used in fresh salads. Today, the leaves serve this purpose. Nasturtium (*Tropaelum minus*) derives its common name "nose twister" from the Latin *nosus* (nose) and *torque* (twist).

Rose: A popular dish in Asia Minor and India is called gulangabin, a rose (*Rosa*) flower served in honey.

Squash: The blossoms of squash (*Cucurbita*) are considered a gourmet delight. The squash blossoms that fall off the vine without producing fruit are the male flowers. They can be stuffed with ground meat and baked. Any partially opened squash flower can be picked and sautéed in butter or olive oil.

Violet: Many species of violet (*Viola*) serve culinary purposes. The French sugar-coat violet petals to use as cake decorations. Fresh petals are used in soups and salads. Violets also are used to make violet vinegar and a liqueur called *crème de violets*.

Other edible flowers include almond, alyssum, apple, borage, day lilies, dianthus, hollyhock, lemon, lilac, lily of the valley, mimosa, orange, peach, plum, and pansy.

Eat Your Greens

What widely popular vegetable was thought to be poisonous until the middle of the nineteenth century?

There is nothing quite like the taste of a plump, juicy, bright-red, vine-ripened tomato. Our love affair with the tomato, however, is a fairly recent occurrence.

Native to Peru, the tomato (*Lycopersicon esceulentum*) wasn't discovered by Europeans until the Spanish found it in Mexico in the early 1500s. About the size of a large cherry, the early tomato wasn't cultivated but gathered in the wild by the Peruvians.

After the Spaniards brought the tomato back to Europe, it quickly found its way to the kingdom of Naples, a Spanish possession at the time. The Italians embraced the tomato, which they called *pomodorro*, or "golden apple," because this tomato may have been yellow.

Northern Europe didn't warm to the tomato for quite some time. Botanists correctly placed the tomato in the nightshade family of plants, which includes belladonna and mandrake. The tomato's leaves and stems are actually poisonous. It wasn't until the middle of the nineteenth century that the rest of Europe grudgingly embraced the tomato. Early Americans were also suspicious of it. Records show that one brave American publicly ate a tomato on the courthouse steps in Salem, New Jersey, in 1820, to disprove the poison theory. He suffered no ill effects and encouraged others to indulge.

The American appetite for the tomato steadily increased during the early twentieth century and reached its peak in the late fifties and sixties. Then something unfortunate happened. The huge demand for fresh tomatoes led to the production of lower-quality tomatoes. Tomatoes are very perishable when ripe, so new varieties were bred with thicker skins and higher yields. These could be picked while still green and shipped immediately. The green tomatoes are "ripened" (reddened) with ethylene gas. They somewhat resemble a vine ripened ripe tomato, but they are hard and rather tasteless, and have an unnatural color.

Despite this, Americans eat roughly eighteen pounds of tomatoes per person every year, in one form or another. If you can't eat another one of those orange rocks they call tomatoes in the winter, try to find vine-ripened tomatoes grown in Israel. They are quite good. If not, hold on till next July!

Are Brussels sprouts really from Belgium?

Brussels sprouts (*Brassica oleracea gemmifera*) have grown wild on the seacoasts of Western Europe since antiquity. No one can say exactly when Brussels sprouts first came to Brussels, but they have been a source of great national pride for almost a millennium. The rich, loamy soil of Belgium is perfectly suited to their growth. It wasn't until 1820, however, that the Brussels sprout was officially recognized as Belgium's national green.

Brussels sprouts are an autumn crop and are said to be at their sweetest when harvested after the season's first frost. Belgians like their sprouts to be no bigger than a pea. Good luck finding those in this country!

Brussels sprouts are quite nutritious. A cup contains 810 units of vitamin A, 423 milligrams of potassium, and 112 milligrams of phosphorus, along with vitamin C, riboflavin, and thiamine.

Are potato skins really that good for you?

If your mother was like many, she was convinced that the most nutritious part of the potato was the skin. (She probably also said the same thing about your bread crusts.) Raw potato skins have about the same nutrient content of the raw tuber, with slightly higher levels of calcium and zinc. Baking potatoes, however, causes more vitamins to accumulate in the skin. They are also a good source of fiber. So, Mom was kind of right about making you eat your skins. One thing Mom probably didn't know is that potato peels may contain a naturally occurring poison—solanine.

Potatoes (*Solanum tuberosum*), which like tomatoes and eggplant are members of the Solanaceae or deadly nightshade family, contain steroids and toxic chemicals known as glycoalkoloids. These poisons are the potatoes natural defense against soil pests and are therefore concentrated in the peel. After harvest, solanine levels can become toxic if the potato is exposed to too much light. A greening of the potato skin is a telltale sign of too much solanine. Don't panic, however—properly handled, potatoes are a great food source, and their skins are healthful and tasty too. Just don't eat any green-skinned potatoes (see page 110).

Potatoes are our favorite vegetable, along with lettuce and tomatoes. We grow 35 billion pounds per year. They have the undeserved reputation of being fattening, but the average sized potato has about 150 calories. It's the butter, sour cream, and other fattening toppings that add calories. Potatoes are our second highest source of vitamin C.

What are the different kinds of potatoes?

There are several kinds of potatoes available in the local supermarket. You should buy them according to how you plan to use them. The more common potato varieties follow:

Idaho (or russet) *potatoes* are long, with slightly rounded ends, and rough brown skin. They have a low moisture, high starch content, and are best for baking and frying.

Long white potatoes have a thin, pale brown skin with very tiny eyes. They can be baked, broiled, or fryed.

Red round and white round potatoes (also called boiling potatoes) have a waxy skin, with more moisture and less starch than
the russets or long whites. This suits them for boiling, frying, or
roasting.

How did squash get its odd name?

Did early man squash this vegetable before eating it? No. Does
it look as if it has been squashed? No. The word "squash" is
another example of the many Indian words the Colonists changed
because they had trouble pronouncing them. The Naragansett
word for squash was *askatasquash*, meaning "something eaten
green." The colonists shortened it to "squash." This word
referred specifically to summer squash.

What is the difference between summer and winter squash? All
varieties of squash belong to the genus *Corurbita*. Summer squash
ripen in the summer and can be eaten "green," or before fully
ripe. If allowed to ripen, the skin gets hard and the flesh fibrous.
Winter squash mature in the fall and must be eaten ripe. Because
they are harvested fully ripe, they have tough skins. They also
have a stronger taste and higher nutritional values than summer
squash.

Summer squash include yellow crookneck, zucchini, pattypan,
and bottle gourd. These squash can be cooked and eaten whole.

Winter squash include Hubbard, butternut, acorn, and pump-
kin. The seeds of the winter squash are removed before cooking
and the skins are inedible.

What's the difference between a sweet potato and a yam?

For some reason supermarkets seem to use the names "sweet
potato" and "yam" interchangeably. Botanically, they might as
well be calling apples oranges.

Yams and sweet potatoes are entirely different "animals." The
yam (*Dioscorea*) is a dark orange tropical herb that is a native of
Africa and can weigh up to a hundred pounds. (Try fitting one

of those on Granny's table!) No yams are grown in the United States, except for a very few found in Florida. The sweet potato (*Ipomoea batatas*), on the other hand, is a lighter colored member of the morning glory family, and is a native of the West Indies. The two taste nothing alike. The yam is more starchy and less sweet than the sweet potato.

The reason for the confusion can be traced back to the time of the African slave trade. The slaves, never having seen a sweet potato before, erroneously called it a yam, after their familiar African vegetable, which it somewhat resembled. (You might be interested to learn that the word *yam* means "to eat" in many African dialects.) The sweet potato that Columbus encountered in the West Indies was called *batata* by the natives. This name later evolved into "potato," another crop native to the Americas.

The sweet potato that we know today comes in a light and dark variety, and is grown commercially in the United States as far north as New Jersey. In fact, it enjoys a worldwide popularity and is the third-leading vegetable crop in the world. It is a particular favorite of the Chinese. We Americans eat very few sweet potatoes, except on the holidays.

The yam is grown today in Latin America and parts of Florida. You will have a difficult time locating it at the local store. If you simply must try one, look in a Latin American speciality market and you may get lucky.

Is spinach really a good source of iron?

Spinach (*Spinacia oleracea*) worked wonders for Popeye. One can of the stuff and he turned into a man of iron. The same, however, isn't likely to happen to you.

Yes, your mother was right when she said that spinach is full of iron. Unfortunately, it's not in a form readily available to the body, so we don't benefit from it as we could. But don't despair, moms—spinach is chock full of other good things that the body can use. One cup of spinach has a whopping 14,580 units of vitamin A, 583 milligrams of potassium, and 167 grams of calcium.

So, go ahead. You can still force feed your kids spinach and feel good about it!

What do eggplant and eggs have in common?

Nothing, really. But the earliest eggplants, cultivated in China, were small, pearly oval-shaped fruits that resembled bird eggs. It is said that the first Westerner to eat one made the mistake of consuming it raw. He got an acute case of gastritis. This was unfortunate for the eggplant. It was already viewed with a cautious eye, as it is closely related botanically to belladonna, horse nettle, and tobacco—all poisons—and was thought by many to cause madness.

The eggplant eventually moved west to the Mediterranean, where it was bred larger and in the colors we are familiar with today. The stigma attached to the eggplant lasted centuries, and still endures today in its botanical name—*Solanum melogena*, which means "soothing mad fruit."

There are two kinds of eggplant—male and female. You can tell the difference by looking at the bottom (blossom) end. The female eggplant has a straight groove indentation, while the male has smoother, rounder bottom with a round indentation. The female "fruit" contains many seeds, which may be a drawback to some consumers.

What modern leafy vegetable was used as a spoon by the Greeks?

Romaine lettuce (*Lactuca sativa*) originated on the Greek Island of Cos, not in Rome. It is rumored that the great philosopher Socrates took his lethal dose of hemlock from a Romaine lettuce leaf spoon. The plant was named for the way its leaves resembled Roman tablespoons of the day.

What vegetable used to be placed in a vase as a table centerpiece?

Today's humble celery (*Apium graveolens dulce*) was once held in much higher regard. During the early nineteenth century, it was considered a "classy" food, like caviar is now. The celery stalks would be served from their very own special pressed-glass vase, which was placed in the middle of the table as a centerpiece before serving. So common was this practice that glass celery vases were the "in" wedding gift in America of that time.

What vegetable, popular in the Southeast, will cause a red rash if not harvested carefully?

This vegetable came from Africa with the slaves and is well loved in the Deep South, but hasn't really caught on in the rest of the country. It's okra (*Hibiscus esculentus*). Okra isn't a vegetable at all, but an edible pod of the mallow family.

Okra was known as *ngumbo* in its native Angola and hence gumbo in the American colonies. The slaves made stew from it, modeled after a dish prepared by Native Americans, which they also called gumbo. Gumbo is still a popular dish in the South; okra itself, however, is one of the least liked vegetables, due to its mucilaginous, slimy quality. When cooked long enough, it loses this property.

One must wear long sleeves and gloves when harvesting okra. Just one touch of its leaves can cause a red rash that lasts for weeks.

Why are onions found in so many recipes?

The obvious answer would be that they taste good. While that may be true, the answer goes much deeper. It's not just the way the onion tastes, but the way it makes other foods taste.

Onions stimulate the taste buds. Like hot peppers, onions contain astringent oils, which irritate the mouth's membranes, making the taste buds more sensitive to flavor. Not only this, these oils are aromatic and carry the aroma and flavor of the food to the real taste center of the body—the nose.

Why do onions make you cry?

Onions are actually the leaf stalks of the *Allium cepa* plant tightly balled together in layers to form an underground bulb. Onions make you cry because they contain aromatic sulfuric compounds that are released into the air when you chop them. Most of these noxious compounds are located at the root end of the bulb. If you want to avoid some of the tears while chopping onions, cut up the root end last. Or wear a scuba mask!

What is the difference between a scallion and a shallot?

Many people use the two words interchangeably; however, they are two different species of plants. Scallions are simply immature onions. Farmers often plant too many onion seeds, and when it is time to thin the crop soon after germination, many small onion plants are pulled up and bunched for sale. The green onions are called scallions.

Shallots (*Allium ascalonicum*) are another bulbous member of the lily family. Like onions, shallots have bulbs whereas scallions do not. Shallots taste similar to onions, but milder.

Another perennial plant related to the onion is the chive (*Allium shoen-oprasum*). A grasslike bulbous herb with hollow stems, chives are often grown in pots. Because it has a delicate flavor and does not stand up well to cooking, the chive is often served chopped raw on foods.

Name a well-loved vegetable that comes from a perennial plant.

Almost every common vegetable that we eat comes from an annual plant (i.e., one that lives for a single growing season). One popular vegetable that comes from a perennial plant (a plant that lives for many years) is asparagus.

An asparagus plant (*Asparagus officinalis*) will produce abundantly for up to fifteen years. The stalks that are so highly prized, will grow into a bushy, fernlike plant if left uncut. The stalks are not cut from new plants for two or three years in order to allow the plant to mature. It will then yield succulent tips for six to eight weeks every spring.

Green asparagus stalks are ones that have emerged from the ground and have been exposed to sunlight. White spears are the result of burying the asparagus crowns (roots) eight to ten inches below the ground and harvesting the tips just as they emerge—before they start to photosynthesize. The two leading asparagus-growing states are California, and, surprisingly, New Jersey.

Throughout much of history, the phallic-shaped asparagus spears were thought to be an aphrodisiac and women were thus not allowed to eat them.

Asparagus has one very interesting property that only half of you probably know about—it gives urine a quite distinctive odor. Roughly 43 percent of the population will notice this if they have eaten asparagus within the last few hours. Twenty minutes after consumption, their urine takes on a rather unpleasant smell. Scientists aren't really sure why this happens. The odor is thought to come from a sulfuric compound called methanethiol. Either 57 percent of people have an enzyme which breaks down methanethiol, or they simply cannot smell it.

What are the two basic types of pickles?

We Americans use the word "pickle" when referring to pickled cucumbers. Pickles, however, can be made from a wide variety of fruits and vegetables, as well from eggs, pigs' feet, herring, and other foods. Pickles are preserved in a seasoned brine, which is highly acidic, and retards the growth of bacteria and fungi. There are two basic types of pickles—fresh packed and processed.

Fresh packed pickles make up the majority of pickle sales. They are packed directly into containers from freshly picked cucumbers and covered with a pickling solution. They retain some of the flavor of fresh cucumbers and are a light yellow-green in color. This category includes dills.

Processed (cured) pickles are the part of the summer cucumber crop that is not immediately fresh packed. They are fermented in salt tanks for winter packing. They are darker green than fresh packed pickles and are flavored sweet, dill, or hot.

The most popular pickle is the dill. It is prepared in a vinegar solution that contains dill as well as other herbs and spices, such as cloves, peppercorn, cinnamon, mace, red peppers, allspice, mustard seeds, ginger root, and bay leaves. Other popular pickle varieties are kosher, which does not imply that they are prepared according to the Jewish dietary laws, but that they are flavored with garlic; and sweet gherkins, made with the tiny cucumbers known as cornichons.

Vlasic is the number-one-selling brand of shelf pickles in America. The company markets over eighty-five core items and many regional varieties. According to its figures, 66 percent of all pickles are eaten with sandwiches, and sandwiches make up six out of ten lunch and dinner meals.

Why do pregnant women crave pickles?

It's no old wives' tale—pregnant women really do sometimes crave pickles and other unusual foods. The seemingly irrational cravings of pregnant women actually make perfect sense. They are the body's way of asking for certain lacking nutrients. In the case of pickles, it is salt that the body is craving.

Women have been warned for years to reduce their intake of salt; however, a pregnant woman needs a lot more salt than she normally would require. A pregnant woman needs to make about 40 percent more blood than normal to feed the placenta. The key ingredient to maintaining this higher level of blood is salt. The fetus needs lots of salt, too. It is constantly bathed in a saline solution. All this extra salt has to come from somewhere. By craving things such as pickles, pretzels, and anchovies, the expectant mother is assured of getting enough salt.

Why some pregnant women put pickles in their ice cream is another story!

What is the difference between green olives and black olives?

Both come from the same tree (*Olea europaea*) and are in fact the same fruit. The difference is in the length of ripening. Green olives are immature when picked. Olives left on the tree will turn from green to yellow to purplish brown. While they do change in color, they do not increase in size between the green and the brown stages. The brown, or black, olive has 10 to 30 percent more oil than the green, tastes more mellow, and is more nutritious.

Olives are inedible and quite bitter when picked. They must be pickled to become palatable. Black olives are cooked in a brine solution after harvesting. Green olives, on the other hand, are not cooked, but are cured in lye and then pickled in a brine solution. The green olive remains rather tart after pickling. It is sold whole or pitted and stuffed with a pimiento or, more commonly today, some sort of colored filler. The smaller Spanish variety is more often stuffed.

Olives are native to the Mediterranean and have been cultivated for thousands of years. The ancients relied heavily on olives for food, cooking oil, lamp fuel, and body oil. Olive trees are said to be extremely long-lived. There is one in the Vatican garden that is believed to date to the time of Charlemagne, roughly twelve hundred years ago. Whether this is true or not, olive trees must live a long time to be productive. They do not bear fruit for their first ten years, and do not reach mature production for thirty years. While California and Arizona do grow olives, around 90 percent of the world's crop comes from the Mediterranean.

What are the different types of olive oil?

Olive oil sales doubled between 1985 and 1990. This was due in large part to the suggestion that olive oil may lower LDL (low-density lipoprotein—the bad cholesterol) or may be good for your heart. This, combined with the fact that olive oils contain monosaturated fats instead of the polyunsaturates in other vegetable oils, appealed to health-conscious consumers. There are many types of olive oils. Which is right for you?

Olive oil is produced by pressing the oil out of the olives. The first pressing yields what is called virgin oil. The highest quality oil is known as extra virgin. Below are brief descriptions of the various oil grades:

Extra virgin oil comes from the highest quality hand-picked fruit. The olives are washed, blended, mashed, and squeezed in a hydraulic press at room temperature. The liquid is then centrifuged to draw out the water. The oil must then pass tests for aroma, color, and flavor, and contain less than one percent free oleic acid, which can affect it's flavor. Extra virgin is usually dark green and is redolent of olives. Most extra virgin oils are imported from France or Italy.

Fine virgin oil is from the second pressing of the same olives. It is olive oil that doesn't meet the exacting standards of extra virgin oil, and is less flavorful and more acidic.

Pure oil, which is now simply called olive oil, is extracted from whatever remains in the press after the second pressing. Solvents may be used to extract any free acids or impurities. The oil is also heated to remove the solvents. This leaves a colorless, flavorless oil. Small amounts of extra virgin oil are then added to impart an olive flavor.

Light oil is similar to pure oil that hasn't had any extra virgin oil added. It is produced especially for the American market.

Olives used for pressing oil are usually much smaller than olives for pickling. It takes one hundred pounds of olives to produce about fifteen pounds of edible oil.

Olive oil is sensitive to heat and light and should be stored in a cool, dark place. Properly stored, it lasts about two years.

Olive oil is much more costly than other vegetable oils. Save your extra virgin oil for cold uses, such as in salad dressings. Use the cheaper light oil for frying and as an emulsifier in cakes and brownies.

What's the difference between a rutabaga and a turnip?

The names "rutabaga" and "turnip" seem to be used synonymously. The rutabaga (winter or Swedish turnip) and the common turnip are often both called turnips, but they are entirely different plants.

Rutabagas (*Brassica napobrassica*) are similar to turnips botanically, but do not resemble them in appearance. They have smooth, shiny blue-green foliage, a large tuber that is purplish on top, a long leafy neck, and firm, golden yellow flesh. By contrast, the common turnip (*Brassica rapa*) is smaller and flatter than the rutabaga and has hairy leaves and a white-fleshed tuber.

Store-bought rutabagas have been waxed in hot paraffin diluted with beeswax, resin, or mineral oil to reduce shrinkage during shipping and marketing. Homegrown rutabagas don't bear much of a resemblance to that large, waxy, candlelike vegetable you find in the produce section.

Native to Asia Minor, turnips were probably one of the first foods eaten by primitive man during his scavenging days. They grow in poor soil and keep well, and thus have always been relatively cheap and considered food for the poor.

The rutabaga is of more recent origin, resulting from a seventeenth century cross of the turnip and the cabbage by Swiss botanist Gaspard Bauhin. It did not reach America until 1804, but, being a cool-weather crop, has been a staple of the Scandinavian diet for centuries. The people of Sweden are the largest consumers of rutabagas, hence their other common name— Swedish turnip.

Have carrots always been orange?

No. As a matter of fact, today's carrot (*Daucus carota*) has only been orange for about the last two hundred years. The original carrot, which is probably native to Afghanistan, was purple. Through centuries of selective breeding, the color was gradually changed to white, yellow, and finally orange. It wasn't until they became orange that carrots caught on as a popular food.

Why is there a salad named after Caesar?

Green salads, as we know them today, have only been around since the late 1800s. They certainly weren't eaten during the time of Caesar. How, then, did one of our most popular salads come to be called Caesar? Simple. It's not named for Julius Caesar, but for Caesar Cardini, an Italian immigrant who owned Caesar's restaurant in Tijuana, Mexico, and others in southern California, where salads had become very popular during the 1920s. His romaine lettuce salad with oil and egg dressing and Parmesan cheese became a favorite of Hollywood's stars, and helped immortalize Cardini's first name.

So when did the modern green salad appear in America? Before the Civil War, most salads were made out of cabbage because it stayed fresh and crisp long after other garden greens had been killed by the frost. The first salad common in America was cole slaw, which was brought to the colonies by the Dutch. A typical salad after the Civil War consisted of poultry or seafood and vegetables surrounded by a few leaves of lettuce. With the increased availability of fresh vegetables and fruits grown in California, the eating of salads became more and more common by the end of the century.

What really put salads on tables nationwide was the introduction of iceberg lettuce (*Lactuca sativa*) in 1894. Iceberg was a revolutionary new lettuce developed by the W. Altee Burpee Company. Before iceberg, lettuce was a very seasonal crop, available only in the spring or fall, because the plants went to seed or burned up in the summer months. Once harvested, lettuce had to be rushed to market before it began to wilt. Iceberg, however, was crisp and had a strong root system, allowing it to be grown in hot weather and survive the trip to market. Its name was coined because its tight head kept it "crisp and cool as an iceberg," even in the summer heat.

What does "cole slaw" mean?

We all know what it is, but what does its name mean? Exactly what you may have thought—"cabbage sliced." *Kohl* is the German word for cabbage (*Brassica oleracea var. capitata*). The Saxons changed it to "cole" and added "slaw" for "sliced." Some things do make sense!

Amber Waves

What is the world's most important source of food?

To most of the peoples of Asia and Africa, rice is the staple food. Rice (*Oryza sativa*) feeds more of the world's population than any other food. Sixty percent of the people on earth live on rice as their main food. The Chinese, who have been eating rice for four thousand years, eat about a pound a day per person. In fact, instead of saying "Hello" as a greeting, it is common for them to ask, "Have you eaten rice yet?" It is estimated that some 1 billion people worldwide are involved in the growing of rice, most of which is eaten locally.

Rice is a tropical grass, native to Southeast Asia. It requires a hot, moist climate and freestanding water in which to grow. In Southeast Asia, these conditions occur naturally through the seasonal monsoons. The young rice seedlings are planted in water. They will grow this way in paddies until a few weeks before harvest, when the water is drained off and they produce their loose seed heads. In temperate climates, such as the United States, these special conditions are created through irrigation techniques.

Rice cannot be grown in latitudes north of Peking, above what is known as the rice line. North of Peking, wheat is widely cultivated and is the local staple crop.

Rice first came to America in 1685 and was widely cultivated in South Carolina. It remained that colony's most important crop until the introduction of cotton. The center of American rice production has since moved to Arkansas, Texas, and Louisiana, but the "Carolina" variety of long-grained rice (i.e., rice which has grains four or five times longer than they are wide) is still one of our most popular rices.

Why is brown rice brown?

All rice is brown before milling. Brown rice differs from white rice in that it has not had its brown outer layer of bran polished off. Once the bran is removed, the white endosperm beneath is exposed. Aside from making the rice tan in color, the bran layer also makes it more nutritious, chewy, and nutty in flavor.

What is wild rice?

Wild rice is not rice at all, but the brown seed of an entirely different plant. Wild rice is an aquatic grass plant (*Zizania aquatica*) native to North America. It can be found growing in freshwater or brackish swamps in most states east of the Rockies. It is most commonly found along lakes in Michigan, Wisconsin, and Minnesota, where two thirds of the world's supply is grown. It is now grown commercially in California as well.

Native Americans enjoyed wild rice, which they harvested in canoes. Until recently, the Chippewa Indians harvested much of the crop this way. When the white settlers arrived, they ate wild rice, but were not really all that fond of it. This soon changed, however, and wild rice was so intensely harvested that it was on the verge of extinction. Happily, conservation efforts and harvesting regulations have saved it from doom.

Wild rice has a nutlike taste and a chewy texture. Nutritionally, it is closer to wheat than rice. It has more protein and lysine than either white or brown rice. Unfortunately, due to the difficulty in harvesting it, it is quite expensive. The cultivated California variety is larger grained and somewhat less expensive.

What is converted rice?

There are two types of Carolina rice—polished and converted. Polished, or regular, rice is milled to remove the hull, germ, and most of the bran. Converted rice, also known as processed rice, has the vitamins and minerals from the hull, bran, and germ forced into the starchy part of the grain before polishing. Converted rice is more nutritious, but cooks up less fluffy than regular rice.

Was there ever a real Uncle Ben?

The original Uncle Ben was a black rice farmer who lived in Texas. His rice crop was renowned among the rice millers in and around Houston for being of the highest quality. His rice was so good that the other farmers proudly compared their rice to his, claiming it was "as good as Uncle Ben's."

In the late 1940s, two of the founders of Converted Rice, Inc. (forerunner of Uncle Ben's, Inc.) were having dinner in their favorite Chicago restaurant, discussing how to better market their "converted" rice in the United States. They both were familiar with the Uncle Ben quality story and decided to call their product Uncle Ben's Converted Brand Rice and manufacture it in the rice growing area around Houston, where Uncle Ben farmed.

The restaurant's maître d'—Frank Brown—was a close friend of the two men. They talked him into posing for the famous Uncle Ben portrait that is still on the boxes today.

What popular "instant" American food product was developed by a cousin of the king of Afghanistan?

Minute Rice is the product with royal connections. Ataullah Durruni, cousin to the king of Afghanistan, came to America to work as a research chemist. His ambition was to create a rice that could be prepared quickly and easily—not a strange desire for a man whose native country's staple food is rice.

Durruni's success did not exactly happen in a minute. He toiled for eighteen years in his kitchen, experimenting until he had a fluffy, Southern-style rice that could be prepared in a few minutes. He took his creation, a dehydrated precooked rice, to the people at General Foods. They were duly impressed with Durruni's product. The General Foods research department made further developments and improvements, and in 1946, Minute Rice debuted in American stores.

Minute Rice has been continually improved over the years. In 1958, it set a new record for speedy preparation of rice—five minutes. (They should have named it Five Minute Rice!) Minute Rice is enriched with important vitamins and is guaranteed to come out white, fluffy, and tender every time—Durruni's dream come true.

Why does popcorn pop?

Popcorn (*Zea mays everta*) is a kind of corn called flint corn. It has small hard kernels that contain only a small amount of soft starch. Each kernel has a moisture content of about 13.5 percent. The kernels contain a food storage layer known as the endosperm. This tough, elastic layer resists the buildup of steam pressure within the kernel when heated. When the temperature reaches a critical point, around 400° F, the kernel expands up to thirty-five times its original size and the endosperm violently ruptures.

Popcorn is a relatively minor crop. It is grown primarily in Indiana, Iowa, Illinois, and Ohio. Unlike sweet corn, popcorn is harvested after it has matured and dried on the corn cob. While dry, unsalted popcorn may taste like Styrofoam, it actually has the same nutritional content of sweet corn.

The popcorn you buy at the movies may be popped in coconut oil, which is very high in fat. When you add that imitation butter, one of those huge tubs of popcorn at the movies has more fat than several Big Macs!

What famous man turned a 4-H project into America's best-selling premium popcorn?

Orville Reddenbacher, one of our most unlikely TV stars, is the great 4-H success story. As a youth, he grew popcorn in 4-H and sold it to stores at a profit. In college he did research on popcorn breeding and went on to become the world's largest grower of hybrid popcorn, after buying an agricultural business in 1952. In 1965, after years of cross-breeding, he finally developed a yellow corn that popped twice as big and left very few "old maids" (unpopped kernels).

At first no one wanted to buy premium popcorn and he traveled the Midwest peddling his higher priced "Red Bow" (named for his trademark bow tie). It wasn't until he put his face on the label and changed the name to Orville Reddenbacher's Gourmet Popping Corn that sales started popping. By 1975, he had the best-selling popping corn. In the process, he helped spread the popularity of homemade popcorn from the South and Midwest to the entire nation.

Orville sold his business to Hunt-Wesson in 1976 for millions. Today, he remains the company's chief spokesperson, along with his son, Tim.

What grain, common in birdseed mixtures, is a staple food in Africa?

In ancient times, millet (*Panicam miliaceum*) was eaten extensively by the poor. The Romans ground it into a porridge or gruel. It is still widely cultivated and eaten in Africa.

One advantage of millet over other grains is that it does very well in adverse growing conditions, such as drought and infertile soils. Also, it does not need to be processed after harvesting, and it keeps a long time.

Millet gruel and flatbreads are the staple foods in countries with poor growing conditions, like Ethiopia. While millet was the main Western grain in prehistoric times, barley and wheat eventually displaced it. Today, while many countries hold millet in high regard, we relegate it to birdseed and animal feed.

What food crop led to the civilization of man?

Most probably, it was wheat. Its cultivation by neolithic man directly led to his settling down and abandoning his nomadic ways.

Agriculture began around 7000 B.C., when man started farming wheat. Before this, early man roamed the land, following the animals he hunted and gathering wild fruits, nuts, and roots. With the advent of farming, he had no need to wander, settling in fertile areas. This fostered mutual cooperation and the beginnings of modern civilization.

No one knows the exact origins of modern wheat (*Triticum aestivum*). It is probably the result of mutation and selective breeding of plants somewhere in Asia. No wild wheat can be found anywhere today, however.

Wheat is just as important to civilization now as it was nine thousand years ago. It is the number-one crop in terms of acreage planted and production. Along with rice, and to a lesser degree corn, it supplies roughly 50 percent of all calories for human consumption.

You might think that America, with her amber waves, is the largest grower of wheat. We, however, rank third to the former Soviet Union (mostly the Ukraine) and China in total wheat production. But we are by far the leading exporter of wheat. Interestingly, the former Soviet Union and China, the biggest growers, are also the leading importers.

What makes wheat such a popular grain? The answer is gluten, the sticky, gray substance that makes dough tough and elastic. Wheat, along with rye, contains large quantities of gluten and is thus the best source of flour.

What are bran, wheat germ, and cracked wheat?

Cracked wheat is made from the whole wheat kernel. It is cracked by steel blades. It can be eaten cooked as a breakfast cereal or in pilafs, stuffings, and whole wheat breads.

Wheat bran is the outer coating of the wheat kernel, which is removed during milling. Valued as a source of fiber, it is used in muffins, cereals, and breads.

Wheat germ is also removed from white flour during milling. It is rich in oil and protein and is sold as a nutritional supplement in health food stores.

What are Graham crackers made of?

The obvious answer would be graham, but what is graham? Graham crackers are made of graham flour; graham flour is simply whole wheat flour. It was promoted by a nineteenth-century Presbyterian minister named Sylvester Graham, who was very active in the temperance movement. Graham felt that eating a healthful diet could cure alcoholism and lead to a more wholesome lifestyle. He traveled through the United States preaching the evils of eating meats and fats, which he was sure led to sexual promiscuity. His answer to man's lack of virtue was a diet of vegetables, fruits, and unsifted whole wheat flour in place of white bread. His many followers helped make the use of "Graham" flour popular, and his legacy lives on today in the form of Graham crackers. So if you ever feel the need to cleanse your soul, get a box of Graham crackers and a glass of milk, and think pious thoughts!

What are the different types of flour?

All-purpose flour is a mixture of soft and hard wheats, which can be used for cakes and breads.

Self-rising all-purpose flour has added baking powder.

Enriched flour is made through the addition of vitamin B and iron, which are lost when the wheat germ and bran are removed during milling.

Whole grain flours have the wheat germ and bran added back after milling.

Milled flour has a light yellow color. White flours are bleached, after milling usually with chlorine dioxide.

To speed the aging of flour, which enhances its baking qualities, flour is chemically treated with potassium bromate or iodate.

What is semolina?

Semolina, or durum flour, is coarsely ground from the endosperm of durum wheat, which is the hardest wheat. *Durum* is the Latin word for "hard." "Semolina" is from the Latin word *similia*, meaning "finest wheat flour." Farina is the rough granulation of any other high quality hard wheat.

Wheats are classified as either hard or soft depending on their gluten-starch ratio. Soft wheats have a low gluten content while being high in starch. Hard wheats are just the opposite—high in gluten, low in starch. Gluten is the elastic substance formed when wheat flour is moistened. It allows bread dough to trap gases and hold a shape.

Soft wheats are good for cakes and pastries. Bread flours, on the other hand, are blended from hard wheats. Their high gluten content produces a stronger flour. The strongest flour—durum— is used to make pasta. It is the gluten that allows pasta dough to be rolled and stretched into noodles.

Durum flour is enriched with B vitamins and iron. About three quarters of the durum wheat grown in the United States comes from northeastern and north central North Dakota. This area has a combination of rich, black, loamy soils and a semi-arid climate that is perfect for durum wheat cultivation. The winters are long and severe, while the summers are mild. The rainfalls come mainly in spring and summer, during the growing season. Durum wheat was bred specially to thrive under these conditions.

Who first brought pasta to America?

As with the eggplant and ice cream, it is Thomas Jefferson who helped establish pasta in this country. Jefferson was a celebrity in Europe and traveled there often. He was always open to new ideas and often tried to introduce foods that were popular in Europe to the United States. Macaroni was all the rage with the European upper classes of the time, and Jefferson thought this "exotic" dish would be a big hit here. He sent to Naples for a macaroni machine, but received a spaghetti machine instead.

The English song "Yankee Doodle" poked fun at the "simple" colonists for trying to be as cultured as the Europeans by doing such things as wearing fancy clothes, putting feathers in their hats and eating "classy" foods like macaroni. Americans didn't take offense and quite enjoyed singing the song.

Pasta evidently caught on. America's first pasta factory was opened in Brooklyn in 1848 by a man named Antoine Zerega.

How many different kinds of pasta are there?

We all have our favorite kind of pasta—spaghetti, lasagna, ravioli, ziti, cannelloni, linguine, macaroni, manicotti, rotelle, rigatoni, fettuccine, or tortellini, among many others. So how many different kinds of pasta are there, anyway? More than you could ever remember! Depending on where you live, you may be able to find many of the several hundred different shapes of pasta manufactured.

Shape is the main difference between the myriad types available. Because pasta is made from hard wheat paste (hence its name), it can be molded into almost any shape imaginable.

Italians eat pasta as a first course, not usually as the main dish. The following are the Italian meanings of some of the more popular pastas:

Linguine means "little tongues."

Manicotti means "small muff."

Macaroni, according to one legend, was named by a thirteenth-century king. Upon first tasting elbow noodles he was so pleased that he exclaimed, "Macaroni!" meaning "the little dears" or "how very dear."

Ravioli are stuffed pasta "pillows."

Rotelle means "small wheels."

Spaghetti means "strings." In Italy, spaghetti is never served with meatballs.

Tortellini means "little twists."

Vermicelli means "little worms." This is the southern Italian name for spaghetti. In America, vermicelli is a very thin spaghetti.

Why do runners eat pasta before a marathon?

If you follow the Boston or New York City marathons, you know that the runners like to load up on carbohydrates before the race by eating pasta and other starchy foods. Eating foods like pasta helps to store carbohydrates in the muscles.

The actual carbohydrate-loading regimen starts eight days before a race, when the athlete begins a high-protein, high-fat, very-low-carbohydrate diet, while maintaining the usual training schedule. This low-carbohydrate diet results in the muscles becoming carbohydrate-depleted. Three days before the race, the athlete switches to a high-complex-carbohydrate diet, while reducing the amount of training. This "tricks" the muscles into storing away two to three times the normal amount of carbohydrates as glycogen. These added carbohydrates provide energy reserves during the long marathon.

What is buckwheat?

More people probably know *who* Buckwheat is than know *what* buckwheat is. Buckwheat is not a kind of wheat but a completely unrelated plant in the genus *Fagopyrum*. It is a sprawling Siberian herb that serves as a base for many Russian dishes, such as kasha, a pilaflike dish of braised buckwheat kernels.

What is malt?

Unless you are a beer connoisseur or a culinary buff, you may not know. Where does malt come from? There isn't a malt plant, is there? Malt is obtained mainly from barley (also corn and wheat), or barley seedlings to be more precise.

Barley grain is steeped in cisterns for two or three days. It is then spread out and allowed to germinate. The seedlings are then roasted, which converts their starch to maltose. Additionally, a fair amount of the enzyme diastase is formed. It is this enzyme, which converts starches into sugar, that makes malt commercially important.

By using malt in making beer or Scotch, no sugar need be added. Any starchy ingredient—grains or potatoes—will produce the sugars needed for fermentation with the addition of malt.

Malt on its own isn't a popular food item. You may have had some in a malted milk shake. Powdered malt is added to a chocolate malted to give it a toasty flavor.

What were the first cultivated grains?

Along with wheat, barley (*Hordeum vulgare*) is the oldest cultivated grain. It was first grown in Egypt around 6000 B.C. and remained the number-one grain of Europe up until the sixteenth century. One of the reasons for its early popularity is that it can grow under harsher conditions and at higher latitudes than any other grain.

There are three types of barley—six-row, two-row, and hull-less. The six- and two-row varieties are the commercially important ones. (The term "row" refers to the kernel arrangement on the seed head.)

Because of its low gluten content, barley is not suitable for making flour. Its main use in the past was in porridge and gruel for the poor. Today, barley, which is the fourth most cultivated grain, is used in animal feeds and the making of malt for brewing.

Barley was such a part of life in Old England that the barleycorn actually became a unit of measure in 1324. One inch was equal to three grains of barley laid end to end. The longest "foot" (thirteen inches) was equal to thirty-nine barleycorns. The U.S. shoe industry adopted this form of measure in 1888, when manufacturers declared that a size 13 shoe (the longest standard size made) would be equal to thirty-nine grains of barley.

Did you ever have a bowl of hot groats?

It would be surprising if you didn't. Every time you eat a bowl of oatmeal, you are actually eating groats. This is the name of the edible part of the oat plant (*Avena sativa*), which is obtained by removing the hull, or shell, from oat kernels.

What do the Quakers have to do with the Quaker Oats Company?

Absolutely nothing! The Quaker man was America's first registered trademark for a breakfast cereal, but has no connection with the real Quakers.

In 1877, a partner in the Ohio-based Quaker Mill Company, one Henry Seymour, was flipping through an encyclopedia and found an article on the Quakers. He felt that the qualities they possessed—integrity, honesty, purity—provided a perfect identity for his company's oat breakfast cereal. He registered the figure of a man in Quaker garb holding a scroll that said "Pure" to let customers know that his product was different from the others.

How was it different? While most other oats were sold out of large open barrels in the general store, Quaker Oats were sold in individual packages. In 1900, a historical event occurred when the round Quaker Oats box was introduced. It still endures today, as does the Quaker man.

He was revised three times over the next century. In 1946, the original standing Quaker man was replaced by the familiar smiling Quaker head portrait. This image was updated with the addition of colors in the late fifties. The portrait of the Quaker man adorning the Quaker Oats boxes today was painted by John Mills in 1972.

A modern corporate logo was created in 1970 to identify the entire line of Quaker products. This stylized "shadow" image of the Quaker head portrait can now be found on all of the company's products (usually on the back or side corner of the label), including Gaines and Ken-L-Ration, Gatorade, Aunt Jemima, Van Camps, Rice-A-Roni, and Celeste Pizza.

What cereal is kids' favorite?

Considering the tons of money Kellogg's, General Mills, and Post pour into advertising their vast array of colorful, sugar-flavored, cartoon-character-shaped cereals, you might think it would be Froot Loops or Count Chocula. Hard as it may be to believe, good ol' Cheerios is number one with kids.

Introduced in 1941, Cheerios has tried to keep up with kids' tastes ever since. This plain, slightly sweet oat cereal in the boring yellow box has offered prizes, games, cutouts, and contests reflecting the changing spectrum of interests that capture children's imaginations. From the Lone Ranger to *Star Wars* to the *Lion King*, Cheerios has stayed in step with what kids like.

Cheerios was originally called Cheerioats, until the Quaker Oats company sued General Mills, claiming that it had exclusive rights to the word "oats" as a registered product name. Cheerios became General Mills' best-seller anyway.

Can you guess what their second best-seller is? Honey Nut Cheerios, introduced in 1979. Multi-Grain Cheerios came out in 1992. One half of all American homes are regular users of these Cheerios products. They're not flashy or exciting, they just taste good!

Why do Rice Krispies go Snap! Crackle! Pop!™?

People have been enjoying this cereal's breakfast serenade since its introduction in 1928. It has been a big seller for Kelloggs ever since. What gives Rice Krispies its unique crackling ability? It has to do with the way the cereal is processed during manufacture.

Obviously, rice is the basic ingredient in Rice Krispies. Like the rice we cook at home, this milled rice has the bran and germ removed, leaving a polished white grain. The rice and added malt flavoring, salt, sugar, vitamins, and minerals are steam cooked under pressure, dried, and tempered. Tempering means that the cereal is allowed to sit for a while to equalize its moisture content. It is then slightly flattened by rollers. The rice is tempered again, then quickly toasted by hot air, which causes each grain to expand to several times its original size.

Each toasted puff of rice is filled with tiny air bubbles of varying size. When milk is added, it is unevenly absorbed, which causes an uneven swelling of the kernel's starch structure. The swelling of one part of the rice puff causes an increased pressure and subsequent breakage of the surrounding starch structure. This breaking action results in the friendly Snap! Crackle! Pop! sound that greets us at breakfast time.

How was America's favorite cereal inspired by a broken tooth?

Cold breakfast cereals haven't been widely popular all that long. In fact, it was less than a hundred years ago that a guy named Kellogg came along and changed all that.

Dr. John Harvey Kellogg wrote several diet books before he was hired to be the director of the Western Health Forum Institute in Battle Creek, Michigan, in 1876. The sanitarium, as health resorts were known then, was opened in 1866 by a religious zealot named Sister Ellen Harmon, founder of the Seventh-Day Adventists, who once sat in a basket on a hilltop in Maine, waiting for God to come and shuttle her and her followers up to heaven. After tiring of that, she headed west to open a haven for those wishing to purify the body and soul.

Kellogg changed the name to the Battle Creek Sanitarium and instituted his dietary regimen. He was a strong believer in hard, dry foods being good for the teeth. One day while eating some brittle zwieback, a patient broke her false teeth. Because of this episode, Kellogg set about to create a less crunchy health food. The eventual result was Corn Flakes. (Actually, he first came up with a wheat flake cereal called Granose in 1895, but later invented the now familiar Corn Flakes in 1898.)

Another patient of the sanitarium was a guy named C. W. Post, who was there to help cure an ulcer. While Kellogg did nothing for his stomach problems, he did inspire Post to create his own line of cereals.

Corn Flakes were sold by mail order, but Kellogg refused to compromise his medical ethics by selling them in stores. Enter his brother, Will Kellogg. Will was a capitalist and purchased the commercial rights to Corn Flakes from his brother in 1906. He improved their taste, adding malt, sugar, and salt. John Kellogg didn't take kindly to his brother spoiling the purity of Corn Flakes and filed several lawsuits against Will, all to no avail.

To distance his cereal from its many imitators, and his brother, Will had his signature emblazoned on every box—"W. K. Kellogg." Corn Flakes remains one of America's best-selling cereals today.

Other popular Kellogg's cereals followed—All-Bran, in 1916; Rice Krispies, in 1928; Sugar Corn Pops, in 1950; Sugar Frosted Flakes, in 1952; Sugar Smacks, in 1953; Special K, in 1955; Kellogg's Product 19, in 1963; Nutri-Grain, in 1981; Crispix, in 1983; Just Right, in 1985; and Müeslix, in 1987.

The word "sugar" was dropped from the product names in 1984, resulting in Frosted Flakes, Corn Pops, and Smacks. Kellogg's did *not* remove the sugar, however. Today, there are over two hundred different brands of cereal. Kellogg's makes four of the top five selling cereals—Corn Flakes, Frosted Flakes, Raisin Bran, and Rice Krispies. General Mills' Cheerios, at number two, rounds out the list.

What are Grape-Nuts?

If you have ever eaten them, you must have wondered. They contain neither grapes nor nuts. Little Pebbles might be a better name! There is, however, some convoluted logic behind the name.

Grape-Nuts are essentially very hard bread crumbs containing whole wheat, malted barley flour, salt, and yeast. These ingredients are baked into loaves, crumbled, and baked again, very slowly. Then they are crushed into the familiar Grape-Nuts "pebbles."

C. W. Post, the Grape-Nuts inventor, thought that the double-baking had converted the bread starches into dextrose, also known as grape sugar. The hard pebbles reminded him of nuts. Hence the name Grape-Nuts.

Post was a native of Illinois who worked in the hardware business and real estate until a stomach ulcer forced him into Kellogg's Battle Creek Sanitarium in 1891. His stay with Kellogg helped convince him that there might be a big demand for healthful foods. Post stayed in Battle Creek, which was to become the national cereal capital, and in 1895, produced a hot cereal beverage that was supposed to be a coffee substitute. He called his creation Postum Cereal Food Coffee, later shortened to Postum Cereal. Through heavy promotion, he had Postum on store shelves from Maine to Colorado within eighteen months. Prompted by Postum's success, he quickly developed Grape-Nuts.

Grape-Nuts, when introduced in 1897, was the first nationally distributed cold cereal. Post had created it for his own digestive problems. The wheat husks that were removed from the kernels for Grape-Nuts were used as the bran for Postum. Post was a frugal man!

His frugality is also seen in the size of the Grape-Nuts box. It is smaller than most other cereal boxes because Post maintained that Grape-Nuts is a "concentrated" cereal.

The original box was brown and tan. It contained a copy of

his thoughts on health, "The Road to Wellville," which of course recommended eating Grape-Nuts for breakfast, for lunch, and as a salad topping for dinner.

Another Post creation—Post Toasties—was one of the two most popular cereals of the first half of the twentieth century, (Corn Flakes was the most popular). Created in 1904, this corn flake cereal was originally called Elijah's Manna, until religious objections forced the name change.

Post Cereals incorporated in 1929, forming the company we all know today—General Foods.

The Staff of Life

When was bread first sliced?

How many times have you heard that expression about "the best thing since sliced bread"? So when did sliced bread come about? More recently than you may think.

Before it was sold pre-sliced, Wonder Bread was already one of America's most popular brands. In 1925 the Continental Baking Company bought out its maker, Taggart Baking Company of Indianapolis. Continental Baking made a number of significant changes that revolutionized not only the shape of bread, but its nutritional content.

It was the introduction of pre-sliced, soft white bread—the sandwich loaf—that popularized the eating of sandwiches. But while it is the convenient pre-slicing of bread that is remembered today, it is the addition of vitamins and minerals to bread in the late 1930s that was truly a great innovation. It came as a response to a national concern that large segments of the population were undernourished. Known as the quiet miracle, this enrichment of bread is credited with eliminating the crippling and fatal diseases of beriberi and pellagra in America and with bringing essential nutrients to the poor, who otherwise could not afford nutritious food.

The sale of white bread began to decline thirty years ago. In 1963, nine billion pounds were consumed; by 1990 sales had dropped to 5.6 billion pounds. Apparently, whole grains started making a comeback with health-conscious consumers. So the next time you have the urge to refer to some wonderful new invention as "the best thing since sliced bread," reconsider. Perhaps you should say "the best thing since nutritionally enriched bread"!

What is America's largest baker?

To know their products is to love them! What started as a home bakery in 1898 has grown into today's largest bakery—Entenmann's. The horse and wagon that William Entenmann first drove to deliver baked goods in Brooklyn, New York, now adorns the millions of boxes of baked goods Entenmann's sells nationwide. The company went national in 1982, after its purchase by General Foods.

What are its best-selling products? Chocolate chip cookies, chocolate frosted doughnuts, golden pound loaf, raspberry Danish twist, and crumb coffee cake top the list.

Where is Pepperidge Farm?

We all known Pepperidge Farm is a huge food company. Most of us, however, probably don't know that it got its start on a small Connecticut farm.

Unlike most major corporations, Pepperidge Farm has the distinction of having been founded by a woman—Margaret Rudkin. Born as Margaret Fogarty in 1897, she had a comfortable middle-class upbringing in New York City. She worked for six years in the brokerage and banking business before marrying Henry Rudkin in 1923. They did well and left the battle of the city for a country home with orchards, stables, and barns in Fairfield, Connecticut. There were many sour gum or pepperidge trees around their home, so they named their new estate Pepperidge Farm.

Determined to serve her family more healthful foods, Margaret began to research old family cookbooks and found a recipe for a whole wheat bread that used only the purest ingredients, such as stone ground wheat, molasses, yeast, and honey. Margaret's first few attempts at baking bread did not go too well. But finally, with practice she could bake a delicious loaf of bread that was also nutritious. On August 17, 1937, she took her loaves of bread to a local grocer and convinced him to sell them for twenty-five cents a loaf. Other breads at the time sold for only ten cents. Before she had returned home, the grocer was calling to order more loaves of Margaret's bread, which had quickly sold out. Within weeks, other grocers were placing orders. Pepperidge Farm bread was born.

In 1940, the baking operation was moved from Pepperidge Farm to a larger facility in Norwalk, Connecticut. With the new facility came new products, such as melba toast, pound cake, and poultry stuffing. The outbreak of World War II caused serious shortages of essential ingredients like butter, flour, honey, and sugar. Products whose quality could not be ensured were temporarily discontinued. After the war, production and product selection increased. Dinner rolls, cracked wheat, and oatmeal breads were introduced. Bowing to consumer pressure, the bakery offered sliced bread in addition to unsliced bread. By the end of the forties nearly 500,000 loaves of bread were sold every week. With the opening of a new bakery in Downers Grove, Illinois, in 1953, bread production rose to one million loaves a week.

In 1961, a new chapter in the Pepperidge Farm story began when the company became affiliated with the Campbell Soup Company. It was at about this time that Goldfish Crackers, Distinctive Cookies, Toasted Thins, and frozen layer cakes debuted. Margaret Rudkin retired in 1966, and her son Bill became chairman of the board.

What's sourdough bread?

Sourdough bread is made from day-old bread dough that is used to start the leavening fermentation process in a new batch of bread, giving it a distinctive yet subtle bite and an acidic taste.

The yeast found in the old ("sour") dough eliminates the need to keep a fresh supply of yeast on hand.

This method of keeping a little dough from the previous day's baking is associated with the days of the Old West. Prospectors could keep the same strain of yeast alive for years by their repeated use of sourdough (yeast, flour, sugar, and water). All they had to do was add a little sourdough to each days new batch of bread dough to get it going.

Don't credit the prospectors too much, though. The use of sourdough is perhaps the oldest form of leavening known, going back to the ancient Egyptians.

Why is thirteen known as a baker's dozen?

Why is it that bakers should be so generous as to sell thirteen of something for the price of a dozen? Well, generosity has little to do with the origins of this centuries-old practice.

The bakers of England formed a trade guild as early as the twelfth century, which later split into the Company of Brown Bakers and the Company of White Bakers. These baking companies were subject to very strict regulations. A law passed in 1266 stipulated that exactly eighty loaves of bread were to be baked from a standard sack of flour. It was illegal to sell loaves of bread that varied from a set weight.

Bakers who sold underweight loaves to retailers could get into big trouble. By adding an extra loaf of bread to every dozen loaves they sold the bakers could ensure that they weren't short-changing the retailers.

Another reason for the baker's dozen goes back to the time when butlers would order all the food for a house. In exchange for the butler's order, the baker would give him thirteen of whatever was being purchased for the price of twelve as a sort of butler's commission.

What "French" roll was first created in Austria?

The croissant is another one of those foods that we associate with France. It was first created, however, by a Viennese baker in 1683. Vienna was under siege by the Turks at the time and the city was on constant alert. Bakers were among the earliest risers, and one particular baker happened to hear the Turks tunneling under the city walls early one morning during his baking. He promptly sounded the alarm and is credited with saving Vienna from the invaders.

In gratitude, the city rewarded the baker with a patent to make crescent-shaped rolls to commemorate how the Viennese had "devoured" the Turks. The shape was based on the crescent moon that adorned the Turkish flag.

Are English muffins really from England?

If you went to England today, you would not be able to find a product called an English muffin. The closest thing you would find would be the crumpet. The creator of the English muffin was, however, an English baker named Samuel Bath Thomas.

Thomas came to America in 1875 with a secret recipe for a specialty bread never before seen in this country. Lacking the capital to open his own bakery, the twenty-year-old Englishman apprenticed himself to an established baker while he scrimped and saved to open his own bakery. By 1880, Thomas had saved enough to open a bakery on Ninth Avenue in New York City.

His secret recipe was simply a variation on the crumpets and scones that were popular at that time in his native England. Crumpets are small cakes of spongy yeast bread, made from batter poured into ring forms on a hot griddle and browned on both sides. English muffins differ from crumpets in that they are made from dough, not batter (which contains more milk than muffin dough) and are rolled in cornmeal before cooking.

The demand for Thomas' unique English muffins grew quickly. Retailers began showing up at his bakery to purchase the muffins, which they then resold throughout the city. When Thomas died in 1919, his daughters and nephews took over and expanded the bakery by opening a new production facility in Long Island City, New York. The company continued to grow and in 1962 opened a new plant at its present Totowa, New Jersey, site. Today, S.B. Thomas, Inc. (now owned by the conglomerate CPC International, Inc.) has regional production facilities throughout the United States.

Thomas' English Muffins, the originals, are still considered by many to be the best.

Did you ever have a coffee and a Viennese?

Sounds like a silly question, doesn't it? How about coffee and a Danish? Makes more sense, right? Well, not really!

The bakers in Denmark belong to a guild. About a hundred years ago, they went on strike. They had been receiving room and board in exchange for their work but wanted to get paid wages. The bakeries hired Viennese bakers during the strike. The Viennese bakers introduced the people of Denmark to their wonderful pastries. When the Danish bakers returned to work, they too began baking these pastries.

Americans got these pastries from the Danes, and erroneously called them Danish pastries. In Denmark, however, they are called Viennese pastries. Whatever you call them, they are a perfect match with a hot cup of coffee!

What is the best-selling cracker in the world?

The one with the classiest name, of course—Ritz!

In 1934, the National Biscuit Company (Nabisco) transformed the ordinary soda cracker by leaving out the yeast and increasing the amount of shortening. A thin coating of coconut oil and a sprinkling of salt topped it off. Consumers found the buttery taste and crispy texture irresistible.

Milk and Honey

How are the various kinds of milk different from one another?

With the wide variety of milks and creams available today, it is easy to confuse the differences between them all. The following should answer any unresolved milk classification questions that you may have:

Buttermilk was originally the milky residue left after churning butter. Today, buttermilk is made by adding bacterial cultures to skim milk. The cultures convert the milk sugars (lactose) into lactic acid, giving buttermilk its tartness. Contrary to popular belief, buttermilk is actually low in milkfat. It contains about 8.5 percent milk solids and has one-fourth the fat content of whole milk.

Condensed milk, which can be either whole or skim milk, has about half the water content of milk and contains not less than 8.5 percent milkfat. Sweetened condensed milk has added sugar. The final product contains 40 percent sugar and 35 percent milk solids.

Evaporated milk is made from whole milk that has been heated to remove 60 percent of its water. It is canned and heat-sanitized. Evaporated milk contains not less than 7.5 percent milkfat. It can easily be reconstituted to approximate the consistency of whole milk.

Low-fat milk is the same as whole milk, except that some of the milkfat has been skimmed away to produce a milk with either a 1 percent or 2 percent fat content, (which isn't all that low if you are concerned with such things).

Skim or nonfat milk has had as much milkfat skimmed off as possible and contains less than 0.5 percent milkfat, but retains all the proteins and minerals of whole milk. Skim milk, however, is deprived of the fat-soluble vitamins A, D, E, and K, which are added back in fortified skim milks. Because of its low fat content, skim milk should not be used for whole milk in recipes.

Whole milk must contain at least 3.25 percent milkfat and 8.6 percent nonfat solids, like proteins, carbohydrates, minerals, and vitamins. Most whole milks have vitamins A and D added to aid in the assimilation of calcium and phosphorus.

Light cream is milk that contains at least 18 percent milkfat.

Whipping cream is milk that contains at least 30 percent milkfat.

Heavy cream is milk that contains at least 36 percent milkfat.

Sour cream is a cultured cream which is mixed with nonfat milk solids and other ingredients. It is high in fat content.

Butter is milk that contains 80 percent or more milkfat.

Regardless of its form, the people of Finland are the milk-and-cream consuming champs. American consumption has been steadily declining since the 1950s, with the increased awareness of fat and cholesterol and the rise in popularity of various juices and soft drinks.

At what temperature is milk pasteurized?

Named after the great French bacteriologist Louis Pasteur, pasteurization involves heating milk to kill bacteria. Milk can be effectively pasteurized at various temperatures for various lengths of time. The higher the temperature, the shorter the heating time.

Temperature	Heating Time
145° F	30 seconds
161° F	15 seconds
191° F	1 second
212° F	0.1 second

What is ultra-high-temperature (UHT) pasteurization?

In recent years, you probably have seen packaged milk that is sold off the shelf at room temperature. This is UHT processed milk. It is ultra-pasteurized at 280° F for two seconds and is then aseptically packaged and sealed. Incredibly, this milk will keep up to six months unrefrigerated.

How is milk homogenized?

We all know that milk is heated to pasteurize it. But how is milk homogenized? While pasteurization kills bacteria, homogenization creates a uniform liquid, one where the cream does not separate and float to the top.

Milk is homogenized by preheating it and forcing it under very high pressure through a mesh that breaks the fat up into tiny globules small enough to remain in suspension in the milk.

Who invented sweetened condensed milk?

The inspiration for sweetened condensed milk came from a man deeply affected by the number of babies who died aboard ship during an Atlantic crossing. On his way home from the London Exposition of 1851, Gail Borden was appalled that so many infants died from the milk of diseased cows on board. He vowed there and then to develop a safe method of preserving milk.

After watching the Shakers in New Lebanon, New York, using a vacuum method to preserve fruit, Borden tried it with milk. This method removed water and condensed the milk. Added sugar acted as a preservative. He adopted the American bald eagle as a logo for his product, which was in heavy demand during the Civil War. Thus Borden Inc. was born.

What is nondairy creamer?

Fifty percent of American coffee drinkers take milk or cream in their coffee.

To many of those people who work in an office with a coffee maker, but no refrigerator, Coffee-Mate and Cremora are life savers.

They lighten and mellow coffee, taste kind of creamy, and never go bad. But what are they? Well, they're basically powdered corn syrup and vegetable oils—sugar and fat. Mixed in are artificial flavors, colors, and various other ingredients.

Listed below are the ingredients found in Cremora Non-Dairy Creamer:

Corn syrup solids, partially hydrogenated vegetable oils (may contain one or more of the following oils: coconut, cottonseed, palm, palm kernel, peanut, or soybean), sodium caseinate (milk derived), dipotassium phosphate (regulates acidity), monoglycerides (prevent oil separation), sodium silicoaluminate (prevents caking), sodium tripolyphosphate (an emulsifying salt), diacetyl tartaric acid ester of mono- and diglycerides (prevent oil separation), artificial flavors, beta-carotene, and riboflavin (artificial colors).

Cremora Lite differs in using only partially hydrogenated sunflower oil (and sugar) and has 85 percent less saturated fats than regular nondairy creamer.

Either way, you're getting eight to ten calories per teaspoon serving, and a lot of chemistry. But to some people, anything is better than black, office-brewed coffee.

Who discovered cheese?

Cheese has been around at least four thousand years. Legend has it that cheese was first created by accident. It seems that some traveling Arab salesman had a calf stomach containing milk slung over his camel while riding across the Sahara on a sales call.

Apparently, the rennet in the calf-stomach container, heated by the sun and stirred by the camel's trot, coagulated the milk into curds and whey. The happy man discovered his good fortune one evening when he drank the whey and ate the curds with his figs and dates.

Cheese is made from the curd of milk from which the whey has been removed. Either raw or pasteurized milk can be used to make cheese. In the case of raw (unpasteurized) milk, lactic acid bacteria in the milk coagulate the casein (protein). Pasteurized milk does not contain these bacteria and a starter culture must be added to initiate coagulation of the curd. Another method used to coagulate pasteurized milk (or to speed coagulation) is to use rennet, an enzyme extracted from the fourth stomach of young calves. When slowly heated, the enzyme aids in the clumping of the milk protein into curds, leaving behind the watery whey.

Curds contain most of the nutrients from milk, including casein, most of the fat, some lactose, albumin salts, and water. The whey is mainly water and contains most of the lactose, some albumin, and a bit of fat.

After coagulation, cheeses are drained of whey and pressed, cooked, ripened, and aged. Ripening agents include bacteria and molds. Mold is the ripening agent in cheeses like blue, Gorgonzola, and Roquefort.

Because raw milk cheese like Parmesan is not pasteurized and can carry diseases, it must be aged sixty days to be sold in the United States.

How are cheeses classified?

There are many classification systems for cheese. The different kinds of cheese are commonly classified by their firmness, as follows:

Soft cheeses (cottage cheese, cream cheese, etc.), also known as fresh cheeses, are uncooked and unripened (or barely ripened). They are not molded and are creamy and milky. Soft cheeses are very perishable because of their high moisture content and most should be used within a week of purchase.

Soft-ripened cheeses (Brie, Camembert, Muenster, Limberger) are uncooked and unpressed. They are cut in large curds and left to drain naturally. An orange cheese rind is created by washing the cheese in brine or alcohol. Some are sprayed with spores of the white mold *Penicillium camemberti* to promote a powdery white fungal rind. Soft-ripened cheeses ripen from the rind inward as the fungus secretes enzymes into the curd. They have a soft, spreadable consistency and can be mild or strong-tasting.

Semi-firm cheeses (cheddar, Edam, Jarlsberg) are cooked and pressed to reduce the moisture content. Some have rinds, some don't. They are firm enough to be sliced and have a wide range of flavors.

Firm cheeses (Parmesan, Pecorino Romano) are cooked, pressed, and aged until dry and hard. After aging they can't be sliced, but must be grated. They can be kept a long time because they are so dry.

So what about ricotta?

Ricotta is not a curd cheese like those above. It is made from the whey of such cheeses as cheddar, mozzarella, provolone, and Swiss. It comes in regular or skim milk varieties, with a fat content of 4 percent and 2 percent respectively. Literally translated, *ricotta* means "twice cooked." This is because it is made by cooking the whey from a previously cooked cheese.

How did cottage cheese come by its name?

Cottage cheese originally *was* made in cottages. Many housewives produced this cheese as a by-product of their homemade butter, and its production was an actual "cottage" industry.

Cottage cheese was made by skimming the milk obtained in the butter-making process and allowing it to curdle. The curds would be strained from the whey using cheesecloth, and the resultant cheese was readily eaten.

What is American cheese?

American cheese does not begin as milk, but as cheese. The terms "process" cheese and "American" cheese are almost synonymous.

However, process cheese is not an American invention. Two Swiss chemists came up with it in 1910 to create a better-keeping cheese.

Process cheese is made by finely grinding one or more cheeses, such as cheddar or Colby, adding water, and heating with emulsifiers for consistency. Seasonings and orange food color are often added. Sorbates and propionates may also be added as preservatives. The cheese is sold unripened.

American cheese is about 90 percent cheese. The rest is made up of the above ingredients and added cream or milkfat. By law, it must contain at least 45 percent butterfat and no more than 44 percent water.

This cheese makes up around 40 percent of the U.S. market. It generally has a cheddar taste.

What is cheese food?

Cheese food must contain not less than 23 percent butterfat, and not more than 44 percent water. Skim milk, buttermilk, and whey can be used in place of cream and butterfat. They need only be 51 percent cheese. Otherwise, it is similar to process cheese.

Cheese spreads, like Velveeta, can contain up to 60 percent water and not less than 20 percent butterfat. Gums and sweeteners can also be added.

What is special about Roquefort cheese?

To be a true Roquefort, a cheese must be aged in the limestone caves of Mount Cambalou near Roquefort, France. By French law, Roquefort cheese must be made from sheep's milk and use the fungus *Penicillium roqueforti* during curing, which lasts two months. Outside of France, these cheeses are called bleu because of the coloration imparted by the mold, and are made with cow's milk in the United States.

Where is Philadelphia Brand Cream Cheese from?

You guessed it, not Philadelphia! A New York State dairy farmer named Lawrence was the first to perfect the use of cream and milk to create cream cheese, in 1872. The name Philadelphia was chosen because at that time the city had a reputation for fine foods.

Who invented ice cream?

You might think iced desserts would be a fairly recent creation due to the problems of refrigeration. The Chinese, however, who had perfected ice storage using the principle of evaporation in the eighth century B.C., were enjoying fruit-flavored ices by the time of Marco Polo's visit in the thirteenth century. He brought the recipe back to Italy, where it has been a favorite ever since. The Arabs and Indians picked up the idea from the Chinese also, and named this delicacy sherbet.

What we call ice cream today was created in the early seventeenth century by a French chef for King Charles I of England. By the end of the century, commoners, as well as the nobility, were hot for ice cream.

First Lady Dolly Madison and Alexander Hamilton's wife, Elizabeth, popularized ice cream in the United States. America's great contributions to the world of ice cream were the invention of the ice cream soda in Philadelphia in 1874 and the introduction of the ice cream cone at the St. Louis World's Fair in 1904.

What is the difference between ice cream, ice milk, and sherbet?

The ice cream business is a $3-billion-a-year industry, and there are many types of frozen dairy products available. How do they differ from one another? Here's a quick summary:

Ice cream is strictly defined by law. Each gallon must weigh at least 4.5 pounds, contain not less than 10 percent butterfat, 2.7 percent protein, and 20 percent milk solids, and contain not more than 50 percent air. (Air must be added to ice cream to make it soft enough to eat.) The less air added, the thicker and richer the ice cream will be.

Most brands actually have 12 percent fat, 11 percent nonfat

milk solids, 15 percent sugar, and 0.3 percent vegetable gum stabilizers. Premium brands have around 14 percent fat, while super-premium brands have 16 percent or more.

Ice milk differs from ice cream in that it must contain between 2 percent and 7 percent butterfat and not less than 1.3 pounds of food solids per gallon. It usually contains too much air to be called ice cream.

French ice cream is a rich ice cream that has a higher fat content and deeper color than regular ice cream. It is made from a custard base with cream and egg yolks.

Sherbet is a water ice made from pulverized fruit pulp, fruit juice, and sugar syrup. (The French call it *sorbet*, the Italians *sorbetto*.) What we call Italian ice is really sherbet. In many parts of the United States, what we call sherbet is pastel-colored and contains milk or cream. Technically this is not sherbet, but ice milk.

The overall quality of an ice cream depends on the amount of air whipped into it as well as on the ingredients. To keep your frozen dairy products at their best, store at 0° F and eat them within two months' time.

What is America's best-selling ice cream?

Breyers! What else? It uses all natural ingredients. If it's not on the label, it's not in the ice cream. Breyers vanilla ice cream, for instance, contains only fresh milk, cream, pure sugar and imported natural vanilla. No preservatives or stabilizers are added.

William Breyer hand-cranked his first batch of ice cream in Philadelphia in 1866. Breyers now sells over 50 million gallons a year. Vanilla is America's favorite flavor, regardless of the brand.

What ice cream factory is the biggest tourist attraction in Vermont?

Ben & Jerry's! Ben Cohen, a Colgate University dropout, and Jerry Greenfield, a lab technician, wanted to start a bagel business in rural Vermont. When they found out how much bagel-making equipment cost, they decided on ice cream.

From the information contained in a five-dollar Penn State ice-cream-making course, they launched Ben & Jerry's in an old gas station in Burlington, Vermont. The two self-proclaimed hippies painted cartoon characters all over the garage and entertained customers waiting for cones with a pianist and movies.

They began selling packaged ice cream in local stores during the cold months to make ends meet. When they tried to expand into stores farther south, not many distributors would touch their stuff. They learned that Häagen-Dazs was blocking their expansion by threatening to pull its own ice cream from any store that sold Ben & Jerry's. Ben and Jerry sued Häagen-Dazs and won. They never looked back.

Why is Ben & Jerry's ice cream so successful? Ben and Jerry mix in all kinds of candies and produce a denser ice cream than the nonpremium brands. In the true hippie spirit, 7.5 percent of Ben & Jerry's pretax profits are donated to charity. It is partly due to the fun, laid-back attitude of the company that makes the Ben & Jerry's factory in Waterbury, Vermont's number-one tourist attraction.

What about Häagen-Dazs and Frusen Gladje?

Where do they come from? With such exotic European names, you might think Switzerland or Holland or Sweden. No such luck! These two brands are totally American.

In the case of Häagen-Dazs, which comes from the far-off land of Teaneck, New Jersey, the name is a fabrication dreamed up by the manufacturer's wife. Reuben Mattus, a Polish immigrant, had been selling ice cream in the Bronx for over sixty years when he decided people would be willing to pay more for a better ice cream, that is, one with less air pumped into it.

He was right. His ice cream was good and it sold for 50 percent more than regular brands. What he really needed to set his product apart and spark the imagination of the consumer was a distinctive name. His wife, Rose, had the inspiration to call it Häagen-Dazs, a word which meant absolutely nothing. This did the trick and sales soared. Häagen-Dazs was bought by the food giant Pillsbury in 1983 for $80 million.

tures be present—*Lactobacillus bulgaricus* and *Streptococcus thermophilus.*

These two bacteria convert the lactose (sugar) in milk into lactic acid, causing the milk to curdle and turn into a custard-like, tart-tasting yogurt. It is the presence of the living bacteria that gives yogurt its healthful properties. Make sure you see the word "active" or "living" cultures on the yogurt container to ensure you are getting good yogurt. Heat-treated yogurts lose their beneficial properties.

Some yogurts, like Dannon, have a third culture added—*Lactobacillus acidophilus.* This bacteria naturally occurs in the body's gastrointestinal tract. It is more likely than the other cultures to survive its trip through the stomach and replenish the body's own beneficial bacteria in the intestine.

All three bacterial cultures help populate the intestines with "good" bacteria, which displace "bad" bacteria such as *E. coli*, *Salmonella*, *Shigella*, *Staphylococcus*, *Listeria*, and *Campylobacter*. These organisms, which are found in food, can cause gastroenteritis and diarrhea. The good bacteria produce lactic acid and antibiotics that inhibit bad bacteria in the body. Yogurt can also stimulate the activity of immune cells in the body, increasing the production of gamma interferon, which fights some viral infections. Yogurt also gives you about the same amount of protein, calcium, minerals, and vitamins as does milk.

Dannon was the first yogurt company, founded in Barcelona by Issac Carasso. Originally, the company was named Danone, after Carasso's son. When he moved the company to New York after World War II, he Americanized the name to the now-familiar Dannon.

What country consumes the most yogurt?

Yogurt is most popular in the country of its origin—Bulgaria. Bulgarians maintain that only a "true" yogurt, made with bacilli from the mountains of Bulgaria, promotes long life and health. Also, the milk must be a combination of water and goat's milk, which is much higher in butter fat than cow's milk.

Maybe you think you like yogurt. Well, the average Bulgarian may eat up to six pounds of this curdled milk a day! It has been a food staple for thousands of years in the Balkans, Mongolia, and the Middle East.

We Americans have only just recently taken a liking to yogurt. It was originally marketed as a diet food. In the 1940s, when the Dannon Company sold plain yogurt, it didn't go over too well. To please the American palate, Dannon added strawberry preserves. With the ever increasing number of flavors produced, yogurt consumption in the United States has continually grown. Today, the two most popular varieties are strawberry and plain.

One reason for yogurt's wide popularity is that 70 percent of Earth's population is unable to digest fresh milk. Many adults, after weaning from breast milk, don't have access to a supply of fresh milk. As a result, their bodies fail to secrete the enzyme lactase, which is needed to digest milk sugar (lactose). Most Americans get an uninterrupted supply of fresh milk and do not develop this problem. In yogurt, however, the lactose is already converted into lactic acid and anyone can consume it.

Why doesn't honey need to be refrigerated?

Honey is one of nature's perfect foods. What other food tastes as good, can be stored indefinitely at room temperature, and needs no refining or processing?

Bees do all the refining and processing for us. They collect the nectar with their tongues and pass it into a honey stomach where salivary enzymes convert the sucrose in the nectar into dextrose and levulose. When the bees return to the hive, they deposit the partially digested nectar into the cells of the honeycomb. "House" bees then work the nectar in their mouths to cause further chemical changes. By fanning their wings they evaporate excess water from the solution. The final product—honey—has a moisture content of about 18 percent.

One of the salivary enzymes added to the nectar by the bees is glucose oxidase. This enzyme retards the growth of bacteria during the evaporation process and thereafter should the honey's moisture content rise. (It is because of this antiseptic property of honey that it was used to dress wounds in ancient times.) If the moisture content of stored honey begins to rise, this enzyme keeps it from spoiling by converting the glucose into gluconic acid and hydrogen peroxide, both of which kill bacteria and yeasts. This is important because honey tends to absorb moisture. The baking and tobacco industries use honey to keep their products fresh and moist.

The most important reason that honey doesn't spoil, however, is due to its high acid and sugar content. Most bacteria and yeasts can't tolerate these conditions. Honey's high osmotic pressure quickly dehydrates microorganisms before they can reproduce.

Pure honey tends to crystallize over time, which raises the moisture content of the nongranulated honey. Certain yeasts can tolerate the high sugar content of honey, if the moisture content rises too high, it will begin fermentation. To return crystallized honey to a liquid state, simply heat the jar in a pan of water. To prevent granulation, store honey in a dark, dry place.

When did honey come to America?

There were no honeybees in America until around 1640, when they were introduced from Europe. By the early 1800s they had spread as far west as Texas. The movable bee hive wasn't invented until the mid-nineteenth century by an American, L. L. Langstroth. The average hive contains fifty thousand to seventy thousand bees and produces sixty to one hundred pounds of honey per year. Two thirds of this is removed from the hive; the rest is left to sustain the bee colony.

To produce one pound of honey, bees must gather four pounds of nectar from about two million flowers! One worker bee can collect about a teaspoon of nectar in its three-to-six-week lifespan. Different honey is produced depending on the kind of flowers from which the nectar is gathered. Generally, the lighter in color the honey, the milder its taste.

Each year, Florida beekeepers move their hives slowly up the East Coast, following the warm weather to pollinate the fruit orchards in bloom along the way. North Dakota and South Dakota are the top honey-producing states, respectively.

Soup to Nuts

What is the second most familiar name-brand food product in America?

Coke is number one. What is number two? Coincidentally, it's another product that comes in a red and white can—Campbell's Soup!

Eight out of every ten cans of soup sold in the United States are Campbell's. A June 1992 survey using price scanners of the top ten fastest-moving grocery products, found Campbell's Chicken Noodle Soup, Cream of Mushroom Soup, and Tomato Soup ranked third, fourth, and sixth, respectively.

Incidentally, the red and white Campbell's colors, adopted in 1898, were inspired by Cornell University's football uniforms. Two years later, Campbell's Soup won a gold medallion at the Paris Exposition. The medallion and the original colors have graced the label ever since.

What "French" soup was actually created and named in Manhattan?

What dish could be more French than vichyssoise? In 1910, chef Louis Diat celebrated the opening of the Ritz-Carlton roof garden at Forty-sixth Street and Madison Avenue with a new soup for Manhattan's socialites. It was from a French peasant recipe that his mother used to make—a traditional hot leek and potato soup cooled with rich, sweet cream. It was refined by *le maître* and named vichyssoise after the popular French watering spot at Vichy. It was served for the first time to steel magnate Charles Schwab.

Dr. John MacAdam is known for popularizing what expensive nut?

You may never have heard of him, but his name should be a give-away. Dr. MacAdam was a scientist and early promoter of the cultivation of the Queensland nut of Australia. Thanks to his efforts the nut came to be named after him—macadamia.

Macadamia nuts come from the macadamia tree (*Macadamia ternifolia*), which looks somewhat like a holly tree. The nut itself is very nutritious and, with its hull, about the size of a golf ball. The hull is easy to remove, but the shell requires a hammer or nutcracker to open. The nut resembles a hazelnut, has sweet meat, and is rich in oil. Each nut has about sixteen calories.

The macadamia nut is now grown in many areas outside of Australia, but only in Hawaii is it commercially successful. When the tree was introduced to Hawaii in the 1880s, it was primarily grown for ornamental purposes. It wasn't until the 1920s that scientists learned to remove the nuts from the shells easily, opening the way for large-scale cultivation for food. Hawaii now grows 90 percent of the world's macadamia nut supply.

Why are pistachio nuts red?

To many of us, pistachios just aren't pistachios unless they are red. Originally, Middle Eastern pistachios were coated with a red colorant to hide blemishes. As time passed, people came to expect pistachios to be red. Today, they are still colored, whether blemished or not, to meet consumer preferences. Natural-colored pistachios are also available.

Pistachio nuts are the fruit kernels of the *Pistacia vera* tree.

Their shells open naturally when they are ripe. The leading pistachio producers are Iran, Turkey, and more recently California. Pistachios are high in iron and are 54 percent oil.

Why don't you ever see cashews sold in the shell?

Most nuts—peanuts, walnuts, hazelnuts, almonds, pecans, Brazil nuts—can be bought in the shell. You will never see cashews sold this way, and for a good reason. The oil that surrounds the shell is very irritating to the skin and can cause blisters. (Cashews are in the same plant family as poison ivy.) This makes the harvesting of cashews nasty work. Trying to shell these obnoxious little nuts at home would also be a difficult task. Even roasting the shells off produces a noxious smoke. No one would bother. Hence, the packager does it for you.

Cashews come from the cashew tree (*Anacardium occidentale*), native to Brazil, which produces a double nut. The nut is found on the outside lower end of the cashew apple, a juicy fruit which is eaten locally.

Another interesting thing about cashews is that they can help prevent tooth decay. The oil in the nut is so powerful that it inhibits the growth of plaque-producing bacteria.

Are there any native American walnuts?

The black walnut (*Juglans nigra*) grows in abundance all over the eastern half of the United States. The nuts were a delicious source of food and black dye for the Native Americans and colonists. The nut is covered by a thick green husk that contains an oily black substance, and the enclosed shell is hard to get off. Today, the black walnut is highly prized by the furniture industry for its beautiful, fine-grained hardwood. The English walnut (*Juglans regia*) is the one you find in stores. When it was first introduced to England in the 1500s, it was called a "foreign," or a "wal" nut. Native to southeastern Europe and western Asia, the so-called English walnut actually does not grow very well in England. As a matter of fact, California now grows about two thirds of the world's walnut crop.

Which common "nut" has the most uncommon habit of growth?

America's favorite "nut"—the peanut—is not a nut at all, but a legume. Legumes are plants whose fruits are seed-bearing pods. A nut, by contrast, is a fruit that contains a single edible seed enclosed in a papery inner skin, surrounded by a hard shell. Examples of nuts are acorns, pecans, and hazelnuts. Some other "nuts" that aren't really nuts are Brazil nuts and almonds, which are both seeds.

Interesting, but back to peanuts. The peanut plant (*Arachis hypogaea*) is a vinelike member of the bean family. The plant's flower stalks wither and bend toward the ground after being fertilized. The developing peanut pod is pushed below the soil and matures in the ground. The plant actually plants its own seeds!

Peanuts, which are a good source of fat, protein, vitamin D, iron, and phosphorus, originated in South America and made their way to North America before Columbus arrived. It wasn't until the late nineteenth century that the peanut's value as a food crop was realized, thanks in large part to the work of Dr. George Washington Carver. He eventually came up with 325 different uses for the peanut, 118 uses for sweet potatoes, and 75 for pecans.

The United States produces over one billion pounds of peanuts a year, mostly in Georgia, Florida, and Alabama. This is only 3 percent of the world total. India and China grow over 50 percent of the world's peanuts.

Half of the American crop goes to make peanut butter. Most of the rest is used for oil and cattle feed. It takes about 550 peanuts to make a twelve-ounce jar of peanut butter. Law prohibits manufacturers from adding sugar, artificial sweeteners or preservatives, or vitamins. Very little peanut butter is consumed outside of the United States. Interestingly, folks on the East Coast prefer creamy style, while those of you on the West Coast prefer chunky.

What became of the American chestnut?

At one time, the American chestnut (*Castanea dentata*) was the dominant tree in eastern hardwood forests and a valuable source of food and timber. In fact, one in every four trees in the central Appalachian forests was a chestnut. That was before a shipment of Asian chestnut saplings arrived in Long Island around the turn of the century. These particular saplings contained the fungus *Cryphonectria parasitica*, which is the cause of chestnut blight. This disease quickly spread and killed virtually every American chestnut. No cure has ever been found and only the occasional sucker from still living roots is now seen in the East. A few remote stands, however, survive outside the trees natural range. Most were planted in the Midwest by settlers.

Consequently, our chestnuts today, which are imported from Italy, are sweet chestnuts (*Castanea sativa*). Bigger and meatier than the American chestnut, these nuts are purported to be similar to the American chestnut in taste and are popular at Thanksgiving and Christmas dinners. We import about $20 million worth of chestnuts a year—not that much, really. Two hundred years ago, the American chestnut was a staple of the Indian and colonial diet. Today, we each eat less than an ounce of sweet chestnuts a year.

Through breeding for resistance and introducing a fungus to attack the chestnut blight fungus, the American chestnut may one day return.

Why are hazelnuts also known as filberts?

Hazelnuts and filberts (as they are known in parts of the country) are the same thing! The filbert (*Corylus avellana*) is so named because it ripens in England on August 22, St. Philbert's day. The day commemorates the French saint Philbert of Burgundy.

Hazelnut flowers bloom and are pollinated in the winter, unlike those of any other nut or fruit. In the spring, the pollen germinates and grows to fertilize the ovary.

Most of our domestic filberts, or hazelnuts, are grown in the Willamette Valley in Oregon. Other major growers are Italy, Spain, and Turkey.

Junk Food

Why do we like sweets?

Why do we prefer sweet tastes to bitter ones? It's simply a matter of evolution. Most things found in the wild that taste sweet are good to eat. On the other hand, most bitter things are poisonous or just not good for you. Over the course of human history, the people who preferred sweet things tended to survive better than those who ran around eating bitter things. Thus, through natural selection, human beings have evolved into a sweet-loving species. Please pass the sugar!

What is the origin of chocolate?

It was Columbus who first brought the cacao bean to Europe, but it was Hernando Cortés, the Spanish conquistador, who realized its commercial potential when he brought it to Spain in 1519. There its secrets were kept for one hundred years.

Cortés found that the Aztecs enjoyed a drink called *chocolatl*, their word for "bitter water," which was prepared from cocoa beans. By adding vanilla, nutmeg, cinnamon, cloves, and allspice, and serving hot, the bitter drink was made more appealing to European tastes. The popularity of this new drink spread to England in the middle of the seventeenth century.

The invention of the cocoa press in Holland in 1828 improved the taste of the beverage. By squeezing out part of the cocoa butter from roasted ground beans it gave the chocolate more of the smooth texture and flavor that it has today. In 1847, an English firm combined cocoa butter with chocolate liquor (meaning liquid, not alcohol) and sugar to make eating chocolate. Milk chocolate was invented in Vevey, Switzerland, by Daniel Peter in 1876 when he combined milk solids with chocolate liquor (see pages 104–5).

The first chocolate factory in America was Baker's Chocolate, opened in Dorcester, Massachusetts, in 1765.

How is chocolate made?

Chocolate could be America's favorite flavor. We don't ever make it at home because the chocolate-making process is so involved.

Chocolate and cocoa come from the cacao tree (*Theobroma cacao*), an evergreen with large, glossy leaves that only grows in hot, rainy, tropical climates. (Cacao is unrelated to coconuts or coca, the source of cocaine.) Cacao trees, which are cultivated to a height of fifteen to twenty feet, begin bearing fruit in their fifth year. They cannot stand the hot tropical sun and are thus planted among banana and rubber trees, which provide shade, and additional income for the growers. Interestingly, the green, yellow, or red football-shaped fruit pods, which contain the cocoa beans (seeds), sprout directly from the trunk of the tree and the main branches. Like coffee, cocoa does not acquire its rich taste and aroma without a good deal of processing and roasting.

The pods are harvested by *tumbadores* (pickers) using machetes. They are then hacked open to reveal anywhere from twenty to fifty cream-colored beans. It takes about four-hundred dried beans to make one pound of chocolate. Exposure to the air turns the beans a lavender or purple color. The cocoa beans are then boxed or piled under banana leaves and allowed to ferment from three to nine days. As they ferment, they heat up and lose some of their bitterness. During this process, the sugars contained in the beans are converted to lactic and acetic acids. The heat produced during fermentation, up to 125° F, kills the germ of the bean and activates the enzymes which will form the compounds that produce the chocolate flavor when the beans are roasted.

The beans are now dried and cleaned, then roasted in large rotary cylinders. Roasting lasts from thirty minutes to two hours, at 250° F, to bring out the characteristic flavor and aroma. The beans are next cracked, dehulled and winnowed, leaving them in small pieces, or "nibs."

The nibs, which contain 53 percent cocoa butter, are then blended and ground. The frictional heat of the grinders is hot enough to liquify the cocoa butter into an oil known as chocolate liquor. When chocolate liquor is solidified, it becomes unsweetened, or bitter, chocolate.

Up to this point, the manufacture of chocolate and cocoa is the same. The process now diverges. To make cocoa powder, the chocolate liquor is pumped into gigantic hydraulic presses to remove any cocoa butter desired. (The pressed cocoa butter is collected and saved for later use in chocolate manufacture.) The "cake" that is left after removal of the cocoa butter is dried and pulverized into cocoa powder. Cocoa powder has between 10 and 24 percent cocoa butter content. Some cocoa powder is "dutched" with an alkaline solution that reduces its natural acidity and darkens it. It is called Dutch chocolate because it was invented by J. C. van Houten of Holland.

Chocolate is made by adding back cocoa butter to the bitter chocolate (chocolate liquor). The mixture is then "conched," a process that involves the mechanical kneading of the chocolate mass in huge containers. The conches, as the machines are known, are equipped with heavy rollers, which plow through the chocolate for a few hours to several days, at temperatures ranging from 130° F to 180° F. This process modifies and enhances flavor. The chocolate now goes through a tempering interval of heating, cooling, and reheating before being molded for sale.

Still want to make your own chocolate?

What is white chocolate?

It doesn't look like chocolate and it doesn't really taste like chocolate. Is it chocolate? No, technically white chocolate isn't chocolate. Here's a quick overview of the main types of chocolate:

Baking chocolate is simply pure chocolate liquor that has been molded and chilled. Also called bitter chocolate, it contains roughly 53 percent cocoa butter, the same amount present in the nibs before they are ground.

Bittersweet chocolate is semi-sweet chocolate with added sugar and cocoa butter. Also known as "dark" chocolate, it must contain at least 35 percent chocolate liquor.

Sweet chocolate is made of 15 to 35 percent chocolate liquor, with more added sugar and cocoa butter than bittersweet and other flavorings such as vanilla, vanillin, salt, oils, cinnamon, and cloves.

Milk chocolate is made of chocolate liquor, cocoa butter, milk, sugar, and flavorings. American milk chocolates all contain at least 10 percent chocolate liquor and 12 percent whole milk.

White chocolate is not real chocolate at all, because it contains no chocolate liquor. It is cocoa butter with sugar, milk, and flavorings added.

Chocolate flavored syrup is usually corn syrup and cocoa with added preservatives, emulsifiers, and flavorings.

Americans tend to prefer milk chocolate to dark chocolate, while Europeans really go for dark chocolate. Regardless of the type, the Swiss eat the most chocolate—nineteen pounds a year.

What's that whitish color that sometimes appears on chocolate?

At temperatures above 77° F, chocolate begins to melt and the cocoa butter in it begins to rise to the surface. This causes a whitish streaking to appear, which is known as a cocoa butter "bloom." Under normal conditions, this discoloration does not affect the chocolate's quality. Prolonged exposure to heat, however, can result in loss of flavor.

What best-selling candy had its origins on the battlefields of the Spanish Civil War?

On a trip to the south of Spain, Forrest E. Mars, founder of Mars, Inc., met soldiers who were eating a unique candy that melted in the mouth, but not in the hand. Chocolate pellets covered with a hard sugary coating, these candies stood up to the heat of the southern climate, while other candies could not.

Upon returning to the United States in 1939, Mars joined forces with R. Bruce Murie, son of the Hershey's Chocolate president. They called their company M&M (Mars and Murie), Ltd., and set up shop in Newark, New Jersey, in 1941. With Murie on his board, Mars was assured a steady supply of chocolate throughout the war.

The first M&M's were slightly larger than today's, and came in six colors—brown, green, orange, red, violet, and yellow. They did not have the trademark "M" on them, but they were an instant success. American GIs in particular ate them, as had the Spanish soldiers, and production remained at a maximum until 1945.

It is another MARS product that is the number-one-selling candy—Snickers. M&M's come in at number two. The other top-selling candies, in descending order, are Reese's Peanut Butter Cups, Kit Kat, Butterfinger, Nestlé's Crunch, Hershey's bars, and 3 Musketeers.

The Dutch are the world's great candy lovers. They each eat sixty-four pounds of candy a year. By comparison, we Americans eat a paltry twenty-one pounds a year.

Do the different color M&M's really taste the same?

We all seem to have our own favorite color M&M, and many of us are convinced that we can taste a difference between each color. The M&M/MARS Company assures us that this is not possible. All the colors have identical flavorings.

M&M/MARS conducts consumer preference tests to determine which color assortments satisfy the greatest number of people and create an overall pleasing effect. On average, M&M's Plain Chocolate Candies contain 30 percent browns, 20 percent yellows, 20 percent reds, 10 percent oranges, 10 percent tans, and 10 percent greens. M&M's Peanut Chocolate Candies contain a ratio of 20 percent each of brown, green, orange, red, and yellow. After recently conducting a consumer poll, the company has decided to add a new M&M color—blue.

How did Hershey Kisses get their name?

Not many American towns are named after a company, but such is the case with Hershey, Pennsylvania. Actually, it's more accurate to say that the town is named after the company founder— Milton S. Hershey.

You could call Mr. Hershey the original "Candy Man." By the age of thirty, he already had fifteen years of candy-making experience, but was financially unsuccessful. The most important thing he had learned about candy was that milk dramatically improved the taste of caramel. He sold his caramels on the streets of his hometown, Lancaster, Pennsylvania, until one day in 1886 when by chance he met an English merchant who placed a big order. From then on business boomed, and he sold out for $1 million in 1900.

He moved to Derry Church, Pennsylvania, because of its proximity to dairy farms, and opened a chocolate factory. The first Hershey's Milk Chocolate bars rolled off the production line in 1905. Hershey's Kisses, named for the puckering sound they make when extruded from the candy-making machine, followed in 1907.

Hershey became fabulously successful and was very generous. He gave all his stock in the company to the Milton Hershey School in 1918. He built a local water and electric company, stores, homes, a bank, and a trolley system.

Today, Hershey is the largest user of almonds in the country and uses as much milk a day as does the city of Philadelphia.

Who was Reese?

Reese's is now owned by Hershey. An ex-employee of Hershey, Harry "H. B." Reese, who managed one of Hershey's dairy farms in 1917, invented Reese's Peanut Butter Cups. He gave up dairy farming to follow in Milton Hershey's footsteps. He tried numerous candies, but it wasn't until he mixed creamy peanut butter and milk chocolate that he came up with a winner in 1923. He bought his chocolate from his ex-employer. After Reese's death, Reese's was bought out by Hershey.

What candy once helped support the John Birch Society?

Robert Welch, a Cambridge, Massachusetts, candy vendor, created the Sugar Daddy candy in 1925. He was also the founder of the John Birch Society.

The Sugar Daddy was originally called the Papa Sucker, because it was the "papa," or longest-lasting, of all lollipops. It wasn't really a lollipop, though, but a hunk of caramel on a stick. Welch named it the Sugar Daddy in 1932, after a popular slang term of the time. Robert Welch and his brother James went on to create other successful candies, such as Sugar Babies, Pom Poms, and Welch's Junior Mints. Nabisco bought out the James O. Welch Company in 1963.

The money Welch made in his business helped him found the ultraconservative John Birch Society in 1958, after he had left the candy company. So, if you bought any of Robert Welch's candies in the 1950s, you indirectly helped fund his fight against Communism and the fluoridation of water.

What classic American dessert is made from animal skin and bones?

Jell-O gelatin is basically purified glue. They are both made from the same stuff—boiled animal hooves, bones, and hides. Gelatin is just a little more refined.

Since the seventeenth century, people have been boiling down calves hooves to make jelly. After boiling, the liquid was strained, allowed to sit for a day, skimmed of fat, sweetened, flavored, and set in molds. Powdered gelatin had been around since the 1840s, but it wasn't until Charles B. Knox of Johnston, New York, packaged it in easy-to-use form in the 1890s that gelatin desserts started to catch on.

The first patent on a gelatin dessert was granted to Peter Cooper, the Tom Thumb locomotive inventor, in 1865. Cooper, however, was too busy with locomotives to make a real go of gelatin. It was a carpenter named Pearl B. Wait of LeRoy, New York, who began selling a flavored gelatin dessert called Jell-O in 1897. The name "Jell" came from Wait's wife, who either thought that gelatin was spelled with a *j* or was referring to the fact that gelatin had to "jell" before being eaten. Either way, the "O" was added because it was a popular word ending of the time. Jell-O sales were less than spectacular, and Wait sold his business to another local resident named Orator Woodward in 1899.

Woodward didn't fare so well at first either. It wasn't until an ad ran in the *Ladies Home Journal* that Jell-O sales started to take off. He had sales of $1 million by 1906. The Jell-O Company merged with the Postum Cereal Company in 1925. It would later become General Foods.

Jell-O is about 85 percent sugar, 10 percent gelatin, and 5 percent artificial flavors. This does nothing to help sales among today's health-conscious consumers. Jell-O sales increased dramatically between 1936 and 1968. Then sales fell sharply until 1990, when Jell-O introduced consumers to "Jigglers," which were made with one-third less water and resulted in a harder, candylike substance that could be cut into shapes with a cookie cutter. Kids loved them and sales rebounded.

Why do Wint-O-Green Life Savers spark when you bite them?

If you clench a Wint-O-Green Life Saver between your front teeth and bite down hard with your lips apart, in the dark you should see a flash of eerie blue-green light when the candy cracks. Spooky, but easily explainable.

When sugar crystals are ripped apart, opposite electric charges are created on either side of the break, causing electrons to leap across the crack in the candy. These electrons excite the nitrogen in the air, causing it to emit blue-green flashes akin to lightning.

What makes Wint-O-Green candy different from other hard sugar candies is the wintergreen it contains. Wintergreen contains fluorescent methyl salicylate, which absorbs ultraviolet light and converts it into visible light.

Unfortunately, while the taste of Wint-O-Green Life Savers is reliable, the candy's sparking ability is not. Any background light can hamper the effect, as can humidity.

How did jujubes get their name?

These jellylike candies once contained the juice of a jujube (*Ziziphus jujuba*), a shrubby tree found in India and China. The fruits are green when young and rusty-red at maturity. The dried jujube is sweet and spongy and is often boiled in honey or candied. The trees are now primarily grown in California.

Today, jujube candies are made of gum arabic and flavorings.

Who was Baby Ruth?

Baby Ruth, the delicious chocolate-covered peanut and caramel candy bar, was first created in 1920 by a young Chicago entrepreneur named Otto Schnering. Working in a small rented room above a plumber's shop, he founded what was to become the Curtiss Candy Company and began developing one kind of candy after another. For several years he struggled to survive, until one day he hit upon the log-shaped Baby Ruth bar.

Curtiss had hit the jackpot. An easily identifiable name was needed for the new candy bar. At the time, Babe Ruth was about the biggest star in the country and the company wanted to use his name. However, the two sides failed to reach a financial agreement. In a stroke of sneaky marketing genius, Curtiss named the candy Baby Ruth after the daughter of former President Grover Cleveland, who had been the darling of the press many years before. The rest, as they say, is history.

Another popular candy named for a little girl is the Tootsie Roll. Leo Hirschfield, a New York candy store owner, created the Tootsie Roll in 1896 and named it after his daughter. The lollipop was also first created commercially around the turn of the century. It was named for a winning racehorse of the time.

What does "Pez" mean?

Pez candies originated in Vienna, Austria, in 1927. The candies, shaped like little bars of soap, were first manufactured in one flavor—peppermint. The name "Pez" derives from a contraction of the German word for peppermint, *pfefferminze*. Pez, which originally was marketed as an adult confection, first appeared in the United States in 1950 and came in a headless dispenser.

In 1952, the Pez Candy Company decided to make assorted fruit flavors and put cartoon heads on the dispensers. Sales increased dramatically. The first Pez-head character was Popeye. Since Popeye, there have been almost 250 different Pez-heads, including Dumbo, Wonder Woman, the Green Hornet, Santa Claus, Tweetie Bird, and assorted animals and fruits. The multitude of different flavors sold has covered everything from anise to eucalyptus.

Pez candies are still big in the United States, selling over one million a year. There are actually Pez fanatics who buy and sell various Pez characters and flavors and hold an annual Pez convention.

What is the world's largest food company?

It's not an American company, but a Swiss one—Nestlé.

Nestlé S.A. is the Swiss parent company of Nestlé Enterprises, Inc., which is comprised of thirteen affiliated companies, one of those being the familiar Nestlé Foods Corporation. The Nestleé organization ranks number one in international food sales.

Switzerland is famous for its chocolatiers and chemists. One of each came into play in the creation of the world's first milk chocolate in 1877. Henri Nestlé, a German chemist living in Switzerland, formulated a unique milk food for infants unable to take mother's milk. In 1866, he established a company to sell his formula. He next began producing sweetened condensed milk. In 1875, Nestlé's neighbor, chocolate manufacturer Daniel Peter, combined some sweetened condensed milk with chocolate, creating the world's first milk chocolate.

A string of new products followed—Nestlé Hot Cocoa Mix in 1935; Nestlé Crunch in 1938; Nestlé Chocolate Morsels and Nescafé Instant Coffee in 1939; Nestlé Quik in 1954; and $100,000 Bar and Taster's Choice Freeze Dried Coffee in 1966. Nestlé now also owns Chunky, Bit-O-Honey, Oh! Henry, Goobers, Sno-Caps, Baby Ruth, Butterfingers, Libby's, Perrier, Hills Bros. Coffee, Coffee-Mate, Contadina, Carnation, Stouffer's, and Beringer wines.

The familiar Nestlé's trademark—a bird's nest—is based on Henri Nestlé's family coat of arms. According to the Neslté Foods Corporation, this symbol was chosen because it evoked "security, maternity and affection, nature and nourishment, family and tradition."

Why is bubble gum pink?

This is one of those facts about food that we all take for granted. Why pink? After all, bubble gum could really be any color of the rainbow.

Before August 1928, lots of inventors had experimented with bubble gums, but no one could come up with one that didn't make wet, flimsy bubbles. That's when a man named Walter Diemer, a gum manufacturer's cost accountant, created a new kind of bubble gum. It blew firm, dry bubbles that peeled easily off the skin after they popped.

His first batch of gum was colorless. To the second batch he added some pink coloring. Why? Because it was the only color he had on hand. When the first bubble gum—Double Bubble—was marketed in 1928, the lucky pink color was kept. And so it has been ever since.

What is the origin of chewing gum?

The urge to chew is believed to be instinctive. Prehistoric man chewed on berries, bark, and blades of grass to pass the time. Throughout recorded history, three thickened resins (the latex of trees) have been the popular gums of choice—mastiche, spruce, and chicle.

The women in ancient Greece used to chew a mastic gum, or "mastiche," to freshen their breath and clean their teeth. Mastiche (pronounced "mas-tee-ka") comes from the bark of the shrublike mastic tree (*Pistacia lentiscus*), which grows in the northeastern Mediterranean regions of Turkey and Greece.

Native Americans in New England used to chew gum from the red spruce (*Picea rubens*), and black spruce (*Picea manana*). When European settlers arrived in North America they adopted the habit. Lumps of it were chewed until early in the nineteenth century, when it was slowly replaced by paraffin gum. Paraffin, is used today for novelty chewing products, such as those little soda-bottle-shaped wax candies that are filled with syrup.

The other great chewers of the past were the Mayans of the Yucatán peninsula. They cut the bark of the sapodilla tree (*Manilkara zapsta*), and collected the milk-white latex resin that ran out of the wounds. By boiling the resin, they obtained a silky smooth, tasteless gum that became known as chicle. The word "chicle" derives from the name of a tribe known as the Chichimee, and inspired the name of one of our favorite gums—Chiclets. The natives who collected the resin from the trees were called *chicleros*.

What famous Mexican general introduced modern chewing gum to America?

The story of modern chewing gum begins in Staten Island, New York. Antonio López de Santa Anna, the Mexican general most famous for slaughtering the Texans in the Alamo, in 1836, came to share rooms with an American inventor named Thomas Adams. The two had become acquainted during the 1860s. When Santa Anna was exiled from Mexico, he moved in with Adams at his Staten Island home.

At the time, Adams was busy trying to invent a less expensive, more durable substitute for the rubber that was used on carriage tires. Santa Anna, hoping to earn capital to finance a triumphant return to Mexico, suggested Adams experiment with the resin of the sapodilla tree, which was popular in his native country. Through friends in Mexico, he arranged to have one ton of chicle sent to Adams. Adams and his son, Thomas Jr., spent about a year trying to blend chicle with rubber to create a new super-rubber, but their experiments all ended in failure. Disheartened, Thomas Sr. was about to dispose of his remaining chicle when, purely by chance, he had a great inspiration.

While he was waiting to make a purchase in a New York drugstore, at the corner of Chambers Street and Broadway, in walked a little girl to buy a penny's worth of chewing gum. It occurred to Adams that his chicle, which he and his son had chewed on during their experiments, might be made into chewing gum to salvage the money he paid for it. He soaked chicle in hot water until it had the consistency of putty. The chicle changed in color from brown-black to grayish-white. With the help of his son, he wrapped small pieces of the flavorless chicle in colored tissue paper and placed them in boxes. On each box was a picture of New York City Hall and the name "Adams New York No. 1." Modern chewing gum was born!

What is chewing gum made of?

Gum brands, like Wrigley's, are made with four basic ingredients—chewing gum base, sweeteners, softeners, and flavorings. The various chewing gum ingredients are discussed individually below.

Gum base: Gum base makes the gum smooth, soft, and chewy. Historically, gum bases have been made from natural resins and latex, such as chicle, jelutong, and sorva. These natural ingredients have become rather scarce, but some brands still use resins naturally derived from pine trees in the southern United States. New synthetic gum base materials that allow for long-lasting flavor, improved texture, and reduced tackiness have been used increasingly in recent years. These synthetics must meet the strict standards of the United States Food and Drug Administration because even though we don't swallow it, chewing gum is classified as a food product.

Sweeteners: Powdered cane and beet sugar, as well as corn

syrup, is used to sweeten gums. The powdered sugar also helps provide an appealing texture and is used to coat the gum to prevent it from sticking to the wrapper. The corn syrup not only sweetens the gum, but also helps keep it fresh and pliable. Aspartame (formed from aspartic acid and phenylalanine), and sorbitol and mannitol (derived from corn) are used in sugar-free gums.

Softeners: Glycerin and other vegetable oils act as softeners. They help not only to blend the ingredients into the gum base, but also to keep the gum soft and pliable by maintaining the proper moisture content.

Flavorings: The most popular gum flavorings in the United States are derived from plants of the mint family (spearmint and peppermint). Mint oils are extracted from the plants through a distillation process. Wrigley's, the largest manufacturer of gum, needs over fifty-three square miles of farmland to supply its annual mint oil demands. Most of the mint is grown in Idaho, Indiana, Oregon, Washington, and Wisconsin. The flavorings for other gums are derived from spice and fruit sources.

How much gum do Americans chew?

Today in the United States there are about twenty chewing gum manufacturers. Wrigley Company is the largest. Domestic retail sales of chewing gum are over $2 billion. On average, each American chomps on over three hundred sticks of gum a year. Wrigley's market share is almost half of chewing gum sales.

So who is chewing all this gum? It seems that folks in the Southeast have a real sweet tooth. More gum, as well as other sweets, is sold in the Southeast than in any other part of the country.

What favorite campfire snack was originally made from the roots of a marsh plant?

The roots of the European marsh plant, marsh mallow (*Althaeo officinalis*), were the original source of the candy. Today, marshmallows are made from sugar, starch, corn syrup, and gelatin or stiffly beaten egg whites.

What snack food company is also the world's largest user of toys?

Cracker Jack began when a German immigrant, F. W. Rueckheim, sold popcorn at a corner stand in Chicago, just after the great fire of 1871. Business expanded as he added specialty flavors. Just before the 1893 World's Columbian Exposition in Chicago, he created the now famous popcorn, peanut, and molasses confection. Introduced at the fair, it was a huge success and sales boomed.

It wasn't called by its present name until 1896, when a salesman munching on the snack exclaimed, "That's a cracker jack!" F. W. seized on this popular expression of the time and immortalized it forever in the English language.

In 1899, Cracker Jack was first marketed in handy-sized boxes, with wax paper lining. The 1908 song "Take Me Out to the Ball Game" helped cement the long-standing association between Cracker Jack and baseball. The words "Buy me some peanuts and Cracker Jack" are still heard echoing throughout ballparks across the land.

The familiar patriotic red, white, and blue stripes were added to the box during World War I. The saluting sailor boy logo was also introduced during the war. Known as Sailor Jack, he was modeled after F. W.'s grandson Robert, who died of pneumonia shortly after the character first appeared on packages in 1918. Sailor Jack and his dog, Bingo, still smile at us from every box of Cracker Jack.

It is the toy prize inside each box that makes Cracker Jack most beloved to children. First introduced in 1912, over seventeen billion Cracker Jack toys have been given out so far. Twenty-five million toys of a particular series are purchased. The toys are rotated and changed each year to provide variety. By 1948, the company was using twenty million toys a month. All of Cracker Jack's prizes are produced in the United States and are child safe. Some old prizes are collectors' items worth as much as seven thousand dollars!

Cracker Jack was purchased by Borden, Inc., in 1964. By 1968, Cracker Jack was the fastest-moving item in the confectionery section of all major grocery chains, and is still popular today.

Who invented potato chips?

It was a Native American who invented potato chips. As the story goes, an Adirondack Indian, George Crum, was a cook at the Moon Lake Lodge resort in Sarasota Springs, New York, in 1853. One day a particularly fussy guest who had just returned from Paris sent back an order of fried potatoes because they were not "properly thin" fried potatoes. Crum prepared a thinner batch, which was also sent back. Mr. Crum took exception to this criticism of his cooking and promptly whittled a potato into transparently thin slices, which he deep fried and salted. He sent the ridiculously thin potato slices back to the persnickety customer. Instead of being insulted by the super-thin "chips," the customer loved them. Since Saratoga Springs was the "in" resort for the rich and famous of that time, the popularity of "Crum's Saratoga Chips" soon spread from coast to coast.

Today, the potato chip is the number-one selling salty snack in the United States. We each eat some 6.1 pounds a year!

Why are some potato chips green?

Opening a bag of fresh, crunchy potato chips is a wonderful thing. Golden crispy potato chips are a joy to eat. Every once in a while though, you come across one of those "mutant" green chips. Most of us make a face and toss it back in the bag for some other unsuspecting snacker. Where do these alien chips come from?

Green potato chips are the result of something called sunscald. Potatoes are supposed to grow under the ground. Once in a while, however, part of the tuber might poke above the soil and be exposed to the sun. Being a chlorophyll-containing plant, the potato begins to turn green below the spots that were in the sun. While chlorophyll isn't bad for you, the solanine (see page 41) produced may not be that great for you. There are no studies of how many green chips it would take to make you ill, but you may as well play it safe and toss them back in the bag anyway.

Sometimes you'll find another kind of strange chip in the bag—the dark brown one. This chip is harmless. They are simply from potatoes that stayed in storage too long and built up high levels of sugar. The excess sugar turns brown during cooking.

What company makes eight out of the top ten best-selling snack chips?

Dallas-based Frito-Lay, Inc., is the king of the chip world. With eight out of the top ten best-selling snack chips, it doesn't have much competition. In fact, it's Doritos Brand Tortilla Chips are the second best-selling dry goods item overall in grocery stores.

The Frito-Lay empire began with Fritos Brand Corn Chips. A San Antonio, Texas, native, Elmer Doolin, discovered them in a local diner in 1932. He bought the recipe for a hundred dollars.

At the same time, Herman W. Lay was starting an Atlanta, Georgia, potato chip business—H. W. Lay and Company. After several years of close affiliation, the two companies joined to form Frito-Lay and Company in 1961. PepsiCo acquired the snack food giant in 1965.

Today, Frito-Lay uses 1.6 billion pounds of potatoes and 600 million pounds of corn a year.

Who eats the most pretzels?

In recent years, pretzels have been rediscovered by health-conscious consumers. Baked pretzels are low in fat. A one-ounce serving contains about one gram of fat and 110 calories. An equal serving of potato chips has ten grams of fat and 154 calories.

Pretzels were first baked by monks in southern France and northern Italy from leftover bread dough. They were twisted into the unique pretzel shape to represent the arms being folded in prayer. The monks used the pretzels as rewards for children who had learned their prayers. In fact, the word "pretzel" is from the Latin *pretiola*, meaning "little award." As the snack became popular in Austria and Germany, *pretiola* evolved into *bretzel*. The Austrians and Germans brought the pretzel to America when they immigrated. Julius Sturgis opened the first American commercial pretzel bakery in Lititz, Pennsylvania, in 1861.

Special "pretzel salt" is mined on the Gulf of Mexico. It has large, flat, regular crystals that are perfectly suited for coating pretzels.

The pretzel-eating capital today is not far from that first American pretzel bakery. Philadelphia is considered the "Super Pretzel Heartland." Each Philadelphian eats about three pounds of pretzels a year! Currently, 60 percent of U.S. pretzel sales are in the Northeast and North Central regions.

Who invented Twinkies?

Twinkies were introduced to the world in 1930 and quickly became a best-selling product. Jimmy Dewar, a Chicago area manager for Continental Bakeries, saw the need for a new low-priced snack cake during the Depression era. His company's shortcake pans were only used about six weeks of the year, during strawberry season. The rest of the year they sat idle. Dewar's idea was to inject the shortcakes with a filling and sell them throughout the year. They were sold two to a nickel pack.

Reportedly, during a business trip to St. Louis, Dewar saw a billboard advertising a brand of shoes called Twinkle Toe Shoes, and from this the name Twinkies evolved.

Dewar claimed to have eaten two Twinkies a day since he first created them. He lived to be eighty-eight years old. So much for junk food being bad for you!

Where did pizza originate?

Pizza is now the second most popular fast food in America. We all know that pizza is Italian, but, it originated in Greece. The Greeks came up with the idea of the edible plate, which is really what a pizza is—a big, delicious plate with many kinds of food served on it. The Greeks made a bread trencher (see page 218) with a rim around it to hold the food toppings. They took this idea with them to southern Italy, where it caught on.

In northern Italy, the Etruscans would bake a gruel of grains into a flat "bread" on the stones beneath the ashes of the fireplace. They seasoned these cakes with spices and oils. The Romans took a liking to this creation and dubbed it *focaccia*, or "bread from the floor of the fireplace." (Focaccias are still popular today.)

The pizza we now know, resembles both of these early breads. The word "pizza" comes from the Latin *picea,* meaning "the black ashes from the floor of the fireplace."

It was during the sixteenth century, following the discovery of the tomato in the New World, the Italians began adding tomato sauce to these edible plates, creating one of our favorite fast foods.

Sugar and Spice

Why doesn't pound cake weigh a pound?

Traditionally, pound cake was made with one pound of flour, one pound of sugar, and one pound of butter. Hence its name!

The same logic is true of cupcakes. They are so named because the original recipe called for one cup of each ingredient. And you thought it was because they are baked in those little paper cups!

Why do doughnuts have holes?

There are several stories about who first put the hole in doughnuts. One commonly accepted theory is that they originated in Rockport, Maine, in 1847. Supposedly, a local boy complained to his mother that her doughnuts were too greasy and had her cut out the center. Another story credits an unknown sea captain, who had his cook bake doughnuts with holes so that he could slip them over the handles of the ship wheel and thus keep both hands free in rough seas.

Prior to this, doughnuts were solid, rather oily, cakes. In fact, the Dutch first brought the doughnut to America in their colony at New Amsterdam. They were called, appropriately enough, *oylkoeks* or oil cakes.

Regardless of the inventor, there is no doubt that doughnuts with holes were popularized by the Salvation Army during World War I, when they were served to American troops in France. Apparently, the GIs liked them because they could carry several on their gun barrels and keep their hands free.

What is the world's best-selling cookie?

Chips Ahoy! and Fig Newtons are both big sellers, but the most widely loved cookie is the Oreo. Introduced in 1912 by the National Biscuit Company (Nabisco), the Oreo was first known as the Oreo Biscuit. It became the Oreo Sandwich in 1921, the Oreo Creme Sandwich in 1948, and the Oreo Chocolate Sandwich Cookie in 1974.

No one knows for sure how the name Oreo came into being. One popular theory is that the name is derived from the French word for gold, *or*. The original package labeling had gold scrollwork on a pale green background, while the name Oreo was printed in gold. The dark brown sandwich cookies are still imprinted with the original corporate symbol of the National Biscuit Company—an oval surmounted by a cross with two horizontal lines. Nabisco's first chairman, Adolphus Green, happened upon the symbol one night while flipping through an old book of Italian printer's symbols. It is supposed to represent the triumph of good over evil.

The Oreo has been very good to Nabisco, becoming the best-selling cookie in the world today. Over 200 billion have been sold to date. If stacked one on top of the other, they would reach all the way to the moon and back three times over!

Can you name the seventeen different animals found in Animal Cracker boxes?

Barnum's Animal Crackers are based on a late-nineteenth-century English design. The great showman, P. T. Barnum was used to promote the product when it debuted in the United States in 1902. The small rectangular box, picturing a circus cage filled with wild animals, was very appealing to children, as was the string handle. The short string was not meant to be used for carrying around the box, as you know if you ever tried to pick one up. Originally, parents hung Animal Crackers boxes from Christmas trees as ornamental presents.

We all enjoyed Animal Crackers as kids, and even as adults, but how many of us can name all the various animal characters? There are seventeen in all—a bear (sitting and standing), a bison, a camel, a cougar, an elephant, a giraffe, a gorilla, a hippopotamus, a hyena, a kangaroo, a lion, a monkey, a rhinoceros, a seal, a sheep, a tiger, and a zebra.

Who invented fortune cookies?

You may have thought that fortune cookies were as old as the Great Wall of China and as Chinese as Confucius. Actually, fortune cookies were created in 1916 by Los Angeles noodle manufacturer David Jung. He drew his inspiration from ancient Chinese rebels who used to exchange secret messages inside buns. Jung's messages were pseudo-Confucian in nature. As time went by, the adages became more whimsical and funny.

For years, the Chinese spurned the fortune cookie. Today, however, they are being introduced to mainland China with sayings printed in Chinese and English.

Who was Newton and why is there a cookie named after him?

No, they weren't named for Sir Isaac Newton, or anyone else named Newton for that matter. They were named after the city of Newton, Massachusetts. Today's third best-selling cookie was actually created in nearby Cambridgeport, in 1895. But the name Fig Cambridgeport would have been a mouthful in itself, so the inventors opted for Fig Newton.

Why are chocolate chip cookies known as "Toll House" cookies?

As with every good thing that we take for granted today, someone had to invent chocolate chip cookies. You might have thought that chocolate chip cookies have been around for quite a while. Not so. They were first created by Ruth Wakefield in 1930.

Wakefield and her husband owned an historic inn outside of Whitman, Massachusetts. The inn was known as the Toll House because it sat directly across from the tollgate of the Old Boston–New Bedford Turnpike. One day while baking butter drop cookies, Ruth found that she was out of nuts and instead broke up a Nestlé Semi-Sweet Chocolate Bar and added the pieces. It was a beautiful marriage! Instead of melting into the cookie dough as she had expected and forming chocolate cookies, the bits of chocolate had only softened, resulting in a delightful creamy texture.

She called her creation Chocolate Crispies, and it was a big hit at the inn. When a Boston newspaper ran her recipe, it sparked a huge increase in the Nestlé bar's sales in New England.

Nestlé, seeing a good thing, agreed to print Ruth's recipe on the wrapper of the chocolate bar and called the treats Toll House Cookies. In 1939, Nestlé introduced chocolate morsels to save consumers the trouble of chopping up chocolate bars.

What are the two main sources of table sugar?

Sugar cane (*Saccharum officinarum*) is native to Southeast Asia and was first brought to Europe by the Arabs in the eighth century. It thrives in moist tropical climates that have uniform annual rainfalls of around eighty inches and an average temperature of 75°F. Sugar was a food of the rich until Columbus brought it to the Caribbean, where it flourished. In the late eighteenth century, sugar had become affordable to the common man.

Sugar cane must be refined to remove the sucrose from its tissues. A reedy plant, sugar cane contains about 15 percent sugar by weight. When the plant reaches six to ten feet it is cut and stripped of its leaves. At the refinery, its juice is extracted by press-ing or diffusion. The juice is boiled several times, purified with lime water, and centrifuged to produce sugar crystals and molasses.

The leading growers of sugar cane are Brazil, Cuba, the Dominican Republic, Hawaii, Puerto Rico, and tropical Africa.

The other major source of sugar is the sugar beet. It was first grown on a large scale by Napoleon and allowed temperate coun-tries like France to produce their own sugar. The sugar beet (*Beta vulgaris*) is a variety of the common garden beet. It was not grown for its high sugar content until a British blockade of France in 1810 forced Napoleon to develop the sugar beet industry to meet France's sugar needs.

Refining sugar beets involves cutting them up, diffusing them in hot water, and evaporating the water to yield a thick syrup. Cen-trifuging the syrup separates the sugar from the molasses. Beet sugar must be further refined to become palatable. The former Soviet Union, long isolated from the cane sugar market, is a big grower of sugar beets and is also the world's largest producer of sugar.

What is table sugar?

There are several kinds of sugars used in the kitchen, the most common being table sugar. Granulated table sugar is almost pure (99.9 percent) sucrose derived from sugar cane and sugar beets. Sucrose is made of two simple sugars—fructose and glucose. In America, we prefer sugar cane for home cooking. Sugar beets are usually saved for commercial uses. Despite its recent decline in favor by some people, sugar is one of the most important foods in cooking and in nutritional value. Sugar cane produces more calories per acre than any other crop.

Who uses the most sugar in America? The Coca-Cola Com-pany. We Americans consume 128 pounds of sugar a year in one form or another.

What is brown sugar?

Brown sugar is simply a mixture of granulated sugar and molasses. The darker the sugar, the more molasses it contains and the stronger it tastes.

What are the three kinds of molasses?

Light molasses is a by-product of the first boiling of sugar cane juice. It can be used to top pancakes and hot cereals.

Dark molasses is from the second boiling of sugar cane juice. It is used to flavor and darken dishes and to lengthen the keeping time of breads and other baked goods.

Blackstrap molasses is from the third boil. It has a high mineral content and can be found in health food stores and is also used in cattle feed.

What Is NutraSweet?

More than 200 million people look for the familiar red and white NutraSweet swirl when purchasing any of the hundreds of foods and drinks that now contain it. But what is NutraSweet?

NutraSweet is a brand name for the sweetener aspartame, which along with saccharin is the most successful artificial sweetener. Powdered NutraSweet is sold under the name Equal, while powdered saccharin is marketed as Sweet 'N Low.

Saccharin, a petroleum derivative that is three-hundred times sweeter than sugar, was accidentally discovered in 1879 by a scientist, Constantine Fahlberg, at Johns Hopkins University. (For you chemists out there, its formula is 2,3 dihydro-3-oxobenziososulfonazle.)

In the early 1900s the government restricted its use and more or less considered it to be an adulterant. Sugar shortages during the two world wars eased restrictions, however, and saccharin was used in more and more foods. By the 1970s numerous studies proved that saccharin can cause cancer in very large quantities. This led to the warning labels found on Sweet 'N Low today.

Aspartame, developed by G. D. Searle and Company in 1965, is 180 times sweeter than sugar. Aspartame isn't technically an artificial sweetener, since it is a combination of two naturally occuring amino acids. Searle obtained FDA approval to market it in 1974; however, legal challenges limited its use to a table sweetener until 1981, when it was approved for use in dry foods. The big boost for aspartame came in 1983, when the FDA allowed it to be used in carbonated beverages. Seventy percent of all NutraSweet used today is found in soft drinks, and the NutraSweet Company, owned by Monsanto, makes over $800 million a year.

These sugar substitutes taste so sweet because they fit specialized sweetness receptor sites on the tongue, as a key fits a lock. They do a good job of sweetening, but to the discerning palate, they in no way equal the appealing sweetness of sugar, and they leave an unpleasant aftertaste. NutraSweet also breaks down when heated, so it can't be used in cooking.

What's so good about NutraSweet then? It does not promote tooth decay, and it contains only four calories per every two teaspoons of sugar sweetness it provides.

One more thing: Cans of soft drinks containing NutraSweet float. Cans of regular soda don't. So on your next whitewater rafting trip, you might want to bring along Diet Coke!

What breakfast syrup honors one of America's greatest presidents?

American table syrups of the 1880s were made from corn syrup and molasses. The local grocer ladled the syrup out of big wooden barrels. Maple syrup, which had been used by Native Americans for centuries, was too expensive and hard to obtain. P. J. Towle, a Minnesota grocer who didn't like the way table syrups of the day were made or handled, decided to blend and pack his own.

Towle knew that the consumer would prefer the taste of maple syrup. He was determined to make it available to the general public. So in 1887, he came up with a formula that blended the best Vermont and Canadian maple sugar with sugar cane syrup. He sold it in small, individually sealed containers to ensure its purity.

In honor of his boyhood hero, Abraham Lincoln, who was born in a log cabin, he named his syrup Log Cabin Syrup and packaged it in a tin container shaped like a log cabin. His flair for marketing paid off, and soon Log Cabin Syrup was on breakfast tables across the country.

The Towle Syrup Company joined General Foods in 1927. The company moved from St. Paul, Minnesota, to Hoboken,

New Jersey, two years later. The only change in the product came in World War II, when a scarcity of tin resulted in Log Cabin Syrup being sold in glass bottles. But the Log Cabin logo has remained.

What is the difference between an herb and a spice?

There is no hard and fast definition of either. The following are the general guidelines, however, used to distinguish between the two:

Herbs are the aromatic leaves of plants and come primarily from temperate regions of the world.

Spices consist of the seeds, buds, fruit or flower parts, and bark or roots of aromatic *and* pungent plants, usually from tropical regions.

What are the only three spices native to the Americas?

The three native spices are chili peppers, vanilla, and allspice. Of the three, allspice has remained a New World plant. For some reason, it can't be grown commercially outside the Caribbean or Central and South America.

Allspice isn't a blend of several spices. The evergreen pimento tree (*Pimenta officinalis*) produces the peppercornlike allspice berry, named so because it tastes like a combination of cloves, cinnamon, and nutmeg. The pimento tree has nothing in common with the sweet pepper pimiento that is often used to stuff green olives.

Jamaica is the leading allspice producer. Once it has taken root, the pimento tree lives up to one hundred years and needs little attention.

What seed spice is illegal to grow in the United States?

Poppy seeds come from the Middle Eastern opium poppy (*Papaver somniferum*), which is illegal to grow in the United States. The poppy's narcotic alkaloids are found only in the milky sap of the unripened fruit capsules before the seeds develop. Once the capsules and seeds ripen, the narcotic effects disappear, and the seeds can be imported into this country. While the seeds have no narcotic effect, they do, however, contain trace amounts of morphine, which can show up on routine drug tests. So take it easy on the poppy seed bagels before the next company physical.

What common household spice is also a powerful hallucinogen?

When not on eggnog or in pies and cakes, nutmeg can be a hallucinogenic drug. It contains myristin, which has properties similar to mescaline. If taken in large quantities, it produces hallucinations and a feeling of euphoria. Such large quantities of nutmeg, however, tend to make one nauseated and induce vomiting. Don't worry, though. In culinary portions, nutmeg has no adverse effects.

What is the most expensive spice in the world?

Since prehistoric times, saffron has been as precious as gold. Native to Greece and Asia Minor, this spice is the threadlike stigma of a violet-colored crocus (*Crocus sativus*). The Phoenicians are said to have taken it to Spain in the tenth century, where it is grown extensively now.

Saffron is so rare and precious because the crocus blooms for only two weeks each autumn. Each flower has only three stigmas, which have to be picked by hand at dawn before the sun gets too hot and the flowers wilt. The stigmas are then dried and lose 80 percent of their weight in the process, which intensifies their flavor. It takes 225,000 individual stigmas to yield one pound of saffron!

Since saffron is so expensive, powdered saffron is often adulterated. This practice is nothing new. Merchants caught adulterating saffron in the Middle Ages were burned at the stake. To be safe, purchase only saffron strands, which are bright orange, not yellow. Saffron has a strong perfume and a bitter, honeylike taste. Strands should be soaked in a cup of warm water to bring out their flavored aroma, and then used toward the end of the cooking process. A single pinch is enough to color or season most dishes.

The second most expensive spice is cardamom.

Did you ever eat tree bark?

If you've ever had cinnamon, you've eaten bark. Cinnamon (*Cinnamomum verum*), native to Sri Lanka, is the world's most important baking spice. The cinnamon plant is a tree in the laurel family. When the trees are about six years old, branches at least one inch thick are cut from the tree and the outer bark stripped away. Cinnamon comes from the yellow inner bark next to the wood. When removed from the branch, it is allowed to dry for several hours, at which time it turns pale brown and curls up into the familiar cinnamon "quills."

Another kind of cinnamon, known as poor man's cinnamon, is cassia. It comes from a similar tree (*Cinnamomum cassia*), which was developed in China from the Sri Lankan type. It has thicker, darker bark and is dried in chips.

What spice is the dried bud of a tree?

Cloves are the dried buds of a tropical evergreen tree, *Eugenia caryophyllus*. They look like little nails, which is how they got their name. The French word for "nail" is *clou*. Marco Polo brought cloves back from China. They came from Indonesia and were the object of a trade war between the Portuguese and Dutch.

The caper also is a bud, the flower bud of the caper bush (*Capparis spinosa*). The small, heart-shaped buds must be picked at dawn, before the tuliplike caper flowers, which close tight at night, can reopen. They grow wild in the Mediterranean basin.

What two spices come from the same plant?

Mace and nutmeg are unique in that they come from the fruit of the same plant—*Myristica fragrans*. Mace is the lacy covering of the nutmeg. Orange in color, mace has a sweet, warm, spicy flavor. Nutmeg is the seed of the fruit. Used since the twelfth century, it comes from Indonesia. Nutmeg was so popular during the seventeenth and eighteenth centuries that many English gentry carried their own silver nutmeg graters with them whenever they traveled.

What spice is the fruit of a Mexican orchid?

Many people mistakenly believe that vanilla is native to Madagascar. Although plenty of it is grown there now, the plant is actually native to Mexico. Its name derives from the Spanish word for small sword, which its pods somewhat resemble. Vanilla beans come from the vinelike vanilla plant (*Vanilla planifolia, fragrans*), a rare and beautiful species of pale yellow orchid. The vanilla orchid is an epiphyte, obtaining its food and water from the air while anchored to another plant.

The pods, which resemble green beans, are picked while still green, and initially have no special flavor or aroma. A complex six-month curing process causes the pods to turn dark brown and a crystalline coating to appear. This is a substance called vanillin, which is the essence of vanilla's flavor.

Vanilla extract is obtained by soaking vanilla beans in a solution of grain alcohol and water. After three soakings, the final extract is aged before bottling. Sugar and glycerol are often added.

The extract is bottled in 35 percent alcohol so that it can remain suspended in solution. Vanillin, the main flavor component of vanilla, can be synthesized from wood pulp, oil of cloves, or tonka beans, but the synthetic is inferior to the real article.

Today, Madagascar produces 90 percent of the world's vanilla crop.

What is the difference between black pepper and white pepper?

Pepper is the most popular spice in the world. All true pepper (the spice, not chili peppers) is the dried fruit of *Piper nigrum*, a vinelike plant which is native to the Malabar coast of India. It is trained to grow around trees or stakes and reaches a length of up to twenty-five feet. Pepper can be grown only in tropical regions that receive about one-hundred inches of rain a year, with some periods of dryness. Spikelike stems a few inches long and bearing tiny yellow-green flowers emerge from the vine. The flowers produce clusters of fifty to sixty peppercorn berries, which grow around the stem like grapes.

There are three kinds of pepper sold as a spice—black, white, and green. As the berries ripen, they turn from as yellow to red. The riper the pepper berries become the more pungent their taste. Peppercorns can be picked green and canned whole for use in certain sauces. More commonly, they are allowed to ripen further. Black peppercorns result when the berries are picked slightly underripe and sun-dried until the skin blackens. The black skin is the spiciest part of the pepper. White peppercorns are the same berries, which are picked ripe, soaked in water so the skin can be rubbed off, and then sun-dried. Since there is no skin, there is nothing to turn black.

The extra processing and the weight loss caused by skin removal make white pepper more expensive than black. It is debatable which is spicier. While the black retains the spicy skin, the white becomes more pungent because of its longer period of ripening.

Americans prefer black pepper to white, as do the British. Continental Europeans prefer the white, possibly because the black looks less appealing in white sauces. Americans each consume roughly sixty teaspoons of pepper yearly. As a nation we go through about sixty million pounds of pepper annually.

Pepper is always best when fresh ground. Whole peppercorns won't lose their pungency for years. Ground pepper loses its taste in a matter of months. Pepper tastes the same regardless of where it is grown. So don't spend more money for a pepper because of its place of origin.

Most of today's pepper comes from Malaysia, Brazil, India, Indonesia, and Sri Lanka.

What is red pepper?

Red pepper is the dried pod of a hot *Capsicum* pepper, sometimes called cayenne. This pepper was discovered by Columbus in the New World. Today, it is mostly imported from Asia.

Paprika is the mildest member of the *Capsicum* pepper family. While native to the New World, paprika, like the pimiento, is a red pepper that was developed in Europe. California is the source for most domestic paprika.

What makes chili peppers so hot?

The hottest chili peppers in the world are said to be the Scotch bonnets of the Caribbean. They are shaped like a wrinkled lantern and come in a variety of colors—red, orange, yellow, and green. The habanero pepper found in Mexico is also very hot. All these peppers are members of the genus *Capsicum*. Chili peppers have no relationship to black pepper (*Piper nigrum*). We can thank Columbus for this confusion in naming, as he mistakenly believed that chilies and pepper were in the same family. Before he "discovered" chili peppers, they were unknown in the Old World. After Columbus returned with them, however, they rapidly spread to India, China, and Africa, and were readily accepted and incorporated into local cuisines.

The thing that makes chili peppers so hot is an alkaloid they contain known as capsaicin, which is unique to chilies. Pure capsaicin is so hot that its heat can be detected even at concentrations as low as one part per million. Capsaicin is formed in glands at the tip of the pepper placenta. This is the top part of the partition just below the stem, where the pepper's seeds are attached. Since the capsaicin is more concentrated here, this area of the pepper is several times hotter than the actual pepper itself. If you really want your pepper to be as hot as possible, do not remove the placenta or seeds. Scotch bonnets are so hot that you should wear rubber gloves when handling them, as the capsaicin can actually burn you.

In 1912, a pharmacologist named Wilbur Scoville devised a scale to measure the heat of peppers. He macerated chili in sugar water and alcohol and had a panel of tasters grade each mixture for temperature. His scale was used to determine the temperature of the peppers being used in the muscle salve Heet.

Today, the Scoville scale has been replaced by the far more accurate liquid chromatography test. The lowest rating on the Scoville scale is zero, which corresponds to the heat produced by bell peppers. Jalapeños measure about 5,000, habaneros and Scotch bonnets a fiery 200,000-300,000, and pure capsaicin animpossible-to-imagine 15,000,000.

Pure capsaicin, in fact, is so unbearable that it is used today as a weapon by the police and FBI. When sprayed on an assailant, it causes a reaction somewhat similar to tear gas that lasts at least thirty minutes.

Being an oil, capsaicin is not water soluble. If you have the misfortune to eat a chili that is just too hot to bear, don't try to douse the "flames" with water or beer. Milk and yogurt, which contain caesin, a natural detergent, are better at washing away the spicy oils. Hard candy and bread are also soothing "fire extinguishers."

Chili peppers have evolved to be so hot for their own survival. Rodents, such as rabbits, which can destroy pepper seeds in their digestive tracts, hate chilies. Birds, however, in whose digestive tracts the seeds can safely pass through, seem to love peppers and thus disperse their seeds great distances. The human species apparently is somewhat divided.

Who invented chili?

Chili is a widely popular dish in the United States. Everyone seems to have his own favorite recipes, and countless chili cooking contests are held. Most people feel that the hotter the chili, the better. If you asked the average man on the street, he would probably tell you that chili originated in Mexico or maybe Spain. Chili, however, is as American as apple pie. Mexico and Spain, as a matter of fact, want nothing to do with chili.

Chili was first created in San Antonio, Texas, in 1840. The original chili was a blend of chili powder, beef fat, dried beef, spices, and salt. It could be pressed into a brick that, when dried, was very resistant to spoilage. This made it an ideal food for frontier settlers moving farther west. It could be reconstituted with water and cooked with beans. The Forty-Niners in particular enjoyed this dehydrated food.

San Antonio was known not only for the invention of chili, but also for its "chili queens." These ladies, of questionable repute, would come out after dark with little carts and peddle chili, as well as other things. They were put out of business by the city during World War II.

Why do people in India eat such spicy food?

The favored spice of India is curry, which is actually a mixture of several spices, such as turmeric, cayenne, cardamom, ginger, coriander, pepper, chili, mustard seed, cumin, and cinnamon.

Spices can make bland, unappealing food taste and smell better and improve one's appetite. This, however, is just one of the reasons people add spices to foods. There are other practical purposes for spice. Because spices like curry are hot, they cause the body to sweat and thus help to regulate the body's temperature, making one feel cooler. For this reason, spicy foods are very popular in India, Mexico, and other warm countries. Spices in food also help to kill some germs and aid the digestive process.

Why is garlic believed to repel vampires?

During the Black Death that swept Europe during the Dark Ages this curious belief came into being. The Europeans were totally at a loss to explain what caused the dreaded disease. As was common in simpler days, they attributed it to an evil force—vampires.

The plague was indiscriminate in whom it attacked—rich and poor all were susceptible. All that is, it seemed, except the garlic merchants. There was a decidedly lower incidence of the disease among the men who plied garlic from town to town. The people correctly assumed that there was something special about this herb. Europeans took to eating copious amounts of garlic and wearing cloves strung around their necks. (New England colonists took this practice one step further, wearing garlic cloves on their feet as a cure for smallpox.)

They didn't know it then, but the plague was caused by a bacterium. Louis Pasteur, discovered in 1858 that garlic (*Allium sativum*) contains an antibiotic oil called allicin. Perhaps the garlic merchants' constant contact with this special herb helped to suppress the bacteria in their system. It has been also suggested that the pungent herb *may* have actually helped prevent the plague from spreading by keeping others at a safe distance. It is doubtful, however, that it really was effective in warding off vampires!

Today, we know better, but garlic is just as popular as it ever was. America's real appreciation of this marvelous herb is somewhat more recent, however. Before World War II, garlic was not even grown in the United States. It wasn't until the government needed quantities of dehydrated garlic for the troop's rations that farmers began to raise it. Today, California leads in U.S. production.

What culinary seasoning is used most frequently?

Salt, or sodium chloride (NaCl), is essential to our good health. We need to take in about three ounces a day. Lucky for us, there is no shortage of salt. The seas are full if it and large deposits of salt are found in the ground around the world. One famous ancient salt deposit was mined in present-day Austria. You know it as Salzburg ("salt city").

Salt is about one-third sodium and two-thirds chloride. Modern table salts also contain additives such as sodium silicoaluminate to keep it dry, and potassium iodine as a dietary supplement to prevent goiters. Kosher salt has no additives, is coarse grained, and is half as salty as regular table salt.

The Eskimos, who consume a lot of game meat and milk, both of which are high in salt content, do not use salt. Early man, who hunted to live, didn't have much use for salt either. As civilization moved toward agriculture, salt was needed and much sought after. The Romans so valued it that they paid their soldiers in salt or gave them a sum of money to buy it. This money was known as *salarium,* from which comes our word "salary."

The most obvious use of salt in cooking is as a seasoning to heighten the flavor of food. Another vital use of salt through history is as a preservative. Salt acts to withdraw moisture from bacteria and fungi, and thus retards their growth. Salt used to be the main preservative in bacon and salt pork. Today, other preservatives are used. Salt is added more as a seasoning. Salt is also used when pickling foods to help retard the growth of microorganisms.

Salt also raises the boiling point of water, allowing vegetables to be cooked quicker at a higher temperature. It can lower the freezing point of water, and is thus used in the ice packed around an ice cream freezer.

Is MSG bad for you?

Many Chinese restaurants use monosodium glutamate (MSG). In fact, it is used extensively in many kinds of prepared foods. MSG is simply a flavor enhancer. It stimulates the taste buds and intensifies the taste of food. The Chinese are big users of MSG, the "magic powder of the East," which was originally made from seaweed. It was first isolated in Japan in 1908 from the seaweed kombu (*Laminaria japonica*). The Japanese used the seaweed for centuries to bring out flavor. They are still major producers of MSG today and make it from bean protein. In the United States it comes from cereal protein gluten, wheat, or sugar beets.

MSG has no taste of its own. It enhances the taste of meats or vegetables, but has no effect on fruits, sweets, or eggs. MSG is even used in tobacco products to enhance flavor. When fresh foods are properly prepared, using everyday seasonings, there is not much need for MSG. There is a certain deadening similarity in foods flavored with it. Good cooks believe that foods should stand on their own merits.

Another unappealing aspect of MSG is Kwon's Disease, also known as Chinese Restaurant Syndrome. Some people have an allergic reaction to MSG. In large quantities it can cause headaches, sweating, chills, burning sensations, and temporary paralysis. Unfortunately, most Chinese restaurants do use MSG extensively. It is recommended that you patronize restaurants that will withhold MSG upon request if you are concerned about consuming it. Also, avoid frozen foods, canned and dried soups, and other commercially prepared foods.

MSG is not really a foreign substance in the body. In fact, glutamic acid is a common amino acid in many foodstuffs. This glutamic acid is converted into monosodium glutamate inside the body. At reasonable dosages, MSG should present no danger to most people. We Americans knowingly, or unknowingly, consume some 150 million pounds of the stuff every year.

Saucy!

What was the first spaghetti sauce to be nationally distributed?

There were no nationwide brands of spaghetti sauce until Ragu hit the big time in the 1970s. Spaghetti itself didn't become popular in the United States until the time of the Depression, when a flood of southern Italian immigrants entered this country. It was two such immigrants who gave us Ragu.

Ragu Spaghetti Sauce (translated from Italian, *ragu* means "sauce") was created in the 1920s by Giovanni and Assunta Cantisano, who came to America from Naples. The first batch of Ragu Spaghetti Sauce was made in the Cantisanos' own kitchen in 1937.

Initially, the Cantisanos sold the sauce to friends and later door to door in their neighborhood. Ragu Spaghetti Sauce's popularity increased quickly and in 1946 the Ragu Packing Company was founded in Rochester, New York, to manufacture and distribute this homemade spaghetti sauce. Distribution quickly expanded throughout the Northeast. By the mid-1970s Ragu had become the first spaghetti sauce to be distributed nationally.

Where did ketchup originate and how did it become so popular?

Odd as it may seem, the product we call ketchup had its origins in the Orient. The year was 1690 when the Chinese first concocted a tangy sauce of pickled fish, shellfish, and spices to serve with fish. They called this strange blend *ke-tsiap*. It was a far cry from today's ketchup. Ke-tsiap's popularity spread to Malaya, where English sailors "discovered" it early in the 1700s. They brought this unique sauce back to England, where British chefs had to find substitutes for the inaccessible oriental ingredients. They anglicized the sauce and came up with varieties such as mushroom, anchovy, walnut, lemon, oyster, and even tomato. They also anglicized the name "ketchup."

The publisher of a work called *The New Art of Cookery,* introduced "tomato catsup" to America in 1792. This new tomato sauce did not catch on quickly, however, as it was difficult and time consuming to prepare. The scalding, skinning, seeding, chopping, and blending was tedious work. It wasn't until 1876, when Henry J. Heinz developed a way to mass produce it in Pittsburgh, Pennsylvania, that ketchup became nationally popular.

Is it "ketchup" or "catsup"?

H. J. Heinz used both "ketchup" and "catsup" interchangeably up to the early 1900s, when he chose "ketchup," based on the original chinese *ke-tsiap*, to identify and promote his product. Both words are still in use today. Some brands use the word "catsup," but most major national brands have adopted "ketchup."

Does ketchup need to be refrigerated?

The natural acidity of ketchup keeps most contaminants in check. If ketchup is kept in an area where bakery products or even beer is served, however, spoilage is possible as a result of airborne yeast contamination. So to be on the safe side, refrigerate your ketchup. Restaurants go through their ketchup so quickly that they can leave it out on the tables during business hours with no problem.

What popular hot sauce was originally called "that famous sauce Mr. McIlhenny makes"?

A Louisiana banker and gourmand, Edmund McIlhenny, concocted America's favorite hot sauce in 1868, when he mashed together hot peppers and salt. But not just any salt—Avery Island salt. In 1862, John Marsh Avery discovered that beneath the brine springs of Avery Island, Louisiana, which supplied the Confederate Army with salt, was a huge deposit of rock salt as large as Mount Everest. After the Civil War, McIlhenny married Avery's daughter and created his now famous sauce.

The diet in the post-Civil War South was somewhat less than delectable. A typical Reconstruction-era dinner in the Deep South consisted of such dull fare as cornbread mush, stewed beans, and squirrel meat. To liven things up a bit, McIlhenny created a special sauce. He aged his pepper mash for thirty days, then added French white-wine vinegar, and aged it another thirty days. He strained his spicy potion into little empty cologne bottles and called it " that famous sauce Mr. McIlhenny makes." Later, he came up with a shorter, snappy name—Tabasco sauce (named after the Mexican state of Tabasco, where the peppers where thought to have originated).

Since then little else has changed about Tabasco sauce. Now the mash is aged for three years. It still contains only three ingredients: short, thick-walled Mexican chili peppers, Avery Island salt, and vinegar. In fact, the McIlhenny Company, run by descendants of Edmund McIlhenny, still brews this fiery sauce at the family's estate on Avery Island.

Why are some mustards bright yellow and some brown?

After salt and pepper, mustard is the most popular food flavoring. Man has been enjoying mustard since before recorded history. The Romans made an early form of mustard, crushing the seed in the juice of unripe grapes. Modern mustard was created by an Englishwoman, Mrs. Clements of Durham, in 1729. She ground up mustard seeds and other secret ingredients into a powder that could be mixed with water to make a mustard something like today's version. She sold her powdered mix from town to town on horseback. King George I tried some and became a big fan. Mustard's popularity took off.

Mustard in and of itself has no particular flavor or aroma. But when water is added to crushed mustard seeds and allowed to stand for a few minutes, the mixture comes alive and gets rather hot.

There are three main types of mustard seed—yellow, brown, and black. The brown and black seeds come from black mustard (*Brassica nigra*) and the yellow seeds from white mustard (*Sinapsis alba*). Both plants are native to southern Europe.

The yellow seeds mixed with salt, vinegar, and spices are used to make the bright yellow condiment we know as ballpark or American mustard, which is mild. Turmeric is often added to give it its bright yellow color. The brown seeds, which are stronger in flavor, are mixed with white wine for Dijon mustard. Dijon, named after the capital of the Burgundy region of France, often contains tarragon and peppercorns. Black seeds are used in Indian cooking. A combination of brown and black seeds is used to make powdered mustard.

Freshly mixed powdered mustard is much stronger than bottled mustard, but it loses its potency in a day or so.

What famous French mustard was the creation of an Englishman?

It may surprise you, and cause chagrin for the French, to know that France's most famous Dijon mustard—Grey Poupon—was established by an Englishman named Grey.

Dijon has been the center of the French mustard trade since the seventeenth century. In 1777, Grey began selling a most excellent mustard from his condiment shop in Dijon. He was later joined in the business by a Frenchman named Poupon who provided much needed capital to Grey's venture. For two-hundred years the name Grey Poupon has graced the front of the shop. Over the years, the shop has become a kind of mecca for mustard lovers around the world.

Grey Poupon was first introduced to America by Heublin, Inc., in 1946, after U.S. soldiers returned from Europe. Today, it is made in Oxnard, California, by Nabisco and is the best-selling premium-priced mustard in the country.

What is the origin of Worcestershire Sauce?

That most English of sauces—Worcestershire—actually originated in India. The Indians adopted a similar sauce from the Romans, to which they added tamarind and other spices. A nobleman of the county of Worcester brought some of the sauce home with him after a stint as the governor of Bengal. The nobleman, Lord Sandys, took a sample of his sauce to the chemists Lea & Perrins and requested that they make some up for him from a recipe he had. The chemists made up a batch for Lord Sandys, but also kept a couple of jars for themselves. They found the sauce to be unpalatable and put it in their cellar, where it was forgotten. Some time later they came upon the jars and, before throwing them out, tasted the contents again. To their surprise, the sauce was excellent. Like a fine wine, it had matured. They were soon selling the sauce.

Lord Sandys didn't take too well to Lea & Perrins selling "his" sauce. He returned to the chemists' shop and demanded a 10 percent royalty on the sauce he had "discovered." Lea & Perrins invited him to put on a white coat and earn his cut. He refused, and also barred the use of his family name on the label. Hence, the sauce came to be known for its place of manufacture—Worcestershire.

What is in Worcestershire Sauce?

The one critical ingredient in Worcestershire Sauce is tamarind, most of which comes from India packed in molasses. Tamarind (*Tamarindus indica*) is a brownish-red bean that grows on trees and imparts a unique sweet-tart taste.

Peppercorns from Zanzibar, China, and Mombasa are another important ingredient. Other key ingredients used in the aging process include anchovies from Sicily and Morocco, Dutch shallots, chilies from China and Tanzania, unpeeled heads of garlic, unpeeled red onions, and cloves.

The raw ingredients are allowed to mature for three years. The ingredients, which were once top secret, are now listed on the label. The real secret is preparation time and the proper balance of ingredients. Few people know the exact time required for each step. The sauce continues to improve with age. If you find a half-empty bottle in the dark recesses of your pantry, don't fret; it will probably taste better than ever.

Perhaps the most common use for Worcestershire Sauce in the United States is in Bloody Marys and, of course, on steaks. It also makes an excellent browning agent. Just sprinkle some on a chicken before baking, and it will brown beautifully. It is widely used as a hangover remedy, and some people even claim it is an aphrodisiac. It truly is a wonder sauce!

Americans are big consumers of Worcestershire Sauce, and there is an American plant in Fair Lawn, New Jersey. Interestingly, it is only in the United States that the paper wrapper is put on the bottle. Aside from the wrapper, our sauce is identical to the original English product.

In 1988, Lea & Perrins worldwide was acquired by BSN Group, the largest food company in France. Oddly, very little Worcestershire Sauce is sold in France. Old prejudices apparently die hard.

What steak sauce was named by the king of England?

Around 1820, King George IV of England asked the royal chef to come up with a special new steak sauce for him. The dutiful chef went into the royal kitchen and experimented with different mixtures of the royal spices and condiments. When he presented his new sauce to the king, George was very pleased and proclaimed the sauce to be "A-one!" A.1. Steak Sauce became very popular in England and eventually was introduced to the common folk of America in 1906.

Thirst Quenchers

What is the most popular beverage in the world?

Sorry, Coke and Pepsi, it's not a cola. It is tea!

Today, tea is the most popular drink in the world, except for water. In the United States over 187 million pounds of tea are consumed each year. That's about thirteen gallons per person.

The following should explain everything you ever wanted to know about the world's favorite drink.

It is said that tea was discovered by the Chinese emperor Shen-Nung around 2737 B.C. (The word "tea" comes from the Chinese *t'e,* pronounced "tay.") Legend has it the emperor accidentally discovered it when the wind blew some tea leaves into a pot of boiling water.

Since that time, tea has been attributed with many healing powers. It eases upset stomach and indigestion, relieves fatigue, and stimulates mental ability. The Japanese have a cult called "teaism," which has actually raised the art of making and drinking tea to a near religious experience.

Tea has been popular in Asia since Shen-Nung's time. It wasn't until the seventeenth century, however, that Europeans became aware of this oriental drink. The Dutch East India Company first brought tea to Holland in 1610, and by the 1650s it was imported into Britain. Coffee was the most popular drink in England at the time, but tea soon displaced it, despite the high taxes levied on it by the British government to protect the coffee industry. Tea later followed the colonists to America.

Tea (*Camellia sinensis*) is a perennial evergreen shrub, a relative of the flowering camelia, that can live for a hundred years and reach a height of fifty feet. Tea grows in tropical and semitropical areas receiving between fifty and three hundred inches of rainfall annually, at anywhere from sea level to an altitude of eight hundred feet. It prefers a well-drained acid soil. The best-flavored teas grow in the cooler climates of the higher altitudes. The resultant slower growth produces a smaller, more flavorful tea. Thus, the finest teas are called high grown.

Although there are many varieties of tea, they all come from the same plant. Differences in taste result from the varying conditions under which the plants are grown, such as climate, soil condition, altitude, or rainfall. The way the tea is packed and processed also is a key to its taste.

Tea is almost always picked or plucked by hand. There is an art to tea plucking. In finer teas, the plucker only takes the youngest leaves—the top two leaves and the leaf bud. Medium-grade teas include the next two leaves, and lesser grades use the next lower leaves. To facilitate easy plucking, tea plants are not allowed to grow above three feet in height. Tea is grown commercially in some thirty countries. India and Sir Lanka are the leading exporters.

What are the different types of tea?

While there are over 3000 varieties of tea, there are three broad tea classifications—green, black, and oolong. They are all crushed, dried, and fired. Differences in their withering and fermentation processing result in three distinct teas.

Green teas, such as gunpowder, are not withered, but are steamed immediately after plucking to prevent fermentation. Asians prefer their greenish color and slightly bitter taste. It is mainly grown in China, Japan, and Twiwan.

Oolong teas, such as Formosa, are withered and only partially fermented. It is primarily grown in Taiwan.

The more fermentation a tea leaf undergoes, the more its chemistry is altered, producing the essential oils that are key to its taste and aroma.

Black teas, the most popular tea in the West, is withered and fully fermented (oxidized). Black teas have dark coppery red leaves, which are graded according to size. Pekoe, orange pekoe, and souchong are common black teas.

The differences between the thousands of tea varieties has to do with the exact location of their origin, how they were grown, and how they were picked. At any one time, a tea bag may contain over forty different teas. These teas are blended together under the supervision of expert tea tasters. A true tea connoisseur can tell with one sip where a variety of tea was grown, when it was picked, and how it was processed.

How did tea become so popular in England?

Tea is almost a national obsession in England. This, however, was not always the case. In fact, during the seventeenth and eighteenth centuries, coffee was king in England. There were thousands of coffeehouses throughout London, where people from all walks of life could congregate. As alcoholic beverages began to creep into the coffeehouses, they became rowdier and a lower class of clientele took over. The social elite and businessmen began to take refuge in private clubs or in their offices.

At roughly the same time, the nobility started taking a liking to tea. The British East India Tea Company was making huge profits rushing the tea harvest to England aboard the speedy clipper ships of the day, and really pushed the consumption of tea. Not only that, tea was much easier to prepare than coffee—one could simply add boiling water. Coffeehouses became associated with post-Restoration England, while tea became the drink of the modern day.

Coffee has been the drink of Americans ever since the Revolution. Starting with the Boston Tea Party and the high taxes imposed on tea, we have found coffee to be the more patriotic and energizing drink. The Dutch and French helped us down this road by supplying us with cheap coffee beans during our tea-boy-cotting years.

How did four o'clock come to be "tea time"?

The rural working class of England got out of work at around six o'clock and would then have their main meal of the day. This meal typically included potted meats, fish, cheese, salads, sweets, and, of course, tea. This became known as "high tea."

"Low tea," which still survives today as traditional tea time, was at four o'clock. The Duchess of Bedford is credited with its origin. In about 1840, she began taking tea with a light snack at four o'clock to ward off "that sinking feeling" one gets late in the afternoon. Since the upper classes ate such late dinners, a small meal of tea and cakes was perfect to tide one over. Her practice soon took hold in England and became one of its most sacred traditions.

The Irish are actually the biggest consumers of tea, ahead of the English. Surprisingly, the people of Qatar are number three, followed by the peoples of Turkey, Hong Kong, and Iran.

Who invented tea bags?

Tea bags were created by New York tea wholesaler Tom Sullivan around 1900. He wrapped his tea samples in little silk bags, never thinking his customers would brew the tea, bag and all!

How can you tell fortunes by reading tea leaves?

Ancient man believed that ringing bells could drive away evil spirits and examined the insides of bells for omens. The Chinese viewed a bowl or teacup as an inverted bell and studied the tea fragments left behind to predict the future. The practice of tea reading was developed into a high art. Anyone can "read" tea leaves, if he knows how.

The teacup should be unfluted, narrow at the bottom and wide at the top, with a white interior. One person drinks the tea (made from steeped leaves, not tea bags!) while concentrating on a question or making a wish. When about a teaspoonful of tea remains, he takes the cup in his left hand and swirls the contents three times to the left. He then inverts the cup to drain. The reader picks up the cup and studies the patterns formed by the leaves, while concentrating on the other person. The reading takes place from the left of the handle and progresses around the cup. Symbols farther from the handle represent people or events more distant from the questioner. Images close to the rim represent the near future; the bottom of the cup represents things in the more distant future.

As in reading of Rorschach ink blots, the reader's imagination must take over to envision hidden symbols. Some symbols, such as a bouquet, portend good luck; others, like a small cross, forecast bad luck. There are hundreds of symbols and combinations of symbols, which must be understood and interpreted by an experienced tea reader.

How did coffee come to be called java?

Coffee was first cultivated in an Ethiopian town called Kaffa sometime around the sixth century. Supposedly, its stimulating properties were discovered by the locals who noticed the effect of wild coffee berries on grazing goats. Coffee's "kick" is what made it appealing to the Arab world during the spread of Muhammadanism. Since Islam forbade the consumption of alcohol, coffee became their main drink.

Up until the late 1600s, almost all coffee came from Arabia. The Arabs enjoyed their monopoly for centuries by prohibiting the export of seed and banning foreigners from the coffee plantations. Eventually, however, Moslems making the pilgrimage to Mecca were able to smuggle some seeds out to India. Dutch traders managed to steal whole coffee plants from the Arabs and start their own plantations in Java, giving the Western world its first nickname for coffee.

The Dutch distributed coffee plants to botanical gardens around Europe. One such plant found its way to the Jardin des Plantes in Paris in 1714. The royal botanist was quite proud of this rare plant and kept it closely guarded. Several years later, an entreprenurial French sailor, Gabriel Mathieu de Clieu, who had been stationed in Martinique, had the bright idea to grow coffee in Latin America. When he approached the royal botanist, he was jealously rebuffed. After some behind-the-scenes intrigue, de Clieu managed to make off with the plant and sailed for the West Indies.

The French soon had a thriving coffee industry in the Caribbean. It was now Brazil's turn to covet the highly prized coffee plant. The Dutch and French colonists in the New World were forbidden to export coffee plants or seeds, under the penalty of death.

When a border dispute erupted between neighboring Dutch and French Guiana in 1727, the Brazilians saw a unique opportunity. The two coffee-producing colonies asked Brazil to step in and mediate a settlement. A handsome Brazilian lieutenant colonel who had a way with the ladies was chosen for this delicate mission. He spent his mornings in negotiations and his afternoons with the wife of the governor of French Guiana. Apparently the afternoon negotiations went as well the morning's. When the dispute was settled, he returned home to Brazil with several coffee-plant cuttings supplied by the governor's wife. Thus began one of the world's great coffee empires.

The Brazilian coffee supremacy was assured in the mid-nineteenth century when the devastating coffee disease *Hemileia vastatrix* (coffee rust fungus) virtually wiped out coffee production in Ceylon, India, Java, Sumatra, Malaya, and all of Asia.

While the Arabs still love their coffee, the Finns are now the biggest drinkers of it, at 37.5 pounds per person per year. Worldwide, we consume some 500 million cups of coffee a day.

Why is mountain-grown coffee better?

Coffee is the most valuable agricultural commodity in the world. The United States alone imports $4 billion worth a year.

Most of the coffee we drink comes from the tree *Coffea arabica*. (An inferior coffee is produced from the *Coffea robusta*.) If allowed to reach its full height, the plant would grow to about thirty feet. For cultivation purposes, however, it is pruned to five or ten feet. Coffee, which is mistakenly called an evergreen (it loses its leaves every few years), has small, white, fragrant flowers. From these flowers are produced tiny clusters of green "cherries," which gradually redden and mature. Each cherry contains two seeds, or beans.

Coffee grows best in climates that have a year-round mean temperature of about 70° F. Coffees grown at higher altitudes ("high grown") mature slower than coffee grown at lower altitudes and develop better-flavored oils.

Coffee is still picked by hand. After picking, the coffee must be processed. This involves removing the inner and outer skins and the pulp of the cherry to expose the green coffee bean. Depending on the type of processing, either all the cherries are picked at once or only the ripe ones are picked. For obvious reasons, the latter method yields better-tasting coffee. Countries that pick only the ripened fruit include Colombia, Costa Rica, Kenya, Tanzania, Venezuela, Zaire (Kiva coffee), and the state of Hawaii (Kona coffee). Most Brazilian coffee is processed fruits in varying stages of ripeness and is therefore not of the same high quality as Colombian coffee. (While Brazil leads the world in coffee production, Colombia produces the most consistently high-quality coffee. About half of the Colombian crop comes to the United States.) Green coffee beans look and smell nothing like the coffee we purchase at the store. Roasting causes the beans to shrink in weight, increase in volume (the beans actually pop like popcorn), and turn from green to dark brown. The color changes due to the caramelization of the sugars in the bean. Roasting also develops the coffee's rich aroma and taste.

The best-selling coffee is Folger's regular, which sells more than Taster's Choice regular and decaffeinated combined.

Is any coffee grown in the United States?

Attempts have been made to grow coffee in Florida and Louisiana, but its quality was low and its growth difficult due to frost problems. The only place in the United States really suited to the growth of quality coffee is Hawaii. On the slopes of the active Mauna Loa volcano the excellent Kona coffee is grown. The soil there is composed of hard-packed chunks of volcanic rock. To plant these coffee shrubs, farmers have to dig the holes with pickaxes! Soil from other parts of the island must be packed around the roots and the plants must be fertilized throughout the year. Despite this, the coffee thrives. It receives just the right amount of rain and sun, and the volcano acts as a natural windbreaker. Inexplicably, coffee grown in Hawaii is virtually disease-free. While the yield per acre of Hawaiian coffee is quite high, the total acreage available is quite low. Therefore, Hawaii produces only a tiny fraction of the world's coffee crop.

What is the perfect cup of coffee?

According to coffee experts, a good cup of coffee results when 19 percent of the weight of the coffee grounds is extracted into the brew. For the American palate, a final coffee strength of 1.23 percent soluble solids is desired. You can roughly obtain these coffee specifications by using two level teaspoons (one Approved Coffee Measure) of coffee to six ounces of water.

The fineness of your coffee grind can, of course, affect the outcome. By altering your brewing time you can compensate for grind texture. A fine grind should be brewed one to four minutes; a drip grind, four to six minutes; and a regular grind, six to eight minutes.

How is instant coffee made?

Most people prefer the taste of fresh-ground coffee, but instant makes up 20 percent of sales. Instant coffee is made by forcing atomized strong coffee extract through hot air to dry the coffee into particles.

Freeze-dried coffee is frozen first. Then, with the application of heat, the frozen moisture is vaporized in a process called sublimination.

How is decaffeinated coffee made?

The first decaffeinated coffee was Sanka, which is a contraction of the French *sans caffeine*. For years all decaffeinated coffee was called Sanka, regardless of the brand.

The process of decaffeinating coffee was discovered accidently around 1900, when a shipment of coffee beans became soaked with seawater during an ocean trip and thus lost some of its caffeine. Today, coffee is decaffeinated by first softening the green coffee beans with steam and water, then processing them in a bath of methylene chloride to remove the caffeine. A further steam bath removes the methylene chloride. (Some manufacturers extract the caffeine using carbon dioxide or ethyl acetate). This treatment is repeated up to twenty-four times to remove roughly 97 percent of the caffeine. A newer, more environmentally friendly process uses steam only. Once removed, the caffeine is used in things like soft drinks and pharmaceuticals.

Decaffeinating coffee has a minor effect on its flavor. Decaffeination removes some of the coffee bean's oils and waxes and also alters its structure. Since decaffeinated beans roast differently, they are roasted longer than untreated beans.

What are the different serving styles of coffee?

Today there seems to be a countless variety of ways of serving coffee. The following list of the most common coffee styles should help to remove some of the confusion:

Espresso is a very strong brew, dark-roasted under pressure and served in a tiny espresso cup.

Cappuccino is espresso that is topped with foamy steamed milk and served in a regular-size cup.

Caffe latte is espresso that has a greater amount of foamy steamed milk added and served in a tall glass mug.

Caffe au lait is an equal portion of coffee and hot milk.

Turkish coffee is very strong coffee made by boiling fine coffee grounds, sugar, and water.

Viennese coffee is a strong, sweet coffee, topped with whipped cream and served in a tall glass.

How can a coffee be "Chock Full O' Nuts"?

William Black ran a nut business in New York in the 1920s. When the Depression hit, nut sales fell way off. Black began baking his nuts into date nut bread, which he sold with cream cheese and coffee. His new business, and hence his coffee, was called Chock Full O' Nuts. By the forties, he had several restaurants in New York, New Jersey, and eastern Pennsylvania. His coffee, however, went national.

What is the most recognized product trademark in the world?

Coke is far and away number one. In a recent survey to determine the world's most recognizable brand, the distance between Coca-Cola and the number two brand was greater than the distance between number two and number fifty. Coke's popularity is a direct result of Coca-Cola's long history of intensive advertising.

Its very first ad, in 1886, read, "Drink Coca-Cola." In 1894, the wall of a drugstore in Cartersville, Georgia, was painted with the first of thousands of early outdoor Coca-Cola ads. (If you are really observant and live in an older urban area, you can still find some faded, peeling Coca-Cola advertisements painted on old brick walls.) In 1925, the nationwide use of billboards began.

Norman Rockwell, as well as other top artists, did illustrations for magazine ads that are now famous. One of the commercial slogans with the longest lasting impact was "The Pause That Refreshes," which ran in the *Saturday Evening Post* in February 1929. In fact, in 1931 artist Haddon Sundblom created the modern image of a jolly, red-suited Santa Claus for Coke. Before Sundblom's paintings, Santa had been depicted as everything from a pixie to an elf to a frightening gnome.

Early ads discouraged the use of the word "Coke." Consumers were urged to ask for Coca-Cola by its full name so as not to encourage the sale of substitutes. "Coke," however, had become a part of the vernacular, and in 1941, the company relented and started using the word in advertising. In 1945, "Coke" was registered as a trademark.

Over the years, Coke has continually updated its advertising campaigns to keep up with new trends. You can probably closely

date your age by which   of the following Coke ads you can
remember:

1886	Drink Coca-Cola.
1904	Delicious and refreshing.
1905	Coca-Cola revives and sustains.
1906	The great national temperance beverage.
1917	Three million a day.
1922	Thirst knows no season.
1925	Six million a day.
1927	Around the corner from everywhere.
1929	The pause that refreshes.
1932	Ice-cold sunshine.
1938	The best friend thirst ever had.
1939	Coca-Cola goes along.
1942	Wherever you are, whatever you do, wherever you may be, when you think of refreshment, think of ice-cold Coca-Cola.
1942	The only thing like Coca-Cola is Coca-Cola itself. It's the real thing.
1948	Where there's Coke there's hospitality.
1949	Coca-Cola . . . along the way to anywhere.
1952	What you want is a Coke.
1956	Coca-Cola . . . making good things taste better.
1957	Sign of good taste.
1958	The cold, crisp taste of Coke.
1959	Be really refreshed.
1963	Things go better with Coke.
1970	It's the real thing.
1971	I'd like to buy the world a Coke.
1975	Look up America.
1976	Coke adds life.
1979	Have a Coke and a smile.
1982	Coke is it!
1985	We've got a taste for you. (Coca-Cola & Coca-Cola Classic)
1985	America's real choice.
1986	Catch the wave (Coca-Cola).

1986	Red white & you (Coca-Cola Classic).
1989	Can't beat the feeling.
1990	Can't beat the real thing.
Present	Always Coca-Cola

What best-selling soft drink was originally named Brad's Drink?

A man named Caleb Bradham created a new soft drink in a pharmacy in New Bern, North Carolina, in 1898. Brad's Drink, as he called it, was a unique mixture of kola nut extract, vanilla, and rare oils. Bradham later renamed his drink Pepsi-Cola.

After seventeen years of selling Pepsi-Cola, Bradham went bankrupt and sold his formula. The new owners also failed to make a go of Pepsi. It wasn't until Loft's soda fountain chain purchased Pepsi in 1932 that sales took off.

Today, Pepsi is the best-selling soft drink in the American supermarket and second to Coke in overall sales. Pepsi now holds a 31 percent market share, compared to Coke's 41 percent share. Colas as a group account for two-thirds of the $49 billion carbonated soft drink industry. Pepsi-Cola North America produces some 2.5 billion cases of Pepsi, Diet Pepsi, Mountain Dew, and Slice each year!

What soft drink used to contain lithium?

Feeling a little manic-depressive? How about a quick pick-me-up? Try a nice refreshing bottle of "Bib-Label Lithiated Lemon-Lime Soda." Every popular drink needs a hook, and this one's wasn't its long-winded name!

The soda with the depressant was introduced to supermarkets just before the stock crash in 1929. Its inventor, C. L. Griggs, shortened its name to the now familiar 7-Up, but he left in the lithium until the 1940s. The 7-Up name is said to have been inspired by a cattle brand that Griggs particularly liked and by the fact that the soda had seven ingredients.

Today, sans lithium, 7-Up has taken the opposite marketing approach, emphasizing that it contains no caffeine or artificial flavors or colors. 7-Up is currently the eighth best-selling soft drink, with 4 percent of the market share.

Why is it called root "beer"?

The "root" part you probably figured out—it was originally made from roots. But why "beer"?

Charles Hires was a Philadelphia druggist. While honeymooning in New Jersey in 1875, he tasted an herbal tea containing juniper, wintergreen, and sarsaparilla. Root and berry drinks had been around a long time, but this tea was different. Upon returning to his pharmacy's soda fountain, he worked on creating a similar-tasting carbonated drink. He came up with a mixture of dried roots, barks, herbs, and flowers, which he originally sold powdered as Hires Root Tea.

Hires, a Quaker, tried to sell his Root Tea to the heavy-drinking Pennsylvania coal miners. The miners, however, weren't interested in any drink called tea. So, to make his beverage more appealing to them, he changed the name to Hires Root Beer. Hires began bottling and promoting his root beer and by 1892 more than two million bottles had been sold.

Ironically, Hires fell afoul of the temperance movement in 1895, when the Women's Christian Temperance Union called for a boycott of Hires Root Beer, which they thought actually contained beer. The boycott lasted until 1898, when a laboratory analysis persuaded the misguided do-gooders that Hires Root Beer contained no alcohol.

Who was Dr Pepper?

A pharmacist named Wade Morrison worked at a pharmacy owned by a Dr. Charles Pepper in turn-of-the-century Virginia. Morrison's duties included tending the soda fountain, where he busied himself concocting new flavored soda drinks. He also busied himself courting Dr. Pepper's daughter. The good doctor didn't take kindly to Morrison's affection for his daughter and fired him.

The lovelorn Morrison started his own business—Wade Morrison's Old Corner Drug Store in Waco, Texas. Morrison hired a young English pharmacist named Charles Alderton, who played around with different fruit flavors until he hit on a drink that contained twenty-three different ingredients. It became the local favorite. Morrison's customers, who had heard about his failed romance in Virginia, suggested naming the new drink after Dr. Pepper (maybe to spite him!). One of Morrison's customers was a beverage chemist named Robert Lazenby, who began bottling Dr Pepper.

Morrison never returned to Virginia to marry Dr. Pepper's daughter. He found a local Waco girl to settle down with.

Dr Pepper still has twenty-three ingredients, but the company guards the recipe. All it will say is that it doesn't contain any of the ingredients it's most rumored to contain—prune juice, cherry, or cola.

Today, Dr Pepper is the number-one-selling non-cola soft drink overall, representing 6 percent of the total soft drink market.

What is the difference between caffeine-free and decaffeinated?

Caffeine is a naturally occurring drug in coffee, tea, and cola drinks. Colas do not have naturally high levels of caffeine, however, as coffee and tea do. It is added by the cola manufacturers to give a little zip to their products and to help hook you on the mildly addictive substance. Colas, therefore, are labeled caffeine-free when they contain little or no caffeine. Coffee and tea, on the other hand, are labeled decaffeinated when they have had their caffeine physically removed. Decaffeinated coffees do contain around 3 percent caffeine, however.

Brewed coffee contains up to 180 milligrams of caffeine. Instant coffee contains roughly two-thirds this amount, teas even less. Coffees have varying amounts of caffeine. Philippine coffee has the highest level of caffeine, followed by Brazilian and Colombian. Coca-Cola contains 46 milligrams in a twelve-ounce serving and Pepsi-Cola has 36.4 milligrams. Noncola soft drinks Mountain Dew and Mello Yello contain 54 milligrams and 52 milligrams respectively.

The effects of caffeine in the body are felt within fifteen to forty-five minutes of consumption. After five or six hours, half of the caffeine has left the bloodstream. Children metabolize caffeine at twice this rate.

The best time of day to have a cup of coffee or tea is "tea time," or about four or five in the afternoon. Caffeine belongs to a class of stimulants known as methylxanthines, which block the action of chemicals in the body that act as natural sedatives. Having a cup of coffee in the morning will give you a temporary boost but upsets your biological clock, making you feel sleepy during the day. The caffeine raises your blood sugar levels for about an hour and a half. Then the body reacts by producing insulin, which is a natural sedative, to lower your blood sugar levels, causing you to feel a letdown. Your body's internal clock is peaking around 4:00 P.M. and a cup of coffee at this hour will do the most to charge you up without throwing your body's cycle out of whack.

What best-selling sports drink was created for the University of Florida football team?

Gatorade was developed in the mid-1960s by a University of Florida research team. Their aim was to create a drink that would rapidly replace body fluids lost due to physical exertion and hot weather. What better place to develop a hot weather drink? And who better to test it on than the members of the University of Florida Gators football team, who were experiencing significant loss of body fluids during practices and games?

In 1965, Dr. Robert Dade's research group began testing a formula on ten members of the football team. Hence the name "Gatorade."

That season, the Gators posted a winning record and distinguished themselves by consistently outplaying their opponents during the second half. The coach noticed fewer problems with player dehydration and greater player efficiency and endurance.

In fact, opposing coaches also noticed the difference that Gatorade made on the Gators' performance. On January 1, 1967, after his Georgia Tech team lost to the Gators twenty-seven to twelve in the Orange Bowl, Tech Head Coach Bobby Dodd told *Sports Illustrated* magazine that the reason his team lost was, "We didn't have Gatorade. That made a difference." Word was out.

In 1967, Stokely–Van Camp, a leading producer of fruits and vegetables at the time, bought the rights to manufacture and sell Gatorade. Then, in a stroke of marketing genius, the company signed a licensing agreement with the National Football League (NFL). Gatorade quickly became the drink of choice on the sidelines at NFL games. It wasn't long before other professional athletes embraced Gatorade, which can now be found at virtually all sporting events.

Stokely–Van Camp and Gatorade were acquired by the Quaker Oats Company in 1983. Today, Gatorade is the number-one sports drink in the United States, with an 80 percent market share.

What instant drink owes its success to NASA?

Whenever we think of Tang, somehow the space program comes to mind. That is because these breakfast beverage crystals were made available by General Foods in March 1965. Three months later, the astronauts were drinking Tang aboard the Gemini spacecraft.

Tang was perfect for space shots. It was created by General Foods after years of research and provided a quick, tasty, and nutritious alternative to fresh or frozen orange juice. Able to be stored almost indefinitely, it also contained all the vitamin C and A of fresh orange juice.

General Foods initially marketed Tang on a limited basis, but when it came to the attention of the people at the National Aeronautics and Space Administration, sales "skyrocketed." Being a part of the space program gave Tang instant credibility and national awareness. If it was good enough for the astronauts . . . Tang was on all space shots after 1965, and even landed on the moon. Kids were delighted to know that the drink they had at breakfast was the one their heroes drank in space.

How do juice drinks, ades, drinks, and punches differ?

First off, don't expect much actual juice from any of these drinks. By definition, they all are low in pure juice content. If you are interested in just how little juice is contained in each, read the following:

Juice drinks must contain at least 30 percent juice.

Ades must contain at least 15 percent juice (lemon and lime must contain at least 12.3 percent).

Drinks and juices must contain at least 10 percent juice (lemon and lime must contain at least 6 percent).

Flavored drinks contain less than 10 percent juice.

Artificially flavored drinks require no juice at all.

What about orange juices?

Orange juice is America's favorite juice. The enormous variety of orange juices available today is astounding. Taste varies between varieties and from month to month throughout the growing season. Even oranges picked from the same tree can vary in taste. Those growing lower on the tree and those facing north tend to be less sweet and contain less vitamin C.

Orange packagers eliminate these variations by blending several varieties, picked at different times and in different places, to produce a more consistent-tasting product.

The main reason packaged juice just doesn't taste like fresh-squeezed is heat. Concentrates are evaporated with heat. Most Chilled juices are made from concentrate. The best-tasting orange juices are "premium" chilled juices, not from concentrate, which are squeezed in Florida, packaged in an expandable plastic bottle, pasteurized, and flash (quickly) frozen.

Why does orange juice taste funny after you brush your teeth?

There's nothing like the sweet, fresh taste of orange juice first thing in the morning. If you don't wait a little while, however, the lingering toothpaste in your mouth will foul the taste of your orange juice. Yuck!

There is nothing wrong with your toothpaste or orange juice; the two just don't mix well in your mouth. Most toothpastes contain a chemical detergent called sodium lauryl sulfate (SLS). Any leftover SLS in your mouth will react with the natural acids in orange juice to reduce its sweetness and produce a somewhat bitter taste. Thankfully, SLS dissipates quickly, and in a few minutes orange juice can be fully enjoyed again.

What best-selling grape juice started out as a sacramental wine?

Believe it or not, the Welch's Grape Juice story began with a doctor who set out to make a nonalcoholic wine for sacramental use. Back in 1869, a Vineland, New Jersey, dentist, Dr. Thomas Bramwell, experimented with the newly developed theories of Louis Pasteur to create an unfermented wine that could be used in his church's communion services. With the help of his wife and seventeen-year old son, Charles, he picked forty pounds of Concord grapes (*Vitus labrusca*) from his backyard and cooked them in Mrs. Welch's kitchen. After a few minutes of cooking, the juice was squeezed out and strained through cloth bags into twelve-quart bottles. The bottles were sealed with cork and wax. They were then placed in boiling water for a long enough period of time to kill all of the yeast organisms that are responsible for fermentation. (This was the same method used to pasteurize milk.) The bottles were placed in the family barn to age.

The family waited several weeks for the bottles to explode, indicating that the juice had fermented despite their efforts. To their delight, they had produced the first unfermented, sweet grape juice. Dr. Welch persuaded his pastor to try his unfermented grape juice and began selling small quantities to other churches in south Jersey. He had no idea that he was starting a brand-new industry—the fruit juice industry.

In 1872, Charles Welch, who was studying dentistry in Washington, D.C., at the time, took over the enterprise as a part-time endeavor. He commuted home to Vineland to process and sell the juice. His father admonished him for neglecting his dental interests, but Charles continued to pursue both professions for a few years until he devoted his full time to processing grape juice.

In 1896, he moved his operations to Watkins Glen, New York, to be closer to the grape-growing regions of western New York. The next year he moved the company to Westfield, New York, and built a plant capable of processing six hundred thousand pounds of grapes in its first year of operation. Here, at the center of the great Chautauqua and Erie Concord grape belt, which stretches ninety miles along the southeastern shore of Lake Erie, he started his empire. Over the years, Welch would establish plants in the Finger Lakes region of New York, south central Missouri, southwestern Michigan, northwestern Arkansas, and Washington State's Yakima Valley, all Concord-grape-growing areas.

William Jennings Bryan, the U.S. Secretary of State, served the British ambassador Welch's Grape Juice at a diplomatic dinner instead of the customary wine. The press and political cartoonists got ahold of this and used it to lampoon Bryan. A cartoon of Uncle Sam drinking grape juice ran in the papers with the caption "Grape Juice Diplomacy." Welch's became a household name.

More free publicity came the following year, again courtesy of Uncle Sam. Secretary of the Navy Josephus Daniels ordered the replacement of the sailors' monthly ration of rum with Welch's Grape Juice. Again the press had a field day. Slogans such as "Grape Juice Navy" and "Give 'em Grape Josephus" became popular nationally. It wasn't long before Welch's Grape Juice became known as "the National Drink."

Welch's juice got a huge boost from Prohibition. Since Welch's Grape Juice was the only nonalcoholic fruit drink on the market, sales soared. Like his father, Charles had always been a prohibitionist and even ran for the governorship of New York on the Prohibition Party ticket. The timing of the country's forced abstinence couldn't have been better for the man and his juice.

From Dr. Welch's unfermented wine has sprung a host of grape-related products. Welch's is now the world's largest producer of Concord grape products. It currently enjoys the largest market share in bottled, canned, and frozen grape juice and makes what many consider to be the best grape jellies and jams.

What are the different types of drinking water?

The most essential part of any diet is water. We humans can live for several weeks without food, but just a few days without water and we are in trouble. If we lose 10 percent of our body's water content, we experience severe dehydration. If we lose 20 percent . . . don't ask!

The average man's body contains about twenty quarts of water. The average woman has less, due to her smaller size and higher fat content. So if you are a couple of quarts low, you will definitely not be happy. About 50 percent of our daily water loss is through urination. Another 28 percent is lost through perspiration, 20 percent through respiration, and 2 percent through other secretions. To counter this water loss, we need to add about three quarts a day, although not necessarily in the form of tap water. There is no way you could drink that much water every day. Happily, water comes in many forms.

Many vegetables are up to 90 percent water. Bread is about 35 percent water, and even "dry" foods like cookies and crackers have around 5 percent water content. Milk is 87 percent water, and other beverages are almost all water.

If you prefer to drink your water straight (up to eight glasses a day are recommended by some "aquaphiles"), you have quite an array of choices aside from tap water. Drinking water comes in many forms:

Still water is water without bubbles, including tap water, drinking water sold in large containers, and mineral water such as Evian.

Sparkling water is tap water or underground water that contains carbon dioxide gas, either manmade or naturally occurring in the ground. There are two kinds of sparkling waters, and the labeling can be confusing. "Naturally sparkling water" is water that is naturally carbonated in the ground. When it is brought to the surface, its carbon dioxide bubbles out, but it is captured and added back during the bottling process. Examples are Perrier and Saratoga.

"Sparkling natural water" is spring water that is carbonated with carbon dioxide from another source. One example is Poland Spring Water.

Seltzer is common tap water that has been filtered and carbonated.

Mineral water is any water containing dissolved minerals, whether from an underground or surface water source. "Natural mineral water," usually spring water, contains whatever minerals were in it when it came out of the ground. Mineral water not labeled "natural" may have had minerals added or removed before bottling.

Club soda is carbonated water that has had mineral salts such as bicarbonates, citrates, and phosphates of sodium added.

The French are the bottled water drinking champs—14.5 gallons per person per year. The Belgians, Swiss, and Germans aren't far behind. Americans bought 2.7 billion gallons of bottled water last year.

What Frenchman made bottled water fashionable in America?

Perrier was the first European bottled water to make it big in the United States. It was named after a Dr. Perrier, who operated the spring at Vergèze in the South of France. The spring was purchased from Dr. Perrier by an English newspaper man, St. John Harmsworth, around the turn of the century. After Harmsworth was injured in an auto accident and paralyzed from the waist down, he turned his full attention to bottling Perrier. The now familiar bottle was designed to resemble the Indian clubs that he used as exercise weights during his rehabilitation.

Perrier didn't become an American hit until 1977, when its French owner, Gustav Leven, spent millions on promotion in the United States. Up until that time, most American bottled water was simply processed tap water. Only Deer Park from Maryland, Poland Spring from Maine, and Mountain Valley from Arkansas were bottled at the source; and only Mountain Valley was nationally distributed. Then along came Perrier. Now there are countless bottled waters sold here and abroad.

Originally, Perrier was bottled right at the source and the water lost much of its natural carbonation. Now the water and gas are tapped separately and reincorporated at bottling. The Perrier spring feeds a constant flow of water at the rate of twenty-one thousand gallons per hour.

Perrier's American company, Great Waters of France, purchased Poland Spring and has made it a national success.

What is the best-tasting water in the country?

Whether you are talking about any of the hundreds of brands of bottled water, or tap waters around the nation, the one water judged to taste the very best in a 1980 *Consumer Reports* survey was New York City tap water.

New York's finest (the water, not the police) was rated excellent, beating out other popular still waters such as Great Bear Natural Spring (very good), Poland Spring Pure Natural (very good), Deer Park 100% Spring (good), and Evian Natural Spring (good).

Among the sparkling waters, Canada Dry Club Soda, Saratoga Naturally Sparkling Mineral, Canada Dry Seltzer Pure Sparkling, Poland Spring Sparkling Pure Natural Mineral, and Perrier Naturally Sparkling Mineral all rated good. Schweppes Sparkling Mineral, Deer Park Sparkling 100 percent Spring, and Safeway Bel-Air Sparkling Mineral all rated fair.

You shouldn't be surprised at this survey's results. It is estimated that up to 25 percent of bottled water is in fact just tap water, in a bottle.

What is hard water?

Hard water, which comes from artesian wells, has a high mineral content—120 mg of minerals per liter. These minerals include calcium and magnesium salts, or ferrous iron.

Soft water, on the other hand, has a low mineral content and is said to be better tasting. Rainwater is naturally soft.

Cheers!

Why are hops used in making beer?

The English first used hops in beer brewing sometime during the fourteenth century. The hop plant (*Humulus lupulus*) is a common vinelike perennial found growing wild in the United States and Europe. It is the conelike female flower that is of interest to brewers. The female flowers have glands that contain two resins vital to brewing—hammulin and lupulin. These resins give beer its bite. They also inhibit the growth of unwanted bacteria and help a beer hold its head. Hops are known as the "spices" of beer and add their own special aroma.

What is the best-selling beer in the world?

Budweiser is the world's best-selling beer. In 1991, Budweiser alone outsold the next four competitive brands combined. Bud has been Anheuser-Busch's best-selling beer since 1890. Thanks to Budweiser and its other brands, Anheuser-Busch is the number-one U.S. brewer, with a whopping 44 percent share of the market and an annual production of 86 million barrels!

The top ten selling beers in America are:

1. Budweiser
2. Miller Lite
3. Bud Lite
4. Coors Lite
5. Busch
6. Miller Genuine Draft
7. Natural Lite (Anheuser-Busch)
8. Milwaukee's Best (Miller)
9. Miller High Life
10. Old Milwaukee (Stroh)

Who were Anheuser and Busch?

In 1852, Eberhard Anheuser loaned his friend George Schreider, owner of the Bavarian Brewery of St. Louis, money to keep his foundering brewery afloat. By 1855, the brewery was in financial straits again, and Anheuser suddenly found himself the owner. At about the same time, a newly arrived young Bavarian immigrant, Adolphus Busch, began to court Anheuser's daughter Lilly. Anheuser decided to give the twenty-two-year-old Busch a job as a salesman for the brewery.

Busch had no qualifications, but was exceptionally gregarious and friendly. He made new friends wherever he went. The young Bavarian also came up with gimmicks to make clients remember him. In place of the standard business card, Busch would leave potential customers a handy pocketknife bearing the company name and a peephole at one end with a picture of Eberhard Anheuser inside. He also purchased showy draft horses and delivery wagons, which have since become widely recognized company symbols. This rising star was soon president of the Bavarian Brewing Company and later founder of Anheuser-Busch.

Company image and sales gimmicks are all well and good, but there has to be a superior product to back them up. Busch next set out to raise the quality of his beer above that of his many competitors. In 1876, he began adding a small amount of diluted sugars obtained from malt during the fermentation to the beer as it was beginning to age, or lager. This process, known as kraeusening, is a very old European technique that causes a second fermentation of the beer and imparts a natural carbonation to the final product.

Busch also added beechwood chips during aging, thus establishing the company trademark "beechwood aging" process that is still practiced today. The ingredients for this new beer were to be the best available (see page 162). This new beer was christened "Budweiser," after the Czech town of Budweiser where its formula originated. It was the first nationally distributed American beer, and perhaps the best. Bud took top honors at the 1876 World's Fair in Philadelphia and at similar competitions in Europe.

Busch was determined to create an even better draft brew; one for the real connoisseurs of beer. By adding more hops to Budweiser he came up with Michelob, which was quickly accepted in the marketplace.

Busch died in 1913, leaving his son August with a very successful business. Then in 1919 Prohibition was enacted by Congress. So much for the successful beer business! What do you do with a brewery during Prohibition? Aside from making a nonalcoholic beer called Bevo, Anheuser Busch diversified into the production of bakers' yeast, corn products, and even truck bodies and refrigeration units. It also bided its time, waiting for the inevitable end of Prohibition. The day Prohibition was repealed, in December 1933, a glorious Anheuser-Busch wagon, pulled by eight Clydesdale horses, paraded up Fifth Avenue in Manhattan. Public response to the Clydesdales was so great that the company started a breeding farm to preserve this wonderful ancient Scottish horse and to promote Budweiser. The year after the repeal of Prohibition, August Sr. died and his son August Jr. took over.

During the following years, breweries were opened in Newark, New Jersey; Los Angeles, California; Houston, Texas; Tampa, Florida; Columbus, Ohio; Jacksonville, Florida; Fairfield, Connecticut; Merrimack, New Hampshire; and Williamsburg, Virginia. In 1955, the first new beer since Prohibition was introduced—

Busch Beer. It was targeted to the lower-income end of the beer market.

August Jr. died in 1974 and was succeeded by his son August Busch III. With the 1970s came a new company strategy targeting women beer drinkers. Two new lower-calorie light beers— Natural Lite and Michelob Lite—were introduced to satisfy weight-conscious quaffers. Women soon accounted for 40 percent of light beer sales, double their percentage for regular beer.

Despite all the changes in the company during the last century, the one thing that has remained constant is Anheuser-Busch's commitment to quality ingredients and brewing methods.

What ingredients go into Budweiser?

The Budweiser label boasts that only the "Choicest Hops, Rice and Best Barley Malt" are used in its "all natural" brewing process. Just what are the finest domestic beer-making ingredients anyway?

All Anheuser-Busch beers vary in the type and mix of ingredients used to obtain their unique and distinctive characteristics. However, they all are alike in that no artificial ingredients, additives, or preservatives are used. Their ingredients are described below:

Malt: Malt is the "soul" of the beer, and Anheuser-Busch uses more malt per barrel of beer than any other leading major brewer in the country. Its malt begins with golden barley from the fields of Minnesota, the Dakotas, Idaho, Washington, Wyoming, Colorado, Oregon, Montana, and California.

There are two types of malting barleys. One produces two rows of kernels on each stalk; the other, six rows. The flavor of the two varieties differs, with two-row barley malt being a choicer ingredient because it produces a smoother-tasting beer. Anheuser-Busch beers contain varying amounts of two-row barley malt, with Michelob containing the highest percentage.

In a carefully controlled malting procedure, the barley is cleaned, steeped, germinated, and kilned. Malt is a natural source of carbohydrates, enzymes, and flavor compounds. Most enzymes are produced during the malting process. During brewing, the complex malt carbohydrates are broken apart by the enzymes.

As a result, simple sugars are formed. These sugars are used by the yeast as an energy source during fermentation.

Hops: Hops, the cone-shaped flower clusters from the vinelike hop plant, are the spice of the beer. They add their own special aroma, flavor, and character. Anheuser-Busch uses imported and domestic hops from Europe, Washington, Oregon, and Idaho.

Rice: Rice from Texas, Louisiana, Mississippi, Missouri, Arkansas, and California adds lightness and crispness to the Budweiser brand, while the other brands use either rice or corn to obtain their desired flavors.

Yeast: The special brewer's yeast used by all the company's breweries is decades-old and comes from one carefully maintained pure culture.

Water: Pure water is an essential ingredient to brew a great beer. The water is checked often for purity and is treated when necessary to maintain Anheuser-Busch's standards.

How is Budweiser brewed?

Budweiser beer starts with the best ingredients, but it is through the actual brewing process that this American favorite acquires its own special personality. The steps in the Budweiser brewing process follow:

1. The malt and rice are coarsely ground in huge mills.

2. The ground malt and rice are mixed with water in separate tanks, the malt in a mash tank and the rice together with some of the malt in a cooker. Then the mixtures are combined in the mash tank. During mashing, enzymes in the malt break down starch into fermentable sugars.

3. The grains are strained, leaving a clear, amber liquid called wort.

4. The wort moves through the grant, which controls the rate of flow into a brew kettle.

5. In the brew kettle, the wort is brought to a boil and natural hops are added.

6. The spent hops are strained.

7. The wort is cooled to the right temperature to receive the yeast.

8. As the cooled wort flows into the fermentation tanks, yeast is added.

9. For up to six days, the yeast converts the fermentable carbohydrates into carbon dioxide and alcohol, and the wort becomes beer.

10. The beer is transferred to lager tanks. A portion of freshly yeasted wort is added and allowed to ferment and age (this is the kraeusening process). This second fermentation matures the flavor and is a natural way of carbonating the beer. (All Anheuser-Busch beers are naturally carbonated.) Most brewers do not use a second fermentation, but instead add carbon dioxide to their beer before packaging.

    The beechwood aging process is also part of the second fermentation. All of Anheuser-Busch's beers are beechwood-aged. A layer of beechwood chips is placed on the bottom of the lager tank. The chips have been cleaned and rinsed before use. The beechwood chips provide more surface area for the action of the yeast, which settles on the chips and continues to work until the beer is completely fermented. Anheuser-Busch is the only major brewer in the world to use the traditional beechwood aging process.

11. The beer is transferred to a chill-proofing tank and natural tannin is added. The tannin combines with certain proteins, forming particles that settle to the bottom of the tank together with the added tannin. As the beer flows out of the tanks, the protein-tannin particles are left behind. Chill-proofing keeps the beer from becoming hazy when cooled to drinking temperature.

12. The beer is filtered and sent to the packaging area.

The entire brewing process takes at least thirty days or more.

What makes Killian's beer red?

George Killian Lett of Enniscorthy was the last independent brewer in Ireland. In 1981, Coors Brewing Company entered into an agreement with Killian and the Pelforth Brewery of Lille, France, to brew and distribute Killian's Red. Killian's unique red color is derived from a slow roasting process that caramelizes the malt, imparting the distinctive red-amber hue. No colors or additives are used.

Red is becoming the hot color for new brands of beer. Within the last year or so, several brewers have latched onto this latest trend in the beer business, introducing such imaginatively named brews as Red Wolf, Red Dog, and Boar's Head Red. For some reason, however, not all of these new brews are actually red!

Why does France produce such great wines?

The greatness of French wines is a result of geography and history. France's geography has blessed it with a variety of climates, all suited to growing different types of grapes.

Historically, France's neighbors, especially to the north, have imported her wines. This high demand for French wines encouraged the refinement of growing and production techniques. Other wine-growing areas, like Spain and Portugal, historically had Moslem trading partners, whose religion forbids the drinking of wines. Consequently, Spain and Portugal's wine production was primarily for domestic use and thus they lagged behind in refining their wines.

How are red, rosé, and white wines different?

All grape juice is clear after pressing. The colors of various wines are imparted by allowing the juice to stay in contact with the grape skins for varying lengths of time during the fermentation process. The alcohol produced in the wine will slowly extract coloration from the skins.

Red wines owe their color to a long period of contact between the juice and skins, in which the skin pigment—anthocyanin—is extraccted. Rosés are removed from their skins after one or two days, whites almost immediately. Rosés can also be made by blending white and red wines or by fermenting pinkish-red grapes with their skins.

Reds are fermented at about 65° F for about two weeks. Rosés and whites are fermented at colder temperatures for three to six weeks. Cooler temperatures slow down fermentation and thus lengthen the process. The longer a white wine is fermented, the drier it will be. A short fermentation will result in a sweeter white wine.

Most reds need a maturation period before being bottled to lose their tannic bitterness. Maturation is usually carried out in 225-liter oak wood barrels. The wood of the barrels gives off various flavor-enhancing substances—vanillin and tannin—that give wines their individual tastes. Newer barrels impart more flavors than do older barrels. Reds are matured in barrels for anywhere from three months to three years.

Whites are generally not matured long. They are bottled and drunk young. Most whites are bottled with as little contact with oxygen as possible. Whites that are matured, such as German chardonnays and Rieslings, have improved flavor and complexity.

Rosés are seldom put in barrels, as it does them little good.

How does one properly drink a glass of wine?

Perhaps you go to the store, purchase a bottle of wine, throw it in the fridge, remove it sometime later, pull the cork, and down a couple of glasses. As long as it tastes good, you're happy. Life should be so easy! Drinking wine is not meant to be this simple. There is a complexity to the proper handling and drinking of wine.

A good bottle of wine always tastes better after it has rested a few days. After you bring a bottle home, let it stand before opening.

You may try smelling the cork of the bottle. The cork should smell like wine, not cork; otherwise the wine is said to be "corked." The cork must be sniffed the instant that it is pulled, because the wine on the surface of the cork evaporates almost immediately. Smelling the cork in a fine restaurant after the waiter hands it to you is of no practical value. The wine will have already evaporated.

Many old bottles of wine, mainly reds, have dregs at the bottom and should be decanted before drinking. This is done by letting the bottle stand upright for at least an hour to allow the sediment to settle to the bottom. The wine is then carefully opened and slowly poured into a decanter, stopping before the sediment begins to come out. It can then be served after a brief period of breathing. Be careful not to decant more than an hour before drinking. Decanting too early can dissipate the flavor due to excessive breathing time.

Breathing is a somewhat controversial subject to wine lovers. There is disagreement as to how long different wines should breathe. Wine "breathes" when it comes in contact with the air. Many of wine's four hundred or so various compounds begin to react with oxygen when the bottle is opened. Reds in particular should be allowed to breathe. It is best to decant the wine right after opening and then let it breathe in the glass. Each wine is different and so is its optimum breathing time. Allowing wine to breathe in the bottle does very little, as only the surface of the contents actually comes in contact with the air in this way.

The wineglass should have a large bowl and taper toward the top, so that when you swirl the wine, fragrance and perfume collect at the top. Also, make sure your wine is at the proper temperature. Reds should be at about 60° to 65° F, while whites and rosé should be at a cool 50° F. Generally, the lower the quality of the white wine, the cooler it should be served. Some reds, like Beaujolois and Loire, are better slightly chilled.

Hold up the wineglass to the light and check for the wine's clarity and depth of color. Next, swirl the wine releasing the aroma and bouquet. Take a good long sniff. Now you are almost ready to actually drink the wine. But not quite yet!

There is an art to tasting wine. Take some wine in your mouth and breathe out through your nose. If possible, try to draw some air through your lips. This will help carry the wine's aroma into your nasal cavity, which enhances the sense of taste. Next "chew" the wine, moving your jaw up and down. Notice the taste of the wine after a few moments. Then swallow, experience its taste, and a few seconds later its aftertaste.

You bought the wine, let it rest, removed the cork, decanted, poured into the proper glass, checked the color, smelled it, "chewed" it—now you must know how to hold the glass properly. (Nothing is simple with wine.) Unless you want to be put down as a boor, you should hold the glass by the stem. This prevents the warming of the wine and, just as important, keeps those unsightly finger smudges off the glass, which interfere with our full appreciation of the wine's color and clarity.

Down the hatch!

What is "real" champagne?

To be a true champagne, it must come from Champagne, near Reims in France. The vinters of this region learned long ago that by fermenting a wine a second time in the spring, they could transform ordinary wine into a sparkling delicacy.

It wasn't until a Benedictine monk named Dom Perignon came along in the seventeenth century that champagne was truly perfected. He developed the modern *methode champenoise* that is responsible for making wine sparkle. He also learned that the blending of wines from different vineyards produced a champagne superior to that derived from any single wine. Not only that, he was the first to use a cork stopper that resisted the internal pressure of the champagne. Before Dom Perignon began using corks, vintners used wax, oil, or wooden pegs to seal bottles.

To create champagne, the grapes are pressed and fermented, then stored in casks for the winter. The cellar master decides which wines are to be blended in the spring. Up to one hundred different wines can be used in a single blend. A little sugar and yeast are added to the blend to start a second fermentation that will produce the tiny carbon dioxide bubbles. This second fermentation takes place in the bottles, which are tilted downward. After several years, a *remuer* (today a machine is used) twists the bottles vigorously each day to make the sediments settle down on the cork. They are then carefully removed and the now sparkling wine has more sugar added to adjust its dryness before recorking.

What are the different categories of champagne dryness?

Brut is the driest and most popular champagne in America. It has the least sugar added after the second fermentation.

Extra Dry, the next driest, has between 1 and 2 percent added sugar.

Dry (or Sec) has 3 to 6 percent added sugar.

Demi-Sec has 7 to 10 percent added sugar.

Sweet Douce (or Doux) has 10 to 15 percent added sugar.

Most champagnes are made from black and green grapes, such as Pinot Noir, Pinot Meuner, and chardonnay. Champagnes made from green chardonnay grapes are called Blanc de Blancs.

In California, sparkling wines called champagne are made in a manner similar to the *méthode champenoise*, differing in that the second fermentation does not take place in the bottle, but in large glass containers.

Since champagnes are made from blends of wines, no vintage is found on the label. Champagnes are ready to drink when bottled, and should be consumed within a few years of purchase. They do not improve with age.

Why do champagne bottles have that deep indentation at the bottom?

The deep indentation at the bottom of champagne bottles is there for a practical purpose, not just to cheat you out of a little of the bubbly. There are three main reasons for the indentation (referred to as the punt).

The first relates to traditional design. It was found that a recessed cavity in the bottom made pouring from the bottle much easier, especially for people with small hands. Also, by holding the bottle by the bottom lip, the warmth of your hands does not raise the temperature of the chilled champagne.

The second reason has to do with the history of vinting. Champagne bottles were stored horizontally for fermentation and aging. By laying the bottles end to end, with the top of one bottle inserted into the punt of another, more bottles could be stored per bin.

The third reason has to do with the structural integrity of the bottle. Champagne is under pressure in the bottle, hence the warning labels instructing you to aim the bottle away from people when opening. (One champagne cork was shot a record distance of 109 feet!) By having the indentation in the lower portion of the bottle, the glass is made structurally stronger. You will also notice an indentation on other carbonated drink containers, such as soda cans and bottles.

Next time you pour from a bottle of champagne for your friends, do it by holding the lip of the punt between your thumb and forefinger. If you really want to impress them, tell them why the dent is there!

Why does champagne make one feel so festive?

For some reason, champagne seems to make one feel "good" very quickly—much more quickly than wine. This happy effect is due to the carbon dioxide bubbles that make champagne so much fun to drink.

The carbon dioxide speeds the absorption of alcohol by the stomach wall. This gives the circulation a jump start and rushes the alcohol to the brain, where it produces uplifting, pleasant feelings.

How are cooking wines different from table wines?

Wine serves three main purposes in cooking, acting as a marinating substance used before cooking, as a liquid to cook in, and as a flavoring added after cooking.

Because they are so heavily salted, in order to be undrinkable and thus legal to sell without a liquor license, "cooking" wines are largely unsuitable for cooking as well! You would be much better off buying a decent table wine or sherry for cooking. Better still, cook with the same wine you intend to serve with the meal. The rule of thumb is if you wouldn't drink it, don't cook with it!

When used in marinades, wines not only impart their own flavor, but also help foods absorb the other flavorings. Wine's acidity also acts to tenderize meats.

What is the difference between brandy and cognac?

While all cognac is brandy, not all brandy is cognac. Brandy is a spirit distilled from wine or fruit juice. Its name is from the Dutch *brandewijn*, meaning "burnt [or distilled] wine." Brandy distilled from a fruit other than grapes has the name of the fruit attached to it. Most brandy is made from white grapes, which are distilled and aged for at least two years in wood casks. Applejack is the only true brandy produced in the United States. Other American fruit "brandies" are more appropriately called "cordials," because they are not true distillates.

Since cognac is distilled from wine, it falls into the category of brandy. Cognac, however, is brandy that comes from the Cognac region of France, located in that nation's fertile southwestern area, close to the Atlantic Ocean and the Spanish border. The growing area is divided into six *crus*, or vineyards. The finest crus are Grande Champagne, Petite Champagne, Borderies, and Fins Bois, those closer to the town of Cognac—Grand Champagne (closest) and Petite Champagne—being the best. The farther from Cognac a vineyard is, the lower the quality of its grapes.

The Cognac region in the Charente Valley has over 200,000 growing acres. What makes it so special for growing grapes is its chalky limestone soil, mild, humid climate, and "special" sunlight, which is high in ultraviolet rays.

Cognac, by law, must be double distilled. The grapes are picked in October, before fully ripe. Distillation begins in November and the process must be completed by March 31 to ensure that the white wine produced is still young, fruity, and unoxidized. The first stage of distillation lasts between eight and twelve hours and produces the *brouillis*, a clear spirit. It is then redistilled for twelve hours to produce the *eau die vie*, or "water of life," which has an alcohol content of about 35 percent. After distillation, the cognac is sweetened with sugar syrup and is aged for at least three years. The aging process is done in oak barrels from forests adjacent to the Cognac region. It is the wood from these barrels that gives cognac its distinctive amber color.

The quality of the cognac depends on the length of aging and the blending of cognacs from the various growing regions.

What do VS and VSOP mean?

VS ("Very Special") is the name given by cognac suppliers to their youngest cognac when it is sold in the United States. In other international markets, it is called "Three Star." By law, VS must be aged three years. Most VS cognacs are intended for mixing in cocktails.

VSOP ("Very Superior Old Pale") is the next oldest cognac. It is also known as VSO or VO. VSOP must be aged four years, but most good ones are aged at least six years.

Napoleon cognac must be aged at least six years.

These various quality designations are set by French law. The designation indicates the youngest cognac used in the blend. The reason English words are used in these designations, as opposed to French, is that the English were once the largest consumers of cognac.

Cognac does not improve with age after it is bottled. There is no reason to store it away. Its quality will be the same one hundred years from now. Once a VS, always a VS. After a bottle is opened, it should be consumed within one year.

Who makes the world's most popular sherry?

Harvey's Bristol Cream is the world's most popular sherry. And yes, its creator really was a man from Bristol named Harvey.

In 1796, a British merchant named William Perry established a wine importing business in Bristol. Some years later, the business was taken over by his nephew John Harvey, who renamed the firm John Harvey & Sons. Harvey began importing sherry from Jerez, Spain, blending and bottling it in Bristol.

In the late 1800s the firm had a sherry called Harvey's Bristol Milk. As the story goes, an aristocratic lady sampled this and liked it. When offered a newer, finer sherry Harvey had just created, she remarked, "If that is milk, then this must be cream!" Hence the origin of the curious name Harvey's Bristol Cream.

Why is the alcohol content of a distilled spirit referred to as its proof?

You probably already know that the proof of a distilled spirit is simply double the actual percentage of its alcohol content.

The proof is an arbitrary measure of the proportion of alcohol to water. So why don't we just refer to the alcohol content of a beverage by its percentage? The proof is another one of those old customs that is no longer necessary, but is kept out of tradition.

Early distillers didn't have very sophisticated tests to measure alcohol content. Before the 1700s, they would combine equal quantities of gunpowder and the spirit and apply a flame. If the mixture did not burn, it was considered too low in alcohol content. If it flashed, it was considered too high. The proper amount of alcohol produced a mixture that gave a nice, steady blue flame, and the spirit was said to have been "proved." In the early 1800s, the hydrometer was invented to test the specific gravity of alcohol and water mixtures, and thus the percentage of alcohol, but the term "proof" lives on.

Today there are three different proof systems. The familiar American system uses a scale of 0 to 200, where each degree (number) of proof corresponds with 0.5 percent of alcohol by volume. So a spirit of 100 proof is 50 percent alcohol and 50 percent water. The British system is very complicated. It starts at "proof," which is the equivalent of 114.2 U.S. proof, or 57.1 percent alcohol. Anything over this is OP (over proof) and anything below is UP (under proof). The scale tops out at 175.1 proof, or 100 percent alcohol. The simplest system is the French Guy-Lussac system, which is used by the rest of the world. In this system, the ever-practical French logically assign the proof value as that of the alcohol percentage by volume. Tradition seems to die a little harder in the English-speaking countries.

Spirits consist of alcohol, water, and various flavorings. The lower the percentage of alcohol, the higher the amount of flavorings added. Conversely, the higher the proof, the less flavorings in the distillate. The typical range of proofs run from 40 proof for some cordials to a high of 151 proof for some rums. A distillate at 190 proof is called a neutral spirit. Neutral spirits are used for blending purposes in blended whiskey and as the base spirit in the production of vodka, gin, and many cordials.

Why is Kentucky the traditional home of bourbon whiskey?

In colonial America, Pennsylvania was the distilling center. Farmers in western Pennsylvania had been turning their surplus grain into whiskey for years. Then a few short years after the colonies gained their independence from the heavy-taxing English, the newly formed government immediately slapped a tax on whiskey. The farmers were understandably upset, and they revolted in what became known as the Whiskey Rebellion of 1791. George Washington sent in the militia to quash the uprising, in 1794, after tax collectors met with violent resistance.

The rebellion ended without bloodshed, and many distillers looked for greener pastures to the south. They found the perfect limestone-filtered waters for whiskey making in Kentucky, and there they settled, making some of the finest American whiskeys right up to the present day.

The original bourbon is said to have been distilled by a Bourbon County, Kentucky, minister, Reverend Elijah Craig.

How are American, Canadian, Irish, and Scotch whiskey different?

The word "whiskey" is an anglicization of the Gaelic word for "water of life."

Whiskey is a spirit that is aged in wood and produced from the distillation of a fermenting mash of grain. It can be made from any grain, but the most common are corn, rye, and barley. The main differences between the types of whiskey come from the various types of grain and the distillation techniques used.

The four main categories of whiskey are described below.

1. *American whiskey* comes in one of several types:

Straight whiskey is distilled from fermented mash (crushed grain steeped in hot water to ferment) having a minimum of 51 percent of a grain, at not higher than 160 proof. It is aged in new, charred oak barrels for two years or longer. The proof is lowered to not less than 80 by the addition of water at the time of bottling. Nothing else may be added. Whiskeys are aged about six years and are bottled at 80, 86, and 100 proof. Straight whiskeys include:

- Bourbon whiskey—51 percent or more corn
- Rye whiskey—51 percent or more rye
- Wheat whiskey—51 percent or more wheat
- Corn whiskey—80 percent or more corn

Blended whiskey is just that. At least 20 percent of the blend must be straight whiskey, the remainder can be any other whiskey or neutral spirits. As many as seventy-five different straight whiskeys can go into a good blend.

Light whiskey is distilled to between 161 and 189 proof and is stored in charred, seasoned oak barrels.

Tennessee whiskey is made using the sour-mash process described below. It may have a majority of any grain, but must be distilled in Tennessee.

American distillers use two different yeasting or fermentation processes: sweet mash (yeast-mash) and sour mash (yeast-back).

In the sweet-mash process, freshly made yeast is added to the mash in the fermentation process. No liquid recovered after the alcohols have been stilled off (stillage) is used. The sour-mash process has at least 25 percent stillage added to the fermenting mash to help "start" the fermentation. In this way each successive fermentation batch is "related" to the previous batch.

2. *Canadian whiskey* is believed to use rye as its main source of grain. The actual formulation is a trade secret. There are no straight Canadian whiskeys. They are always blended, and have a characteristic light body. They must be aged at least three years (but the average is six) and are usually sold at 86.8 proof.

3. *Irish whiskey* also has rye as a main source of grain, cured with smokeless anthracite. It is smooth and medium-bodied and

must be aged four years, although seven or eight is more common. It is bottled at 86 proof.

4. *Scotch whiskey* uses malted barley as its chief source of grain. It is almost always blended, but blended straight, with no neutral spirits added. Scotch grain is cured by peat smoke, which imparts a distinctive flavor to the whiskey. Scotch must be aged at least four years (seven or eight is usual) and is sold at 86 proof. Scotch whiskey, along with bourbon, is the most popular whiskey in the United States.

Why is Scotch whiskey more popular than Irish whiskey in America?

Before Prohibition, Irish whiskey was the leading imported whiskey in the United States. While Prohibition was a big blow to most distilleries, Cutty Sark Scots Whiskey turned it to its advantage. With the competition greatly reduced in the American market (bootleggers prospered), Cutty Sark found creative ways of penetrating the black market.

"Rum running" from the Bahamas to the East Coast was a highly profitable business. Perhaps the most famous rum runner was an American operating out of Nassau, Captain William McCoy. At a time when most bootleggers were selling spirits of questionable quality, McCoy was selling foreign whiskey, which he guaranteed was the "Real McCoy."

Francis Berry, the senior partner of Berry Brothers and Rudd Ltd., makers of the new Cutty Sark Scotch Whiskey, visited the firm's former agents in the Bahamas in 1921. While the company had no intention of directly meddling in the internal affairs of the United States by running whiskey itself, it had no problem with selling to various agents in the Bahamas, with no questions asked. Thus, Cutty Sark had become firmly established in the United States by the late twenties. In fact, one famous American gangster, Jack "Legs" Diamond, personally stopped by Berry's shop at No. 3 James Street, London, and took away a large order of whiskey in several taxis.

From such an extraordinary entrance into the U.S. market

during Prohibition, Cutty Sark has gone on to be one of the brand leaders today. Over two million cases are sold each year worldwide.

The brand owners, Berry Brothers and Rudd, remain independent, family-controlled wine and spirit merchants. The exact formula of Cutty Sark is a secret even today.

The unfortunate Irish whiskeys never fully recovered from Prohibition. Nice guys do finish last!

What popular spirit's name means "little water"?

Created in the twelfth century in either Russia or Poland, vodka was originally called *zhiznenniavoda* or "water of life." By the eighteenth century, it was known as vodka or "little water," and was being distilled throughout the Russian empire from potatoes, barley, or corn. Of the several varieties, it was the grain-based Petrovskaya, named after Peter the Great, that came to the Western world. It is said that Peter refined its distillation with techniques that he acquired on a secret visit to Holland.

Russian vodka had character and was meant to be drunk straight. Vodka remained almost exclusively an Eastern European drink until after World War II. The only vodka distilled in the United States at that time was Smirnoff, which was a Russian vodka from 1818 until the Communist revolution in 1917, when the Smirnoff family lost control.

American vodka is distilled from corn or wheat and is, by law, colorless, odorless, and almost tasteless. Charcoal filtering gives it a smooth, clean taste. It is because of these characteristics that vodka became such a popular mixer after the war. In the late forties the Moscow Mule (vodka and ginger ale) was the rage. In the sixties it was the Screwdriver, and later the Bloody Mary. Its reputation as a "clean" spirit didn't hurt sales. People thought vodka could not be smelled on the breath and left no hangover. (This, however, was not the case!)

Vodka went from being an exotic prewar drink to the number-one selling type of spirit in the United States by 1976. Stolichnaya ("Stoli") was America's imported vodka of choice for years until the Russian invasion of Afghanistan prompted an American boycott of Soviet products, then Sweden's Absolut became number one.

What is the significance of the fruit bat on the the label of Bacardi rum?

Bacardi rum began, as many things do, with a man and an idea. The man was Don Facundo Bacardi y Maso, born in Stiges, Catalonia, in northeast Spain in 1816. He was the youngest of four brothers, all of whom emigrated to Santiago de Cuba, Cuba, in 1830. There, in a large coastal town settled with fellow Catalonians, Bacardi prospered as a wine importer and merchant.

Don Facundo's idea, which eventually made the Bacardi name famous, was to "civilize" rum, which up until that time was generally unrefined and pungent. The Cuban economy was heavily agrarian and relied almost entirely on the raising of sugar cane, from which sugar and molasses were produced. Christopher Columbus first brought sugar cane to the Caribbean on his second voyage, and since that time rum has been distilled from the locally produced molasses. The early rum was primitive, and its quality had not improved much during the sixteenth and seventeenth centuries, when it was the drink of choice of buccaneers and adventurers of the Spanish Main. To the cultivated taste of a wine connoisseur like Don Facundo, it had a coarse, harsh taste. He resolved to improve its quality.

He experimented with the processes of distillation and blending until he had perfected a rum that was so mellow, light, and pure that it could be sipped straight. This rum was originally created for his own private use. He served it to guests at his home, who loved it. This might have been the end of the story, but as fate would have it, at the same time a small distillery in Santiago was put on the market. It was not very impressive, just a tin-roofed shed that housed an old cast-iron pot still, some fermenting tanks, and a few aging barrels. The shed also happened to be home to a colony of fruit bats. Don Facundo bought the distillery, bats and all, and opened his Bacardi rum business on February 4, 1862.

The distillery became a family business, and the secret formula for Bacardi rum has been passed from generation to generation to this day. People from the area would come to the distillery with their own bottles and jugs to be filled with the rum. Since illiteracy was great in those days, Don Facundo decided to label his rum with an easily recognizable trademark. At the suggestion of his wife, he registered the name and the famous symbol of the fruit bat in honor of the residents of his tin-roofed shed. The bat still adorns the Bacardi label today.

What is America's most popular liqueur?

Imported from Mexico since the turn of the century, Kahlúa is the most popular and mixable liqueur in the United States. No one knows the exact origin of this coffee liqueur, but countries as diverse as Morocco and Turkey claim ownership. Its popularity in such drinks as the Black Russian (Kahlúa and vodka), the White Russian (Kahlúa, vodka, and cream), and Kahlúa in coffee helped catapult the spirit to the number-one spot in America.

It is bottled at 53 proof and is distilled from coffee beans cultivated in the remote mountains of Mexico.

Who was Tia Maria?

The legend of Tia Maria dates back to the time of the Caribbean colonial wars in the seventeenth century.

When the British navy attacked Jamaica, the Spanish governor and his family had to flee to the back country. The governor's daughter, Adela, had time to save only her precious black pearl earrings. They were wrapped for her in a piece of parchment by the family's maid, affectionately called Tia Maria. Upon unwrapping the earrings days later, Adela found that Tia Maria had hastily scribbled the family's secret recipe for coffee liqueur on the scrap of paper.

The family's Jamaican Blue Mountain coffee liqueur has been known as Tia Maria ever since. In her honor, the secret recipe has been handed down from mother to daughter on the daughter's wedding day since that time. To this day, Tia Maria is made from that same recipe saved by the housekeeper in 1655.

What Scottish liqueur is made from heather honey?

Drambuie is supposedly the oldest of the Scottish liqueurs. It was brought to Scotland from France in 1745 by Prince Charles Edward Stuart, heir to the exiled House of Stuart, when he returned to claim the British crown. He met with initial success, but was eventually defeated by the forces of British King George II at the Battle of Cullodeh. The prince hid out with a group of his Highland allies—the MacKinnon clan—on the Isle of Skye. The MacKinnons eventually helped Charles escape back to France. In gratitude, he gave them his family's secret formula for Drambuie.

The name derives from the Gaelic expression *an dram buidheach*, "the drink that satisfies." Today, Drambuie is made from a blend of Highland malt Scotch whiskey, heather honey, herbs, and spices. It has a half-dry taste and is 80 proof. The MacKinnon family still supervises its production.

What widely popular alcoholic spirit was created by a Dutch chemist's search for a diuretic?

In 1650, Dr. Franciscus Sylvius, a chemist at the University of Leiden in Holland, unintentionally created a new spirit—gin. He combined the medicinal juniper berry with a clear, grain-based spirit. The new spirit was called genever (from the Dutch word for "juniper," *genievre*) and was an instant hit. It was inexpensive to produce because juniper berries were quite abundant. Also, it could be consumed immediately after being produced. Most spirits of the time required aging.

The Dutch and English were seemingly always at war during this era, and it wasn't long before the enemy developed a taste for genever. As is the English way, the word was anglicized to "gin." Another change that would be made over time was the addition of certain herbs like angelica, anise, cassia, and coriander.

The Dutch also had problems getting along with the French. William of Orange was determined to destroy the French brandy trade. To do so, he flooded the domestic market with a glut of cheap gin. At one point there were actually three gallons of gin for every person in the country!

American and British gins do not have a strong flavor and are thus a perfect base for mixed drinks. The Dutch genever has a stronger flavor and is usually served straight. Gin is bottled at between 80 and 100 proof and is usually not aged.

So what is sloe gin? Sloe gin is not gin at all. It has no juniper berries in it, but is a liqueur flavored with the plumlike sloe berry. Sloe gin is bottled at 42 proof.

What's in a Name?

Who was Lorna Doone?

Introduced in 1912, Lorna Doone cookies were named for the British heroine of a novel written by Richard Blackmore. The cookie has proved more memorable than the long-forgotten novel. Lorna Doones were originally used at teas to make little shortcake sandwiches by putting fruit or jelly between them.

Who was Duncan Hines?

Unless you were born before the mid-fifties, you probably think Duncan Hines is some guy who sold cake mix or a creation of Madison Avenue. Those of you who are a little older should know that he was famous long before his name first appeared on cake mix boxes.

Duncan Hines began as a salesman working out of Chicago in the early thirties. His curious hobby was dining at as many different restaurants and diners as he could while driving around on business, and recording what he liked and didn't like about each. He was constantly asking his business contacts, "Where's the best place to eat?" As his copious notes on roadside eateries grew, his business colleagues would consult Hines on where to eat when traveling on various highways.

One day a Chicago newspaper ran an article about the man and his unique hobby. The piece triggered a constant barrage of phone calls from perfect strangers for dining advice. In an attempt to reduce the volume of calls he was receiving, he printed up a thousand copies of a card called "Adventures in Dining" in 1935. On it he listed 167 restaurants he recommended in thirty different states. He mailed these as Christmas cards to all those business associates and total strangers who had bugged him for his advice. Instead of solving his problem, the cards just whetted the public's appetite for more and more cards. A year later, to meet public demand, he expanded his card list into a self-published book, *Adventures in Good Eating*.

He quit his job and devoted his full attention to evaluating restaurants. He logged some fifty-thousand miles per year and often had six different meals a day! Each year sales increased, and by 1939, he was selling one hundred thousand copies a year. He constantly updated his guidebook, and restaurants clamored to be included. Restaurants he liked could obtain a sign reading "Recommended by Duncan Hines" to attract customers. *Adventures in Good Eating* was a publishing phenomenon for twenty-five years until the interstates came along and changed America's traveling and eating habits.

Duncan Hines was well recognized and well respected from coast to coast, and he made a good living from his books. In 1948, however, an even better financial opportunity came along. Upstate New York businessman Roy H. Clark was looking for a personality to front a new line of food products. (Clark was the advertising and public relations director for a farmer's cooperative that is today called Agway.) A survey showed that Duncan Hines was associated with good food, more so than any other American of the time. He was better known than Vice President Alben Barkley. Within a few weeks of their introduction, Duncan Hines cake mixes captured 48 percent of the market.

The cake mixes were different from the other ones being offered at the time. The Duncan Hines mixes, like others, included dried milk, but removed the usual dehydrated eggs. The box had a fatherly picture of Duncan Hines and the saying, "I have found that strictly fresh eggs mean a bigger, better cake ... in appearance, flavor and freshness."

Although Duncan Hines cake mixes are what we know the man for today, there were once actually over two hundred different food items with the Duncan Hines label.

Duncan Hines was purchased by Procter and Gamble in 1956.

Was there ever a real Betty Crocker?

Betty Crocker has been a trusted kitchen friend for over seventy years. Her face has adorned flour and cake mix products for decades and has become associated with quality baking. Betty's friendly persona was, however, created as a public relations aid by a 1920s milling company. The Washburn Crosby Company, a forerunner of General Mills, ran a sales promotion for Gold Medal Flour in 1921. It offered consumers a pincushion shaped like a sack of flour if they could complete a jigsaw puzzle of a flour milling scene. Thousands of entries poured in, many of them with attached questions regarding baking problems.

Sam Gabe, the company's advertising manager, thought it would be appropriate for a woman to answer the letters. Taking the last name of a recently retired company executive, William G. Crocker, and a friendly-sounding first name, Betty, a fictitious person was created to respond to inquiries. A woman from the company with nice handwriting was chosen to sign "Betty Crocker." Her signature is the one still in use today.

In 1924, "Betty Crocker" started doing food service programs on the radio. By 1936, Betty was so popular that a face was needed to go with the persona. A portrait was commissioned from the prominent New York artist Neysa McMein. In the studio, McMein blended the facial characteristics of several of the women working in the company's Home Service Department into a motherly image that was then used for nearly twenty years.

Betty has changed over the years. In 1955, she was repainted into a softer, smiling version of the original image. She was modernized again in 1965 and 1968. In 1972, to keep up with the changing role of women, Betty became more businesslike and stiffer looking, more like an accountant than someone you'd expect to find in the kitchen whipping up a batch of cookies. Her image softened again in 1980 to represent someone all women could identify with. (Apparently men don't buy Betty Crocker's products!)

Was there ever a real Aunt Jemima?

Unlike Uncle Ben, Betty Crocker, and Colonel Sanders, Aunt Jemima is purely fictional. The Aunt Jemima character was created in 1889 by Chris L. Rutt. He wanted a product name that would reflect the "festive spirit" of pancakes. The name Aunt Jemima came from a popular vaudeville song of the time.

The first Aunt Jemima was a Chicago woman named Nancy Green. She was chosen to portray Aunt Jemima at the 1893 Chicago World's Fair by doing pancake-making demonstrations. Over the years several women have represented this now-famous trademark for various promotions, but the trademark portrait is an artist's conceptualization that is periodically modernized. The latest portrait of Aunt Jemima makes her look less like a servant and more like an independent woman. No longer does she wear a kerchief over her head. She now sports a modern hairstyle and pearl earrings. The name, however, still has some negative connotations.

There is some controversy today about the appropriateness of using Aunt Jemima as a logo. Many feel that the figure is stereotypical. Aunt Jemima Pancake Mix, however, has been a successful trademark for over one hundred years and is not likely to be dropped now.

Is there really a Chef Boyardee?

Yes, Chef Boyardee was indeed a real person. He is one of the people responsible for popularizing Italian cuisine in the United States. Prior to the 1930s Italian food was readily available only in restaurants. Chef Boyardee changed all that.

In 1915, Hector Boiardi, age seventeen, immigrated to the United States from his native northern Italy at the urging of family friend Enrico Caruso. He already had six years of hotel and restaurant experience. Boiardi eventually became the head chef of one of New York's finest restaurants and had the honor of catering President Woodrow Wilson's wedding reception. He also opened a very successful restaurant of his own in Cleveland.

This restaurant was unique in that customers entered and left through the kitchen. Boiardi made a habit of asking them as they left how they enjoyed the meal, especially the spaghetti. It wasn't long before people started asking for spaghetti sauce to go. Many of his customers commented that even with his sauce, their spaghetti still didn't taste as good at home. Chef Boiardi then began including a package of his special blend of cheese with each sauce order. Then, so there would be no difference from what people ate at the restaurant, he started to include uncooked spaghetti with the sauce and cheese. Thus was born the complete packaged "Italian Spaghetti Dinner," an instant success.

Chef Boiardi then began selling his new product to stores. This consumed so much of his time that he hired a food distributor to handle sales so that he could still run the restaurant. Salesmen and customers had trouble pronouncing his name, which prompted him to change the name of his product to the "Americanized" Boyardee. The company was named Chef Boyardee Quality Foods.

By 1938, the company had outgrown its three Cleveland plants. Boiardi closed his restaurant and set up new company headquarters in Milton, Pennsylvania. From there grocery stores across the country were shipped the chef's dinners, spaghetti sauce, and canned pasta.

During World War II, the company was a major supplier of the prepared food for Allied troops. After the war, Boiardi sold the company to American Home Food Products, but remained an adviser until his death in 1985 at the age of eighty-seven.

The familiar chef's picture is still on all Chef Boyardee labels.

How did various dishes get named for certain places and people?

Baked Alaska

This dessert of ice cream encased in hot pastry is believed to have been first created by American-born physicist Benjamin

Thompson in the late 1700s. Thompson's experiments with heat led to the invention of the first efficient cooking range, an early percolator, and the dessert we now call Baked Alaska, which uses a cake base and meringue topping to insulate an ice cream center from the heat of the oven.

Different varieties of this dish were popular in America as early as 1800. Originally, it was known as Alaska–Florida, since it is a cold and hot dessert. Later in the 1800s, it was shortened to Alaska (or Baked Alaska) on the menu of the world-famous Delmonico's Restaurant in New York City. Delmonico's was "the" restaurant of the time and it created and named many dishes that are still with us today.

Beef Stroganoff

Here is a dish associated with Russia that was really created by a French chef in the late nineteenth century for a Russian aristocrat named Count Paul Stroganoff. After the Russian revolution in the early twentieth century, the Russian nobility fled the country and beef Stroganoff caught on internationally.

Boston Baked Beans

How did baked beans become so closely associated with the city of Boston (Beantown)? Baked beans and Boston have been together since the days of the Puritans. Work, including cooking, was forbidden on the Puritan Sabbath, which lasted from sundown on Saturday to sundown on Sunday. Beans would be prepared on Saturday in a large pot and kept warm to feed the family over the Sabbath. Many local bakers would call on households on Saturday morning and pick up the family bean pot for baking. It would be returned by Saturday night, usually with some brown bread. The beans and bread were eaten with fish cakes for Sunday breakfast and lunch. This led to a huge baked bean business in Boston that still thrives today.

Buffalo Wings

Buffalo wings really were first created in Buffalo, during the 1960s. The owners of The Anchor Bar, in Buffalo, New York, received an over shipment of chicken wings one day and came up with this hot and spicy way of serving them, in order boost their sales.

Chicken Kiev

A dish strongly associated with Russia today, chicken Kiev also is a French creation. It was first made by French chefs visiting Kiev for the Russian nobility during the czarist era.

Eggs Benedict

Eggs Benedict is an elegant breakfast like no other. A rich dish of eggs, bacon, and Hollandaise sauce, served on an English muffin, eggs Benedict is another famous creation of the cooks at New York's Delmonico's Restaurant. Like other Delmonico's dishes, eggs Benedict was named for a couple of its best customers—a Mr. and Mrs. Benedict. It is probably safe to say that no other American restaurant has created and named such a number of dishes that are still popular today.

Lobster Newburg

It's not from Newburgh, New York. This is another creation of Delmonico's. One of their best customers was a man named Ben Wenburg, who loved lobster. In his honor, the restaurant created a dish called "Lobster Wenburg." Following a subsequent falling out with Mr. Wenburg, Delmonico's changed the name to Lobster Newburg. Sorry, Ben!

New England Clam Chowder

Many centuries ago, when the French fishing fleets would return home, each man put a portion of his catch into a large community copper pot—*la chaudière*. The whole village would feast to celebrate their safe return. The French colonists took this practice to Canada and it eventually became popular in New England, where *la chaudière* became "chowder."

The most famous New England chowder is clam chowder, which always contains clams and salt pork or bacon. Traditional New Englanders recoil at the thought of Manhattan clam chowder, which adds tomatoes and replaces the milk with water. The Maine legislature once passed an actual law forbidding the mixing of clams and tomatoes!

Oysters Rockefeller

It was created in 1899 at the famed Antoine's restaurant in New Orleans by Jules Alciatore, and not for John D. Rockefeller. Its name was, however, inspired by Rockefeller. Upon tasting the dish, one of Antoine's customers exclaimed, "Why, this is as rich as Rockefeller!"

Peach Melba and Melba Toast

Peach Melba and Melba toast were both created and named for the same person—Nellie Melba. She was a popular singer of the late 1880s. One of her most avid fans was a chef named Auguste Escoffier. Melba often performed a role in a Wagner opera (*Lohengrin*) in which she rode a large swan float across the stage. Escoffier loved this particular scene and created a dish in Melba's honor of peaches, vanilla ice cream, and berries, presented on a swan ice sculpture. The singer was delighted with the chef's peach Melba and she ate it often, perhaps too often. Melba began to put on weight and had to watch her diet. The ever-thoughtful Escoffier then came up with a low-calorie dish for the singer—Melba toast.

Salisbury Steak

Salisbury "steaks" are minced meat patties made from trimmings of hind and chuck. They are named for a turn-of-the-century physician and food faddist, Dr. J. H. Salisbury. The good doctor recommended eating these meat patties three times a day, believing that this diet could prevent all sorts of ailments, from asthma to tuberculosis.

The doctor may have been wrong about the Salisbury steak's medicinal properties, but what would the frozen dinner business have done without it?

Welsh Rabbit

As you probably know, there is no rabbit in Welsh rabbit, also known as Welsh rarebit. Purportedly, a Welsh chieftain of old ran out of game to serve his dinner guests. He asked his cook to create a dish using whatever was on hand. The clever cook came up with a cheese dish that he called rabbit so as not to indicate to the guests that the meat supply had run out.

Another story has it that this dish of cheese and beer was served to the Welsh kitchen help while the English gentry dined on rabbit and wine.

Whatever the real origins are, the name has persisted ever since in America, although many cookbooks now attempt to correct the misnomer, using the word "rarebit" instead.

What are the origins of some of the more curious culinary terms?

Al Dente

Al dente, literally translated from Italian, means "to the tooth." It describes pasta and vegetables that are cooked until just done, retaining some firmness and resistance when chewed. The technical culinary term for "al dente" is "percussion."

Cacciatore

"Cacciatore," spelled *cacciatora* in Italy, means "hunter's style." This dish was supposedly invented by a hunter's wife after he returned home with only a handful of mushrooms, olives, and tomatoes. While game is not usually served cacciatore (chicken is), the dish is always served with copious amounts of spaghetti, making it a favorite of outdoorsmen with hearty appetites.

Chop Suey

What dish reminds one more of China than chop suey? Not many! But chop suey is an American dish. It was first created by Chinese cooks in the American West to feed the laborers working on the Union Pacific Railroad in the 1800s. They mixed together a variety of vegetables and pork or chicken and called the dish chop suey, after the Chinese *shop sui*, meaning "odds and ends."

Florentine

"Florentine" in French cooking indicates the use of spinach. In Italian cooking, it simply means that the dish is a specialty of Florence.

It was Catherine de' Medici, who left Florence in 1533 to become the queen of France in 1547, who introduced haute cuisine and a love of spinach to France. She had her royal Italian chefs incorporate spinach into every meal of her day. So profound was her influence on French cooking that any dish containing spinach is so indicated by the addition of the word "Florentine" to its name.

Jambalaya

Jambalaya was originally a ham-only dish, brought to New Orleans by the Spanish in the late eighteenth century. Its name derived from the Spanish word for ham (*jamon*). The French *à la*, meaning "in the manner of," and the African *ya*, meaning "rice," were added to give it a rough translation of "ham with rice." The Creole cooks embraced the dish and added shrimp and crab from the Gulf, as well as numerous other ingredients.

Parmesan

Parmesan cheese is a mixture of whole and skim milk developed near Parma, Italy. It has a hard granular texture and is perfect for grating. Romano cheese is very similar to Parmesan, but has a sharper, more pungent flavor.

Parmesan dishes today generally are covered with tomato sauce and mozzarella cheese, but not always Parmesan cheese. Red sauce dishes traditionally come from southern Italy—Naples or Sicily. Why, then, is a tomato sauce dish like eggplant Parmesan named for Parma, which is in the north? It is believed that the dish is not named for the city of Parma, but for the thatched palm-roofed houses common in southern Italy. These palm roofs are built in layers, much as eggplant Parmesan is built in similar layers. The original name of the dish was probably eggplant *palmigiana*, which later became *parmigiana*, or "Parmesan."

Sukiyaki

The Japanese word for "hoe" is *suki* and the word for "broil" is *yaki*. Sukiyaki has its origins in Japan's ancient history, when the peasant class was forbidden to eat meat. Farmers would quickly cook whatever game came their way whenever they found it—often using their hoe as a skillet!

Teriyaki

This word comes from the Japanese *teri*, meaning "shiny or glazed," and *yaki*, meaning "broiled." In Japanese teriyaki cooking, foods are marinated in a mixture of soy sauce, wine, and spices, and then glazed with the sauce in a frying pan or on a grill. In this country, beef teriyaki is often made on a hibachi.

How's your Spanish?

Burrito is Spanish for "little donkey." It is a tortilla that is wrapped around beef, chicken, or pork, and served with taco sauce.

Enchilada is a Spanish-American word meaning "filled with chili." An enchilada, for those of you who don't live in the Southwest or frequent Chi-Chi's or Taco Bell, is a tortilla folded around a mixture of meat, cheese, chili, etc.

Tostadas are tortillas that are fried until crispy. Their name means "toasted."

What is the meaning of "hors d'óeuvre"?

In France, hors d'óeuvre are not what we are accustomed to in the United States. The French use the phrase to describe cold or hot foods served at the beginning of a meal. Hors d'óeuvre are often a selection of tart foods served *at* the table. In America, we use the phrase to describe finger food passed around during cocktail hour. What we eat really should be called appetizers.

By the way, "hors d'óeuvre" always remains in the singular. It literally means "outside the work" in French. It refers to food eaten before the main meal, and since there is only one meal (d'óeuvre), technically, it should not be written "hors d'óeuvre*s*," although both spellings are commonly used.

How did hush puppies get their curious name?

According to Southern legend, the hounds that would accompany men on their hunting expeditions were always hungry and began to yelp frantically when they caught scent of the fish their masters fried up for dinner. To placate the dogs, the hunters would drop small balls of cornmeal batter into the fish pan and then toss them to the noisy hounds with the admonishment "Hush, puppies!"

Did French fries originate in France?

The French have long enjoyed deep-fried potato slices, which they called *pommes frites*. During the 1800s, vendors began selling them on the streets of Paris. By the turn of the century, they had been introduced to London and served as fried chips with fish.

The introduction of French fries into the United States is somewhat unclear. One interesting (if apocryphal) story has it that the long, thin French fries we are familiar with today came over here during World War I. During the war, potatoes had become the staple of many European countries and several ways of preparing this versatile crop were devised. The Belgians in particular came up with a tasty twice-fried potato snack. While American soldiers were stationed in Belgium, this fried snack became a favorite. The doughboys in southern Belgium, not realizing that they were buying their fries from French-speaking Belgians, took to calling them "French" fries.

Had the doughboys had a better sense of geography, we might all be enjoying "Belgian" fries with our Coke and cheeseburgers today. The term "French" fry is still strictly American. In most foreign countries, they are so associated with the United States that they are called "American" fries.

What is humble pie?

Did you ever eat humble pie? You may have had to swallow your pride on occasion, but you have probably never eaten genuine humble pie. There really is such a dish, and as its name implies, it has something to do with humility.

In old England, the entrails of animals were known as "úmbles." The gentry would keep the venison for themselves and give the innards to the lowly servants. It was customary for the lower classes to make a pie out of the entrails, known as umble or "humble" pie because of their station in life.

How did shoo-fly pie come by its interesting name?

You probably guessed this one correctly. Flies love molasses. The Pennsylvania Dutch bakers who popularized this dessert were constantly shooing flies while preparing the pie.

Who invented the sandwich?

You think you know this one, right? No, it wasn't the Earl of Sandwich. It *was* named for him, but food served between or within bread is as old as bread itself. John Montagu, the Fourth Earl of Sandwich (1718–1792), however, is forever remembered for popularizing his namesake in English high society.

The story goes that the hard-gambling earl didn't like to leave the gambling tables to dine. In order to eat his meal, he had it placed between two pieces of bread. This left his hands free and eliminated the need for a plate, knife, or fork. Sandwiches soon became the vogue in England and on the Continent.

Of course, people have eaten sandwich-like creations for ages, such as the Mexican tortilla and Middle Eastern pita pockets. Even the early European trencher (see 218) was a type of open-faced sandwich.

What is the origin of the word "tip"?

Today a tip is almost mandatory when dining out, regardless of how good or bad the service may be. This was not true, however, before the seventeenth century in London. The 1600s and 1700s saw a vast popularity and profusion of coffeehouses. For one penny you could be admitted and enjoy some sort of entertainment. For two pennies more, a serving wench would bring you a cup of coffee.

A brass box was often put out with the words "To Insure Promptness" printed on it. The wise customer made a donation. Our custom of tipping began here. The word "tip," as you have already guessed, is an acronym for "To Insure Promptness."

How did the "continental" breakfast get its name?

For many of us, a snack of pastry and coffee does not constitute breakfast, although it does at most motel chains. Most Americans prefer an actual meal for breakfast.

The peoples of the European continent, the French in particular, eat a light morning snack, not a full meal, hence the word "continental" breakfast. They are amazed by the tradition in the British Isles of the full-course breakfast. The typical English breakfast is a *real* meal—the cereal and milk or fruit as a first course, the bacon and eggs as the main course, and the toast and jam as the dessert.

Technically, both meals can be classified as breakfasts. The word "breakfast" simply means "to break the fast." Actually, any meal that you eat after several hours of fasting could be called break-fast, regardless of the time of day.

Why do we call drinking to someone's honor a "toast"?

In medieval France the wine wasn't quite as good as it is now. In order to make it more palatable at feasts and weddings, pieces of spiced toast were floated in the wine goblet. It became a tradition for whoever was able to drink his wine the fastest and swallow the toast to have the right to make a short speech. Not surprisingly, these speeches, which often were to thank the host or honor the bride, became known as toasts.

What's the connection between TV Dinners and television?

The "TV Dinner" was first introduced forty years ago by Swanson and sold for ninety-eight cents. Swanson trademarked the name "TV Dinner" and designed the packaging to look like a television set, with knobs along the bottom and food pictured on the screen.

When the first turkey TV Dinner debuted in 1954, television was in its infancy. There were just three or four hours of programming a day, usually in the late afternoon and early evening. Anyone with a new set wanted to watch the new shows, and dinner in the dining room or kitchen took away from precious viewing time. TV sets were large and too heavy to be moved to the room where dinner was being served. The logical solution was to make dinner portable and serve it in the TV room.

The large influx of women into the workforce during and after World War II also created a market for a quickly prepared dinner. The introduction of refrigerators with larger freezers in the fifties was another boost for frozen dinners.

The main hurdle Swanson had to overcome was the guilty feelings women had about serving their families frozen food, rather than making it from scratch. Those feelings of guilt apparently are long gone. Swanson now sells about 85 million traditional, four-compartment frozen dinners a year. Today, with microwave ovens, a frozen dinner can be served in five minutes. It used to take thirty minutes in the old days.

Swanson, now owned by Campbell, competes with several other frozen dinner giants—ConAgra (Healthy Choice), Kraft General Foods (All American Gourmet), Heinz (Weight Watchers), and Nestlé (Stouffer's and Lean Cuisine). In total, the frozen food industry now grosses $52 billion a year!

What are the three most popular frozen dinners? Believe it or not, they are the first three introduced forty years ago—turkey, fried chicken, and Salisbury steak.

What is canola oil?

Canola oil is one of those products embraced by the new health-conscious consumer. It is low in saturated fats and has gained in popularity recently, as have corn oil and sunflower oil. But what is canola?

Canola plant varieties were developed from rapeseed, an oilseed crop in the mustard family. Rapeseed (*Brassica napus* and *Brassica campestris*) has been grown for years for industrial oils. Scientists in Canada were able to breed new varieties of rapeseed that were suitable for cooking. They named their creation canola to honor Canada.

Canola seed contains 40 to 45 percent oil, of which 6 percent is saturated fatty acids. Canola oil contains less fat than any other oil: 50 percent less than corn oil and olive oil and 60 percent less than soybean oil.

How did the Popsicle get its name?

It is said that an eleven-year-old boy named Frank Epperson accidentally created a "Popsicle" when he left a powdered soda pop mixture outside on a cold night with the stirring stick still in the container. The next morning Frank awoke to find his pop frozen on the stick. The boy thought this was kind of neat and showed all his friends. Little did he realize what he had discovered.

It wasn't until many years later, when Frank was running a lemonade booth at an amusement park in Oakland, California, that he saw its commercial possibilities. At first he sold his creation as an "Epsicle." His kids, however, called them "pop's sicles," since their pop made them. The word "Popsicle" was patented in 1923.

Where is mayonnaise from?

It is said that mayonnaise was created from eggs and olive oil in 1756. The Duke of Richelieu's chef supposedly concocted this sauce in honor of the duke's capture of the port of Mahón on the Spanish island of Minorca. The duke called it *mahonnaise*. The word ending "aise" means "after the manner of."

Some food historians believe, however, that the word "mayonaise" actually was associated with the French Duke of Mayenne as early as 1589. Either way, we eat about three pounds of the stuff a year!

What's so devilish about devil's food cake?

If you look closely at devil's food cake, you will notice that it has a slight hint of red. This reddish color is attributable to the combination of baking soda, buttermilk (or yogurt), and cocoa in the ingredients. The baking soda, which is an alkaline, reacts with the buttermilk, which is an acid, to impart a red color to the chocolate. Since red is a color associated with the devil, the name evolved.

Another reason it's called devil's food cake is that this dark, rather heavy cake is the opposite of white light angel cake. Devil Dogs snack cakes are made with devil's food cake, as are Ring Dings.

Dining Out

Who opened the first restaurant?

Throughout most of history, transportation was so slow that most people never strayed far from home, and consequently almost all meals were eaten at home or at a friend's home. Some urban areas had street vendors, but the restaurant as we know it today is of fairly recent origin.

In the France of two hundred years ago, anyone involved in cooking or baking for the public, either in shops or as vendors, was required to belong to guilds. There was a pastry vendor's guild, a bread baker's guild, and a roaster's guild. There was, however, no soup maker's guild. Enter a man named Boulanger. Taking advantage of a loophole in the law, Boulanger began selling sheep's feet cooked in white broth and started a new kind of establishment—the public restaurant.

On the front of his business, Boulanger hung for the first time a sign reading "Restaurant." The word derives from the French for "restore," indicating that his soups had restorative properties.

Who is Dave Thomas?

If you watch television, you know who he is. He appears in a string of seemingly endless but always entertaining commercials. Who is this guy, and why is he so popular?

R. David Thomas was born on July 2, 1932, in Atlantic City, New Jersey, and was raised by his adoptive parents in Kalamazoo, Michigan. When he was fifteen, his family moved to Fort Wayne, Indiana, and Thomas became a busboy at the Hobby House Restaurant. He left school after the tenth grade to devote his life to the restaurant business.

In 1962, Thomas accepted the challenge of turning around four failing Kentucky Fried Chicken carry-outs in Columbus, Ohio. He soon realized one of the reasons the restaurants were failing was because they had no focus. So he cut the hundred-item menu to just a few items, primarily chicken and salads. To increase public awareness, he opted for air time. The restaurants began to prosper and he added four more locations. In 1968, he sold the restaurants back to KFC for $1.5 million, thus becoming a millionaire at the young age of thirty-five.

Thomas soon became regional operations director for KFC, in charge of three-hundred restaurants. During this time, he traveled with Colonel Harland Sanders, learning his business techniques.

While working for the KFC company, Thomas remained "drawn to hamburgers." And although critics were quick to point out that the restaurant industry was considered saturated, Thomas opened the first Wendy's Old Fashioned Hamburgers restaurant on November 15, 1969, in downtown Columbus. He named the restaurant after his eight-year-old daughter Melinda Lou, who was nicknamed Wendy by her brother and sisters.

The first Wendy's menu included fresh, made-to-order hamburgers, chili, french fries, soft drinks, and a Frosty Dairy Dessert. Competitors scoffed at his methods, especially his use of fresh beef for hamburgers. But the business prospered and grew. In 1973, Thomas began franchising the Wendy's concept. Instead of selling single franchises, Thomas pioneered the idea of selling franchises for entire cities and parts of states to experienced restaurant operators with sound financial backing.

Customers responded to Wendy's promise of old-fashioned quality and value, and the new chain grew rapidly, with more than one-thousand units opening in its first one-hundred months. That rapid growth, faster than any other franchise in history, continued, and Wendy's and its franchisees now operate more than four-thousand restaurants in the United States and over thirty countries and territories worldwide.

What's really in McDonald's food?

McDonald's is the largest food service organization in the world. It has sold over eighty billion hamburgers since being founded in 1948. We've all eaten McDonald's food and probably will eat more. So what's in it? Here's a quick overview:

Beef: McDonald's uses one-hundred percent beef that meets the USDA Standard for lean ground beef, that is, at least 77.5 percent fat-free. The ground beef in the McLean Deluxe Sandwich is 91 percent fat-free.

Potatoes: McDonald's french fries and hash browns are made from Russet Burbank potatoes.

Chicken: The chicken in Chicken McNuggets, McChicken Sandwiches, and Chicken Fajitas is USDA-inspected boneless and skinless white meat.

Fish: The Filet-O-Fish Sandwich is made from prime whitefish from the North Atlantic or Bering Sea.

Eggs: All eggs are Grade A large.

Oranges: McDonald's orange juice is from sweet Florida orange concentrate, with no sugar added.

Wheat: All buns are made with enriched wheat flour with added calcium.

Milk: McDonald's serves 1 percent lowfat. Skim milk is the main ingredient in its lowfat milk shakes, and its lowfat frozen yogurts are 99.5 fat-free.

Cheese: Only real cheese is used.

Oils: Only 100 percent vegetable oil is used to cook french fries, hash browns, fish, chicken, and pies.

Sauces: McDonald's has recently reduced by 50 percent the fat in its Big Mac sauce, tartar sauce, and mayonnaise.

If you are watching your weight, consider the following:

- The meal with the lowest calories and total fat content is Chicken Fajitas, with 190 calories and 8g fat.
- A Quarter Pounder with cheese has 510 calories 28g fat.
- McLean Deluxe has only 10g fat. With cheese it has 14g fat.
- Large fries have 400 calories and 22g fat.
- The breakfast sandwich with the worst numbers for dieters is the Sausage Biscuit with Eggs. It has 505 calories and 33g fat.

Where does McDonald's beef come from?

There have been rumors going around the past few years that McDonald's is a major abuser of the environment. Claims are that its cattle ranching enterprises in Brazil are responsible for massive clear-cutting of the rain forests. When one hears these things, one may be reluctant to dine at McDonald's. These claims, however, like most unfounded rumors, need some explaining

McDonald's has recently strived to be an environmentally friendly company. It buys all its beef, whenever possible, in the country where it is sold. In fact, all McDonald's hamburgers sold in the United States come from domestically grown beef. In Canada they are all made from Canadian beef. The same is true of Europe. In Central and South America, its beef is purchased from long-established cattle ranches and ranges that do not use rain forest land. The company carefully checks the origin of all its beef. If it finds a supplier has sold it rain forest beef, it drops that supplier immediately.

This information may not make McDonald's burgers taste any better, but at least you can feel less guilty for eating one.

What about McDonald's solid waste?

The company has finally switched from its environmentally unsound polystyrene packaging to recyclable paper. This step has reduced the volume of its sandwich wrapping by 90 percent. It now recycles or composts everything it can and uses a great deal of recycled paper. All McDonald's tray liners, Happy Meals boxes, napkins, and drink holders are made of recycled paper. All the corrugated boxes used to deliver goods to the restaurants are recycled. Its carryout bags are made from at least 50 percent post-consumer newspapers and its own corrugated boxes.

McDonald's has gone so far as to identify over 250 other items that can be made from recycled materials, such as furniture, desk supplies, and cleaning equipment. For example, it has used nearly 3.6 million pounds of recycled tires to make the nonskid surfaces of its seventeen-hundred Playlands. Its ultimate goal is to divert 80 percent of the solid waste it produces from the American waste stream.

It's nice to see that some of the major corporations are starting to get their environmental acts together.

Is McDonald's food the same the world around?

With more than twelve-thousand restaurants around the globe you might think the Big Mac you get in Peking is different from the one you buy around the corner. Never fear, they are the same everywhere in the world. There are, however, certain foods offered in different countries that you will not find at your local McDonald's.

For instance, the lucky Germans can quaff a "McBeer" to rinse down their McNuggets. In Japan one can order a teriyaki burger, and in Malaysia one can get the ever-popular drink sugar-cane juice.

McDonald's Fun Facts:

- McDonald's has sales of over $19 billion a year, more than double that of Burger King!
- McDonald's is the second-best-known brand in the world.
- McDonald's uses twenty-five-hundred tons of sesame seeds a year.
- One hundred shares of McDonald's stock purchased in 1965 for $2,250 would have grown to 18,950 shares worth $700,000 in 1992.
- Almost seven dollars out of every hundred dollars spent on eating outside the home is spent at McDonald's.

- McDonald's is one of the thirty companies that comprise the Dow-Jones Industrial Average.

What nationwide fast-food chain started in the same year and in the same town as McDonald's?

San Bernadino, California, was quite a place to start a fast food business in 1947. In that year, an ex-Marine named Glen Bell bought a San Bernadino hot dog stand for four-hundred dollars. By 1952, business was so good at Bell's Drive-In that he decided to add hamburgers to the menu. He bought a new stand, and then another.

To differentiate himself from the two brothers named McDonald who also started a hamburger business in San Bernadino in 1947, he switched to Mexican food. Always a fan of tacos, he devised a way to quickly make fresh tacos that could be sold for nineteen cents each.

Today, Taco Bell is the only nationwide Mexican fast food chain. It had twenty-three-hundred restaurants by 1986.

What is the world's largest restaurant system?

It's not McDonald's or Burger King or Subway! It's PepsiCo, Inc., which owns 22,300 KFC, Pizza Hut, and Taco Bell restaurants in 87 countries.

Who was Colonel Sanders?

Born in 1890, Colonel Harland Sanders, founder of Kentucky Fried Chicken, didn't begin franchising chicken joints until he was 62. Just when most people are retiring to their easy chairs, Sanders began one of the biggest food franchises in the world.

When he was six, his father died. His mother had to go to work, and Sanders was left to cook for his three-year-old brother and baby sister. By the age of seven, he had mastered several dishes. As he grew older, he held several jobs. When he was forty he began serving meals at a service station he ran in Corbin, Kentucky.

At first he just served the odd meal on the dining room table in the living quarters of his service station. As more people began coming in just for the food, he moved across the street to a building that could seat 142 people. Over the next nine years he perfected his secret blend of eleven herbs and spices and the cooking method that is still used today.

His chicken was good, but customers had to wait half an hour for it to be skillet-fried. Most of his diners were travelers in a hurry. To speed the cooking process, Sanders devised a way to fry chicken in a pressure cooker.

His fame grew throughout the state of Kentucky. While he did serve as a soldier for six months in Cuba, private was the highest rank he achieved. However, in the 1930s, Kentucky Governor Ruby Laffoon made Sanders a Kentucky Colonel in recognition of his contributions to the state's cuisine.

In 1952, after his restaurant failed, the Colonel began traveling around the country franchising his chicken recipe at established restaurants. He would cook up a batch of his chicken for the owner and employees. If they liked it, he would enter into a handshake deal that stipulated a payment of five cents for every chicken sold. By 1964 he had six-hundred franchises and sold his interest to a group of investors for $2 million. One of the investors was John Y. Brown, who became governor of Kentucky in 1980.

Why did Kentucky Fried Chicken switch its name to KFC?

Not often does a company as successful as Kentucky Fried Chicken just up and change its name, but that is just what it did in 1991. Well, it did have a good reason. Not only was "KFC" shorter and snappier than "Kentucky Fried Chicken," it eliminated the word "fried" from the company name. Not a bad idea considering today's health-conscious consumer.

KFC still fries its chicken the same way, but now the word "fried" is not plastered all over the place. If you like KFC, you might want to note that the Extra Tasty Crispy Chicken has a higher fat content than the original recipe. Also, different pieces have differing fat contents. See the following comparison:

Original Recipe Chicken

Pieces	Calories From Fat	Saturated Fat	Total Fat
Whole Wing	99	3g	11g
Side Breast	135	4g	15g
Center Breast	126	4g	14g
Drumstick	81	2g	9g
Thigh	189	5g	21g

Extra Tasty Crispy Chicken

Pieces	Calories From Fat	Saturated Fat	Total Fat
Whole Wing	153	4g	17g
Side Breast	243	6g	27g
Center Breast	171	4g	19g
Drumstick	108	3g	12g
Thigh	261	7g	29g

What is the largest pizza chain in the world?

Pizza Hut, founded by brothers Dan and Frank Carney, began as a small hut-shaped pizza parlor opened in Wichita, Kansas, in 1958. It has since blossomed into a seven-thousand-plus-unit international chain, becoming the number-one pizza chain in the world by 1971.

In 1977, Pizza Hut was purchased by PepsiCo, Inc., which also owns KFC and Taco Bell.

Some interesting facts about Pizza Hut:

- Pizza Hut serves 11.5 million slices a day in the United States.

- Pizza Hut delivery, which stared in 1986, now has a 25 percent share of the business.

- Pizza Hut has been voted America's favorite pizza chain for the past nine years.

- The busiest Pizza Hut is in Mexico.

- Pizza Hut uses about 350 million pounds of flour each year, or the combined yield of three-hundred-thousand acres of wheat.

- Pizza Hut uses 80 million pounds of tomatoes each year.

- Pizza Hut needs more than 2.5 million hogs and 1.5 million cattle for its toppings every year.

What are America's favorite pizza toppings?

According to Pizza Hut, the top five are:

1. Pepperoni
2. Beef
3. Italian sausage
4. Mushroom
5. Green pepper

Nothing too surprising there, but what toppings are popular in other countries? The following countries offer some rather unique toppings at Pizza Hut:

Russia: A combination of sardines, tuna, mackerel, salmon, and onion called *Mockba*
Germany: Sauerkraut (sauerkraut and onion)
Spinach (spinach, ham, and onion)
Hong Kong: Corned Beef (corned beef, corn, and peas)
Farm House (Canadian bacon, corn, and extra cheese)
South East Asia, Singapore, Australia: Curry

Pepperoni doesn't sound as exciting anymore, does it?

Label Literacy

Are you label literate?

As of May 8, 1994, the manufacturers of packaged, processed foods can no longer play games with the wording on their labels. Thanks to the enactment of the Nutrition Labeling and Education Act of 1990, labels have become standardized and their terminology has been strictly defined. Before this pro-consumer bill was enacted, terms on most labels were misleading at best.

The new label is called "Nutrition Facts," and it lists a standard serving size for each food, that is larger and more realistic than the serving size that most companies used to use.

The most important information on the new labeling is how much cholesterol, fat, fiber, sodium, and nutrients are contained in each serving. Instead of listing them by weight, as they used to, manufacturers are now required to list them as a percentage of a person's daily recommended allotment, based on a two thousand calorie reference diet. Only two vitamins, A and C, and two minerals, calcium and iron, are required on the new label.

Daily Values are the new label reference numbers. They are

set by the government based on current nutrition recommendations. Some labels tell the approximate number of calories in a gram of fat, a carbohydrate, and protein.

The following is a list of descriptive words that you will see on today's packaging and exactly what each means, as defined by the FDA:

Calorie-Free: Less than 5 calories.

Low Calorie: 40 calories or less.

Reduced Calorie: At least 25 percent fewer calories when compared with the reference food; if more than half the calories are from fat, fat content must be reduced by 50 percent or more.

Sugar Free: Less than 1/2 gram sugar.

Light or Lite: At least 1/3 fewer calories or 50 percent less fat compared to the reference food; if more than half of the calories come from fat, fat content must be reduced by 50 percent or more.

Fat Free: Less than 1/2 gram fat.

Low Fat: 3 grams or less fat.

Low Saturated Fat: 1 gram or less fat.

Reduced Fat: At least 25 percent less fat when compared with the reference food.

Percent Fat Free: Must meet low-fat claims.

Good Source: 10 to 19 percent of the daily value for a particular nutrient.

Good Source of Fiber: 10 to 19 percent of the daily value for fiber (2.5 to 4.75 grams) per serving. If a food is not also "low fat," it must declare level of total fat per serving and refer to the nutrition panel when a fiber claim is mentioned.

More: At least 10 percent more than the comparison food.

High: At least 20 percent of the daily value of a particular nutrient.

High Fiber: 20 percent or more of the daily value for fiber (at least 5 grams). If the food is also "low fat," it must declare total fat per serving and refer to the nutritional panel when a fiber claim is made.

Lean: Fewer than 10 grams of fat, 4 grams of saturated fat, and 95 milligrams of cholesterol per serving and per 100 grams.

Extra Lean: Fewer than 5 grams of fat, 2 grams of saturated fat, and 95 milligrams of cholesterol per serving and per 100 grams.

Low Cholesterol: 20 milligrams or less of cholesterol and 2 grams or less saturated fat per serving.

Reduced Cholesterol: At least 25 percent less cholesterol and 2 grams or less saturated fat than comparison food.

Sodium Free: Fewer than 5 milligrams sodium.

Salt Free: Meets requirements for "sodium free."

Low Sodium: 140 milligrams or less sodium.

Very Low Sodium: 35 milligrams or less sodium.

Reduced Sodium: At least 25 percent less sodium.

Unsalted: No salt added during processing. For a product to use this term, the product it resembles must normally be processed with salt.

Why does the legend "Reg. Penna. Dept. Agr." appear on so many food product labels?

Look at virtually any package of crackers in your local supermarket or kitchen cabinet and you will see "Reg. Penna. Dept. Agr." somewhere on the labeling. You may have already noticed this and guessed that it stands for "Registered, Pennsylvania Department of Agriculture." You could buy a box of crackers in Hawaii that were baked in Maine, and still there would be that ubiquitous notation—"Reg. Penna. Dept. Agr." Why is Pennsylvania so special to cracker manufactures and why don't other states make them register?

The answer goes back to 1933. In that year, Pennsylvania enacted the Pennsylvania Bakeries Law, which requires that bakers, including those selling macaroni, spaghetti, pretzels, potato chips, crackers, and snacks made from cornmeal, obtain a Pennsylvania license to sell their goods in the state. The "Reg. Penna. Dept. Agr." legend assures consumers that the product is of good quality and the weight is accurately stated. In order for a manufacturer to get a license, plants must be inspected for cleanliness and employees must undergo periodic medical exams.

This law applies to all baked goods sold in Pennsylvania, not just the ones produced there. Therefore, even foreign bakeries are registered in Pennsylvania and are identified with the familiar legend on the package. As it is impossible for the Pennsylvania Department of Agriculture (PDA) to inspect plants outside the state, working agreements are maintained with similar agencies in other states or countries and inspection reports are filed with the PDA.

So why does the notation appear on packages sold in other states? Simply, baking companies find it cheaper and easier to label all their products as registered in Pennsylvania, rather than have special labels printed for those products being shipped to the state. It is certainly a comfort to know, no matter which state you are in, that your crackers have passed Pennsylvania's strict purity laws.

Why Pennsylvania is the only state out of fifty to concern itself with such matters is another question, for which there may be no good answer.

What is kosher food?

The Jewish practice keeping foods Kosher, or Kashruth (or Kashrut), which means "fit" or "proper." Their dietary code stems from rules originally taken from parts of the Bible (Deuteronomy 14 and Leviticus 11). The law is very specific about what can be eaten, when it should be eaten, and how it should be eaten.

The forbidden foods include animals that don't chew the cud *and* that have cloven hooves (pork), seafood that doesn't have fins (clams, eels, lobsters, mussels, oysters, shark, and shrimp), birds of prey, reptiles, and animal blood.

The ways animals are killed for consumption are also regulated by Jewish law. The animal must be slaughtered under rabbinical supervision. The act must be performed with one clean slash of the throat, which drains the nonkosher blood of the animal. (Blood is the essence of life and should be drained so that it can be returned to God.) The meat is then soaked, drained, rinsed, and re-rinsed. The only part of a four-legged animal that is kosher is the forequarters. So with beef, only the brisket, chuck, plate, and rib are considered clean.

As far as the ways in which the food can be eaten, the main rule is the separation of meat and dairy products. So cheeseburgers are out. (Bacon cheeseburgers are really out!) Some Orthodox Jews keep two sets of dishes, one for meat and one for dairy. The dishes are even washed separately.

The taboo against the mixing of dairy and meat products goes back to the belief that God created milk to sustain life. It would not be proper, therefore, to cook a slain animal in the liquid that was intended by the Creator to sustain life. This practice evolved into a total separation of meat and dairy products. Many foods that are "neutral," or *pareve* (containing neither dairy nor meat) can be eaten with dairy or meat products, and thus are usually so marked on their packaging.

It was during their captivity in Egypt that the ancient Hebrews gave up pork. The Egyptians associated the pig with their god of evil—Set—and considered it unclean. This may have been because pork spoiled easily in the hot Middle Eastern climate. Whatever the reason, the practice was picked up by the Jews. The Jewish nomadic life-style was also contrary to the keeping of pigs. As nomads, they tended sheep and goats. The sedentary pig was not a practical animal to raise. Also, pigs were kept by the Philistines, who lived in Palestine when the Jews arrived and became their rivals. The Hebrew religion forbade the eating of the enemy's foods—pork and shellfish—that also might have had the effect of altering the traditional nomadic Jewish life-style.

Islam, the religion of the nomadic Arabs, also forbids the consumption of pork, probably for similar historical reasons.

Kitchenware

What piece of cookware was originally a Mongol warrior's hat?

If the wok looks like an oriental helmet of sorts, it is no accident. During the Bronze Age, invading Mongolian warriors wore a wok-shaped metal helmet. The helmet not only protected the head, but could also be turned over and used as a cooking pan.

What made the wok so popular in China is that the heat is highest in a small area at the bottom, making for rapid cooking and efficient use of precious fuels.

What is the best-selling brand of kitchenware?

Tupperware! Three generations of busy mothers have cared for their families using these simple yet functional and versatile products. We can thank the postwar plastics revolution and a man named Earl Tupper for this marvelous invention. Tupperware is one of those products, especially if you have kids, that makes you wonder how you ever got along without it. Tupperware was not, however, an easy product to sell in 1945. Consumers were used to glass, metal, and earthenware. They did not understand how to use Tupperware and stayed away from it.

Earl Tupper, a one time DuPont chemical plant employee, first came in contact with plastics before World War II. Tupper was an inventor of sorts and wanted some plastic to experiment with during the war. He could not buy any, as it all was put toward the war effort. He did manage to convince his former employers at DuPont to sell him some leftover polyethylene slag to play with. Tupper then developed a way to purify the slag and inject it into molds to create his wares.

Coincidentally, developments in refrigeration technology made this the perfect time for the debut of Tupperware. Electric refrigerators and freezers, which until then had been luxury items, were becoming commonplace during the post-war economic boom. The iceboxes of the past created cool, damp environments for food storage. Refrigerators, however, maintained dry, low temperatures, which tended to dry out food. Tupperware solved this problem.

Tupperware was designed by function, not form. The unique airtight seal was modeled after the lid of a paint can, only inverted. Tupper's unbreakable, leak-proof containers locked in freshness and saved money on a family's food budget. But they didn't sell.

Tupper originally marketed the containers in hardware and department stores, as well as through catalogs. The problem was that no one knew how to use the revolutionary new seal, so the containers sat on store shelves gathering dust. It wasn't until direct sellers began demonstrating the products using the now famous in-home party plan that sales took off in the late forties. In 1951, Tupper went to an exclusive direct marketing strategy.

Tupperware is now the worldwide leader in the sale of food storage containers with net sales of $1.1 billion in 1992. There are some fourteen-hundred independent distributors in fifty-two countries and 130,000 active sales consultants. A Tupperware party starts once every three seconds somewhere in the world, and nearly 82 million people attend one each year!

Did you ever cook with a salamander?

Not the amphibian—a cooking utensil. The salamander is a heavy iron disk mounted on a wooden handle. It is heated to red hot over a stove burner and used to caramelize the sugar topping of desserts like Crème Brûlée. (It's also called a crème brûlée iron.)

The heat of the hot iron, when pressed on the dessert, browns the sugar and hardens it, but does not melt the custard below. The salamander can also be held just above certain dishes to brown them.

Does it matter which side of the aluminum foil is used?

If your mother was like many, she always wrapped food in aluminum foil shiny side out. She was sure there was a good reason, she just didn't know what it was. Sorry, Mom! Actually, it makes no difference which side of the foil you use.

The dull and shiny sides of the foil have no special meaning; they are simply a result of the way that the foil is made. In the final rolling step of the manufacturing process, two layers of aluminum foil are passed through the rolling mill at the same time. The side that comes in contact with the mill's highly polished steel rolls becomes shiny. The other side, which does not come in contact with the heavy metal rolls, comes out dull.

Shiny or dull, it does not matter. If you're like many of us, however, you still won't be able to wrap your sandwich shiny side in. It just isn't as attractive somehow.

Can aluminum foil be used in the microwave?

Those of us who were around when microwave ovens first came on the market are afraid to put anything metallic inside of one. We're not sure why, but we think the oven will blow up or at least be permanently damaged. This, however, is not the case. Used in small quantities, aluminum foil is harmless.

According to Reynolds Aluminum, small amounts of aluminum foil can be used in microwave cooking. You can use it to shield narrow areas or fatty edges of foods that tend to overcook before the center is done. Aluminum reflects microwaves and protects foods beneath it. It is the reflective property of the foil that has led to the "metal in the microwave" myth.

The guideline for using foil in microwave cooking is to never cover more than half of the food or let the foil touch the sides of the oven's interior. Fully covering the food will prevent it from cooking and may cause the dreaded arcing (sparking) or, as you feared, oven damage.

Do microwaves really cook food from the inside out?

This is a common misconception. Microwaves are a form of electromagnetic radiation with a shorter wavelength than television signals, but a longer wavelength than visible light. One curious property of microwaves is their ability to excite or agitate water molecules but not other molecules. Water molecules have a positive end (hydrogen) and a negative end (oxygen). Most other types of molecules are neutral. Microwaves act like little magnets, attracting and repelling the positive and negative ends alternately, and thus spinning the water molecules. Microwave radiation alternates its field 2.4 billion times per second, spinning the water molecules incredibly fast. All this spinning of molecules creates a great deal of friction, and friction causes heat.

Microwaves' ability to cook food was accidentally discovered by Percy LeBaron Spencer of the Raytheon Company in the 1940s, when he found that a chocolate bar in his pocket had melted during an experiment with microwaves.

Most foods are made up of molecules of carbohydrate, fat, and protein. Interspersed among the food molecules are water molecules. The spinning water molecules heat up the surrounding molecules and cook the food.

Conventional ovens heat up the air surrounding the outer layers of food. The heated outer layers gradually transfer the heat to the inner layers of food, cooking it from the outside in. In microwave cooking all the food molecules are heated at approximately the same time. Since the air inside the microwave oven remains cool, however, the outer layers of food may be cooler than the inner layers, giving the impression that the inside has cooked first.

One common complaint about microwave cooking is that bread products come out soggy, not crisp. In microwaves, the heated water molecules rise quickly to the surface of the food, condensing into water droplets on the surface and making bread soggy. In conventional ovens, the heated water vapor rises more slowly and then evaporates rather than condensing when it hits the hot, dry oven air. Thus, bread will be crisp on the outside and moist on the inside, where some water remains if the bread is not overcooked.

Why do chefs wear tall white hats?

The custom of chefs wearing tall hats with a puff on top goes back to the fifteenth century. Cooks were well paid and respected by the Greeks in Byzantium. When the Turks toppled the Byzantine empire in 1453, the highly regarded chefs had to go into hiding. They found refuge in the monasteries, where they lived with the monks. The chefs adopted the monks' garb in order to blend in, including a tall black hat with a puff on top. Later they changed the color of their hats to distinguish themselves from the clergy.

Apparently they liked the look!

Why don't the British use salt shakers?

Salt shakers, surprisingly, haven't been around all that long. Some are still slow to accept them. Many of the more traditional people in Britain frown upon the use of the salt shaker. At formal dinner parties it is not uncommon for each diner to be given his own little dish of salt, which the guests sprinkle over their food with their fingers. At less elaborate affairs, one can put a small pile of salt on the edge of the plate.

While it is more difficult to control the amount and distribution of salt this way, it does save one the bother of asking others to please pass the salt.

Why do we use saucers with cups? And why is it called a saucer anyway?

If you are like many of us, you rarely use saucers when alone, but trot them out when company comes over.

The saucer was not always placed beneath the cup. Long ago,

in fact, the saucer was just what its name implies—a small dish for holding sauce. It has since moved to its familiar position under the cup and has more or less become a teaspoon or tea bag holder.

Not all that long ago, the saucer served an actual function beneath the cup. It was quite common for one to pour hot tea or coffee from the cup into the saucer to cool. (Saucers used to be much deeper and resembled bowls.) The cooled beverage could then be drunk from the saucer or returned to the cup. There was even a side plate provided to set the cup on while the saucer was full of tea or coffee.

Today, the saucer looks nice and is kept mainly out of tradition, although it may be useful to the particularly sloppy coffee drinker!

When did using a fork become fashionable?

We Westerners take the fork completely for granted and almost assume that it has always been around. How could we get along without it? But in northern Europe up until the early 1700s, the fork was not used as an eating utensil.

The first record of the fork is around A.D. 900. They were rather large and were used exclusively for cooking. Spoons, and more commonly knives and fingers, were the eating implements of medieval times. Most people carried about their own knife and spoon, as the dinner host did not always supply them.

Food was served in large bowls or on platters set in the middle of the table. Diners grabbed their meal off these platters with a knife or with their fingers and placed it on their "plate," which was not really a plate as we know it today. It was called a trencher and was a stale piece of bread about four inches by six inches. This absorbent plate could be eaten at the end of the meal or given to the dog or the poor. (So much for doing dishes!) The trencher was later replaced by a wooden square with a depression in its center sometime around the fifteenth century.

Another present-day necessity, the napkin, was also missing from the medieval table. This made for a rather messy meal, as diners would thrust their whole hand or arm into the often greasy, gloppy communal serving bowl.

The fork probably first came into use in the Middle East in the eleventh century. The Italian nobility are believed to have been the first Europeans to adopt their use, sometime around the fourteenth century. Soon after, much of the European nobility had them.

It wasn't until the eighteenth century that northern Europeans grudgingly began to adopt the fork. The American colonists more readily accepted the utensil, due to the fact that colonial etiquette frowned on the eating of one's peas balanced on the end of a knife. Perhaps the last European group to embrace the fork was the ultra-traditional British navy. Until 1897, they prohibited its use as "unmanly!"

How has the use of the napkin evolved over the years?

When we go to dinner at someone's house, we expect napkins to be supplied for our use. If they are nice cloth napkins, however, we may hesitate to soil them. In our culture, nice napkins are to be kept clean. (Hence the invention of paper napkins.) This is quite silly if you think about it.

In days gone by, before dinner utensils were in vogue, people ate with their fingers. Obviously they had to be wiped somewhere. In Rome it was common for dinner guests to have two napkins, one supplied by the host and one that they brought themselves. One napkin was tied around the neck to catch falling food. The other, the one the guests brought, was used to wrap up extra food to take home. This was perhaps the first doggy bag.

By the Middle Ages, napkins had fallen out of favor. Hosts did not always provide them. Tablecloths served the purpose. In the case of no tablecloth, diners wiped their dirty hands on their clothes, and quite often on their hair!

Late medieval napkins, when used, were rather large affairs, commonly a yard square, with fancy fringes, and were hung over the diner's left shoulder or arm. By the 1650s, napkin wearing had moved back to the neck and chest. In the 1800s, it was considered impolite to hang the napkin from the neck or shirt collar. It was simply laid across the lap.

It was the rise of the use of the fork that made the napkin

more ornamental than functional. The cultured fork user did not make a mess of the hands or lips.

Napkins at one point were used as artwork for the table. At Versailles in the seventeenth century, napkins were elaborately folded into intricate shapes. Everything from birds to fish was fashioned with expensive cloth. One wouldn't have dared to unfold such a thing of beauty. Other napkins were provided for actual use. The folding of napkins has survived until today at many diners and restaurants.

The etiquette behind the folding of the table linen also extended to the tablecloth. Up until the eighteenth century, tablecloths were screwed into linen presses to produce razor-sharp crisscross folds. The creases had to be straight and clean, and laid out in near-perfect symmetry with the table. A wrinkled fold was considered to be bad luck and meant death to one of the diners. The protocol for tablecloths swung the other way in the nineteenth century. Creases were out. Tablecloths were actually rolled on tubes to guard against unwanted wrinkles or folds.

How did chopsticks come into use in the Orient?

To Westerners the thought of using chopsticks may seem a little odd, if not needlessly complicated. To the people of the Orient, chopsticks are the essence of simplicity.

While the people in the West were using their fingers to eat, the Chinese had refined the concept of using the fingers by creating artificial "fingers," or chopsticks. Chopsticks are basically an elongated version of the fingers. They allowed one to dispense with the napkins needed by the finger feeders, and made the dining experience more sanitary and delicate. The Japanese, who use pointed chopsticks, view soiled napkins with disgust. The Chinese, who prefer chopsticks with square ends, consider our use of knives and forks slightly akin to butchering our meal at the table. Oriental food is cut up in the kitchen. One reason for this practice is that wood for fuel is at a premium in the Orient. Small pieces of food cook much faster and help to conserve this precious resource.

The use of chopsticks evolved from the switch to rice as the staple food in China long ago. Originally, millet was the staple of the Chinese diet and it was eaten with spoons. As rice replaced millet in the diet, chopsticks replaced spoons as the main eating utensils. Chinese rice is moist and sticky, which makes it rather easy to manipulate with chopsticks. (Rices eaten in India and the Middle East are drier and not suitable for chopsticks.)

While we might think that chopsticks are a somewhat clumsy way to eat and would slow things down, the opposite is true. Since the Chinese and Japanese serve their food in bite-size morsels, it tends to get cold if not eaten rapidly. Therefore, they eat much faster than the average Westerner would consider proper. (Westerners call the eating utensils "chop" sticks because they are intended to be used rapidly.) In fact, much of Oriental table etiquette differs from our own.

The chopsticks are never to be licked or bitten. One should not fish around in one's bowl with the chopsticks, but just take whatever is on top. A mouthful of rice should be eaten between every two bites of fish or meat, so as not to appear a glutton. Never put anything back in the bowl that was on the chopsticks.

The proper way to eat with chopsticks is to lift the bowl to the face (something considered rude in the West!) with the left hand and quickly sweep its contents into the mouth, holding the two sticks together with the right hand. In the West, we have utensils and plates that eliminate the need to lift the dish to our mouth. Every grain of rice must be eaten. To leave any behind indicates that one does not know one's own appetite and shows disrespect for the rice, which is considered a sacred crop.

The bowl is the key to using chopsticks. One reason Westerners find chopsticks hard to master is because we try to use them with a flat plate. They are not intended for this use. Even the Chinese prefer the use of spoons when confronted with a plate or when eating soups. Oriental children aren't born knowing how to use chopsticks. They use spoons exclusively until the age of three or four. Then chopstick training begins.

Worldwide, some 1.2 billion people eat with chopsticks (not counting those Westerners eating in Chinese restaurants), while 1.5 billion use forks, knives, and spoons. The other 600 million or so use knives and hands or just hands.

What is the origin of the word "spatula"?

Of all the kitchen utensils, perhaps the spatula has the most interesting name. "Spatula" is derived from the same Latin root as are "spoon," "sword," "spade," and "oar." The reason for this is that the spatula functions similarly to all of these other implements. Like a spoon and spade, it can lift and scoop. Like a sword, a serrated spatula can cut. Like an oar, it can dip into soft mixtures to blend them. Spatulas come in all shapes and sizes—short and long; metal, plastic, and wood; flat, angled, and curved. All the different types have their own special uses—lifting, spreading, mixing, turning, etc.

What piece of kitchenware is named for a famous 1930s bandleader?

A man named F. J. Osius invented and patented a blender in the mid-1930s. Osius, however, did not have the means to finance and promote its sale. He convinced a famous bandleader of the time, Fred Waring, to start a company to market his new blender, christened the Waring Blender.

In 1938, Waring took the blenders on the road with his band. At each stop along the way, Waring would set up a mini-bar and begin to mix drinks as a demonstration of the blender's usefulness. The blender became popular for mixing drinks and liquefying fruits. It is still used primarily for the same tasks today.

What's the best-selling steel wool soap pad?

There are two major brands on the market—Brillo and S.O.S. San Francisco aluminum cookware salesman, Erwin Cox, created S.O.S. soap pads in 1917. He originally made the hand-dip pads in his basement. It is said that his wife came up with the S.O.S name because it is the universal call for help and also stands for "Save Our Saucepans." S.O.S was originally an emergency-use product for blackened aluminum pans only. Gradually the pads found more and more uses in the kitchen and elsewhere.

What, you may ask, happened to the third period in the S.O.S abbreviation? (In case you didn't notice, it has only two.) "S.O.S" is a trademark of Miles, Inc., and is registered with no period after the second *S* to legally protect the name.

S.O.S holds about a 60 percent share of the soap pad market, well ahead of number-two Brillo, a Purex Corporation product that has about 35 percent of the market. Interestingly, the soap pad business is much bigger in the large metropolitan markets and in the East Coast in particular.

Soap pads are manufactured by shaving huge spools of special steel alloy wire. The steel wool is shaped and woven with soap (S.O.S uses blue, Brillo pink). The pads also contain detergents, antioxidants (to prevent rust), fragrance, and sodium carbonate (to maintain product consistency). The pads are then dried to prevent them from rusting in the box.

What is the greatest innovation in food technology in the past half-century?

It's not the microwave, or even the vacuum bottle. As a matter of fact, it is the thing that has recently replaced the vacuum bottle in many lunch boxes—the drink box. According to the Institute of Food Technologists, a food industry group, aseptic packaging—drink boxes and foil drink pouches—earns the honor of greatest food-science innovation of the last fifty years.

Drink boxes, first introduced to America in the early 1980s, are sterile inside and out and thus don't require refrigeration. Because the beverage in a drink box (usually juice) is quick-heated before packaging, it loses less flavor and nutrients than do traditional canned juices.

The drink box looks fairly simple, doesn't it? There is more to it, however, than meets the eye. Both drink boxes and foil drink pouches are comprised of six layers—two inner polyethylene plastic layers, a layer of aluminum foil, a middle polyethylene layer, a paper label layer, and an outer coating of polyethylene. These multiple layers keep out oxygen, moisture, and contaminants.

The small, rectangular 8.45-fluid-ounce drink box rejuvenated slumping sales for Hi-C fruit drinks in 1983, when Coca-Cola replaced the bulky forty-six ounce Hi-C cans with the new single-serving boxes. By 1990, over one billion drink boxes a year were sold, with one-third of those used for Coca-Cola products—Hi-C and Minute Maid juices.

While Americans may think this technology is new, it has been available in Europe for decades. Since the 1960s, the Europeans have used aseptic packaging for soups, gravies, sauces, puddings, oils, and yogurts. We are just beginning to catch up. Along with milk and juice, things like liquid eggs, tomato sauce, and wine are now being aseptically packaged in the United States.

Aseptic packages are used in over 130 countries. Almost half of the liquid nonevaporated milk in the world is packaged this way, as refrigeration is lacking in many places or contaminated water supplies preclude the use of powdered milks. For this reason, drink boxes are commonly used by disaster relief organizations, like the Red Cross.

Why did Maine outlaw drink boxes in 1990?

If drink boxes are so marvelous, why did the state of Maine ban their use? Many environmental groups raised a fuss because they believed that drink boxes, which are 70 percent paper, 24 percent polyethylene, and 6 percent aluminum, could not be separated for recycling. They brought pressure to bear. Their fears, however, were unfounded. Drink boxes, along with recycled aluminum, have the lowest environmental cost of any container. (Virgin aluminum cans have the highest.)

Aseptic packages use less material from the beginning—a proportion of 96 percent beverage to 4 percent container—than any other packaging. Drink boxes are also easily recycled. Through a process called hydrapulping, they are broken down along with paperboard products like milk cartons to make pulp, which is turned into things like tissue and writing paper.

Drink boxes truly are a modern wonder. Maine saw the error of its ways and lifted the drink box ban in 1994.

Kitchen Chemistry

Why are nitrates added to meats?

The use of nitrates in meats like bacon, sausage, ham, and corned beef is twofold. The nice pink or red color of many processed meats is due to the addition of sodium nitrite. That alone would be enough for the meat packers to use the stuff. When you add the fact that it's also a preservative, how can they resist?

Sodium nitrate and potassium nitrate (saltpeter) act as antioxidants, which inhibit bacterial growth. These compounds are especially effective at retarding the growth of *Clostridium botulinum*, the cause of botulism. Sounds good, right? Well, potassium nitrate is broken down by bacteria on the meat into nitrite, which can further combine with secondary amines to form nitrosamines, known carcinogens.

Meats that will be fully cooked at home have no need for added nitrites. Cured canned meats that aren't cooked before canning, however, may harbor the deadly *Clostridium* bacteria and require the addition of nitrates. If the use of nitrates worries you, simply avoid them whenever possible.

Can you name a natural leavening that literally falls from the sky?

If you're ever snowbound at home and in need of eggs for leavening in pancakes or pudding, don't make the dangerous trek to the market. You can use the fresh-fallen snow in place of eggs. Even older snow from below the surface will work. Snow's ammonia content makes it a good substitute riser in a pinch.

How does baking soda act as a leavening agent?

One use of baking soda is as a leavening agent. There are three types of leavening agents—steam, air, and carbon dioxide.

Steam leavens when it is released from the moisture contained in doughs and batters. It is commonly used for cream puffs and popovers.

Air, which works by expanding during heating, is incorporated by beating egg whites, creaming butter and sugar, or sifting flour. Air is used as a leavening in omelets, soufflés, and sponge cakes.

Carbon dioxide, which is the most common leavening agent, is a gas produced by a chemical reaction involving baking soda, baking powder, yeast, or bacteria. When heated, baking soda releases carbon dioxide. For those of you who actually paid attention in high school chemistry class, the following illustrates this point:

$$2NaHCO_3 + heat \rightarrow Na_2CO_3 + H_2O + CO_2$$

Sodium Bicarbonate	Sodium Carbonate	Water	Carbon Dioxide

The sodium carbonate produced from this reaction is alkali, which needs an acid salt to neutralize it. For this reason, acidic ingredients such as sour milk, molasses, buttermilk, cream of tartar, lemon juice, and the acid salts in baking powder are used with baking soda to produce a neutral sodium salt residue, which is colorless, odorless, and tasteless.

The rule of thumb is to use 1/2 teaspoon of baking soda with 1 cup of sourmilk, 3/4 teaspoon of soda with 1 cup of molasses, or 1 teaspoon of soda to 2 1/4 teaspoons of cream of tartar.

Where does baking soda come from?

We all know that baking soda is sodium bicarbonate, but where does it come from? Good question! It is either produced chemically or mined. Baking soda is created chemically when carbon dioxide and ammonia are passed into a concentrated solution of sodium chloride. A crude sodium bicarbonate precipitates from this process and is heated to form soda ash (sodium carbonate), which is further refined to sodium bicarbonate ($NaHCO_3$).

The other way of acquiring sodium bicarbonate is to mine it. Believe it or not, most of our baking soda comes from a huge trona mine in the Green River Basin of Wyoming. Trona is a mixture of salts that is easily convertible to sodium carbonate, and then to sodium bicarbonate. There is enough trona in Wyoming to last the soda industry for hundreds of years.

Another American locale critical to the production of baking soda is Syracuse, New York. Why, you ask? Because of the great limestone reserves found in that area. Limestone is the source of the essential carbon dioxide used in manufacturing baking soda.

What about baking powders?

Baking powders are a mixture of baking soda and acid salts, with starch added as a stabilizer. There are three types of baking powders, classified by the acid salt they employ:

1. *Tartrate powders*: the acid ingredients are potassium acid tartrate (cream of tartar) and tartaric acid.
2. *Phosphate powders*: the acid is either sodium acid pyrophosphate or calcium acid phosphate, or both.
3. *Double-acting powders* (also known as SAS-phosphate powders): the acids are sodium aluminum sulfate and calcium acid phosphate. They are called double-acting because they have two rising actions instead of just one. The baking soda begins reacting with one salt in the mixing bowl as soon as the liquid is added. The second rising occurs during baking, when the soda reacts with the other salt when heated. Double-acting baking powders allow you to mix early and delay baking until needed.

How does baking soda deodorize?

Baking soda has many wonderful qualities, not the least of which is its ability to deodorize. Nothing is more popular for freshening refrigerators and cupboards than a simple open box of baking soda. Baking soda differs from most room deodorizers, which are perfumes that simply mask odors, and physical deodorizers like coffee grounds and charcoal, which absorb odors.

Perfumes work quickly and are good for large areas, but only mask the odor instead of eliminating it. Physical deodorizers work well at first; however, as absorbents, they tend to become less and less effective with time. And since they tend to reach equilibrium, they eventually begin to release the odors that they formerly absorbed.

Baking soda is unique in that it neutralizes odors chemically. It is slightly basic, with a pH of about 8.1. Most unwanted odors are either strong acids or strong bases (alkalines). Sour milk, for example, is acidic, while spoiled fish is alkaline. Most pleasant odors tend to be of neutral pH. It takes a while for baking soda to bring acidic and basic odor molecules to a more neutral, odor-free state. The longer the time air is exposed to baking soda, the "sweeter" it becomes.

Not only does baking soda deodorize in its powdered form, but also when suspended in solution. A little dissolved in water makes an excellent mouthwash (garlic and onion are both acidic).

So how long does baking soda work in the refrigerator? About two months is average. It will still work well, however, when dumped down the sink drain or into the garbage pail.

In the fridge, only the soda at the top of the box used to be exposed to the air. Arm & Hammer now sells a box with ventilated sides to increase the air coming into contact with the soda.

What is the origin of the Arm & Hammer logo?

Almost every household has at least one box. The orange and red box with the muscular arm and hammer symbol has been around since 1867. Originally called Arm & Hammer Saberatus (as baking soda was once known), its distinctive logo is one of the world's most universally recognized. But the well-known logo did not start out representing the product it is now famous for.

Actually, the Arm & Hammer logo has roots in an older mustard and spice business in Brooklyn known as the Vulcan Spice Mill. This company's storefront sign bore the arm and hammer symbol in honor of Vulcan, god of fire and metalworking. The company owner, James A. Church, closed down the business in 1867, but kept the sign for sentimental reasons. Church then opened a baking soda business called Church & Company. He sold the soda by the barrel and included paper bags with which to package it. The bags bore various names for his brands of soda—Lily, Tiger, and Eagle.

Church relied heavily on door-to-door salesmen to promote his business. He employed the seven-foot-four master salesman Colonel Powell as his best seller. Powell traveled the countryside dressed in a top hat and elevated shoes, making him appear at least nine feet tall. His wagon was pulled by two enormous horses wearing the company name on their blankets. When he arrived in a town he created quite a spectacle. His entrance into a customer's store was a whirlwind of excitement as he tacked ads for Church's Baking Soda on the ceiling and went into a harangue about the product's many virtues. Powell informed his customer that Mrs. Church had inserted her very own special recipe for Gold Cake inside each bag and that when he next returned he would bring her recipe for Silver Cake.

How could such a flamboyant and memorable sales pitch fail? But fail it did. Church's Baking Soda could not keep up with its competition. Supposedly, one day, sitting discouraged in his office, Church happened to see his old arm and hammer sign sitting in a corner. In a flash of inspiration, he had all his bags printed with the now familiar Arm & Hammer label. The labeling struck the public fancy and the product went on to become a huge success.

What is cream of tartar?

Cream of tartar is potassium acid tartrate in its white crystalline form. It is mainly used as a rising agent in breads, when yeast is not used. Its acid reacts with sodium bicarbonate to produce carbon dioxide gas, which causes dough to rise. For this reason, it is also found in various baking powders.

It is called "cream" of tartar because of the way the crystals are produced. Traditionally, the crystals are isolated from tartar sediments that are deposited in wine casks. These sediments are removed from the casks, dried, and powdered. Upon resuspension in boiling water and subsequent cooling, the potassium acid tartar crystals rise to the top of the liquid and are skimmed off, much like cream.

Why are sulfites added to foods?

Sulfites, or sulfur compounds, are added to foods and beverages for a host of reasons. They act to preserve freshness, retard bacteria, inhibit browning, control fermentation, and serve as antioxidants. Sounds like wonderful stuff, doesn't it? For some people, however, there is a severe drawback to their use.

Some asthmatics have life-threatening reactions to sulfites. These sulfiting agents (sulfur dioxide and inorganic sulfites that release sulfur dioxide) can cause difficulty in breathing, flushing, hives, gastrointestinal trouble, and anaphylactic shock, to varying degrees, in those 5 to 10 percent of asthmatics who are hypersensitive.

If you are sensitive to sulfites, there is a long list of foods and beverages to avoid: avocado and guacamole, baked goods, dried cod, fruit (cut up, fresh, dried, or maraschino-type), fruit juices, potatoes (cut up, fresh, frozen, dried, canned), salad dressings (dry mix), salad bars (notoriously bad), sauces and gravies (canned and dried), sauerkraut, cole slaw, shellfish (clams, crabs, lobster, scallops, and shrimp), fresh mushrooms, wine vinegar, wine and wine coolers, beer, and cider.

That doesn't leave much!

How do meat tenderizers work?

Believe it or not, when you sprinkle meat tenderizer on your steak, you are actually treating your meat with a papaya enzyme. That's right! Meat tenderizers contain papain, an enzyme from the papaya that breaks down meat proteins and softens connective tissue and muscle fibers. Papain does its work during the cooking process. It is most active at temperatures between 140° F and 176° F. As cooking continues, it loses its ability to break down proteins and is destroyed by the heat.

How are saturated fats different from unsaturated fats?

We see a lot of press about saturated versus unsaturated fats. What makes them different? How can you tell them apart? And what are they saturated with, anyway?

Fats and oils are very similar chemically. They are both triglycerides—glycol molecules with three attached fatty acids. It is the fatty acids they contain that determine whether a fat is classified as saturated or unsaturated.

Saturated fatty acids are saturated with hydrogen atoms. Their molecules are composed of hydrogen and carbon atoms joined by single bonds, allowing the carbons to hold as many hydrogen atoms as possible. Saturated fats are almost always derived from animal fats and tend to raise blood cholesterol levels. Animals fats vary in their level of saturation. The following lists animal fats by increasing saturation: fish oils, poultry and veal, pork, mutton and beef. Saturated fats are always solid at room temperature.

Monounsaturated fats have one double bond. Monosaturated fats are plant derived. They include canola, peanut, and olive oil. Monosaturated fats are liquid at room temperature. They are considered to help lower the LDL ("bad") cholesterol levels in the blood.

Polyunsaturated fats have two or more double bonds, and thus less hydrogen. Polyunsaturated fats are plant derived. Listed in increasing levels of saturation, they are as follows: safflower seed, sunflower seed, corn, and sesame. Polyunsaturated fats are also liquid at room temperature. They are also effective at lowering cholesterol, but aren't considered as "good" as the polyunsaturated oils.

Hydrogenated fats are unsaturated fats that are converted into saturated (solid) fats through the addition of hydrogen. They are thus considered undesirable. Included here are coconut and palm oils. Margarines also fall into this category.

What is an emulsifier?

If you ever have eaten mayonnaise, you've eaten an emulsifier. An emulsifier helps indissoluble oils stay suspended in mixtures. Mayonnaise is an emulsion of fat in water. There are other common food emulsions. Butter is a suspension of water droplets in fat. Milk is a suspension of fat droplets in water. In both these cases, the amount of suspended droplets is a small percentage of the total product. In the case of mayonnaise, at least 65 percent of its total weight is suspended oil droplets.

Egg yolks are used as stabilizers in mayonnaise. They contain lecithin, a natural emulsifier. An emulsifier has a unique molecular structure that allows one end of its molecules to bond with an oil and the other end to bond with water, thus allowing oils and water to be mixed together. The egg yolks attach to the oil droplets and form a protective coating around them, so that when they are beaten into smaller and smaller droplets they do not coalesce back into larger droplets.

Lemon juice added to the mixture causes the egg proteins to change and thicken the mayonnaise. Cheaper brands of mayonnaise, or salad dressings, use less egg yolks (they use cooked cornstarch instead) and less oil (between 30 and 45 percent) and add stabilizers such as seaweed extracts or locust bean gums to act as thickening agents.

Many food emulsions, like milk, are homogenized by smashing the mixture into metal surfaces at high pressure to make the droplets smaller and more uniform in size. In milk, the smaller droplets take longer to coalesce and rise to the surface as cream. In good mayonnaise, however, it is preferable not to homogenize, because oil droplets of homogeneous size are not packed as tightly together as droplets of dissimilar size, and a less dense sauce will result.

Why should egg whites be beaten in a copper bowl?

If you ever watch any of the multitude of cooking shows on TV, you know that whenever a chef beats egg whites, he does it in a copper bowl. You may even do so at home. But why is a copper bowl so important?

The idea behind beating is to incorporate air into the egg whites and make them foamy and stiff. This is accomplished using a whisk, preferably a balloon whisk. Beaten eggs expand in the presence of heat and increase the volume of whatever mixture they are added to. They are the leavening agent used in baked foods like soufflés and are used to lighten cold dishes like mousses.

Egg yolks are removed from the whites before beating because they contain fats that destabilize the foam and thus reduce its volume dramatically. The foam with the greatest volume can be made with egg whites at room temperature beaten in a copper bowl. It is believed that proteins in egg whites interact with the copper in the bowl to form very strong bonds, resulting in an egg white–air structure that is more stable.

If you don't have a copper bowl, stainless steel will do. Avoid aluminum, which can discolor the whites gray; plastic, which tends to retain an oily film; and glass or ceramic, both of which are too slippery to allow the whites to fluff up.

Another option, if you don't have a copper bowl, is to use an acid, such as cream of tartar, to help foam your egg whites. It is used to stabilize the beaten whites in angel food cake. Sugar also serves this purpose in meringues. Cream of tartar and sugar, while making the foam less likely to fall, can also slow the foaming process. Therefore, they are usually added after the whites begin to get frothy.

What exactly is "freezer burn"?

How does something frozen burn? Foods left in the freezer too long or poorly wrapped don't "burn" per se. Instead, they dehydrate, causing a loss of color, texture, and flavor.

Who first thought of freezing foods?

If you think it was Clarence Birdseye, think again. The Eskimos have been successfully freezing food, perhaps not by choice, for millennia. Clarence Birdseye, however, did perfect the process in warmer climes and introduced it to the world at large. It was already known that cold storage preserved food, but the freezing methods of the time took all day, and when thawed for use, the food broke down and became mushy and tasteless. While working as a fur trader in Labrador in 1912, Birdeye realized that fast freezing of food, as practiced by the Eskimos, was better for preserving foods. He then devised a process of spraying food with a mist of circulating brine at –45° F. He came to learn that quick freezing inhibited the formation of ice crystals in the food that caused the cell tissues to burst apart. Upon thawing, the cells now remained intact and the food looked and tasted fresh and ready for consumption.

He then started a seafood company in Gloucester, Massachusetts, in 1924. Birdseye eventually declared bankruptcy after trying to manufacture and distribute frozen foods. He sold his process and plants in 1929 to a company that later became General Foods Corporation.

Does hot water freeze quicker than cold water?

Common sense would tell you that cold water, which is much closer to the freezing point than hot water, should freeze a lot quicker. Well, it does. Common sense prevails!

This myth probably has its origin in the old wives' tale that you can make ice cubes in less time by using boiling water. This claim boggles the mind, as well it should. It is such an easy claim to test that one wonders how it persists. Try this simple experiment. Boil some water and pour it into one end of a plastic ice cube tray. In the other end put very cold water. Place in the freezer. Check it in about twenty minutes. The cold water will have frozen over and, wonder of wonders, the boiling water will not have. The boiling water won't ice over until about 40 minutes, depending upon your freezer.

If you have the time or curiosity, you can try one further experiment, which will provide much more interesting, and unexpected, results. Boil some water, allow it to cool to room temperature, and pour it into one end of an ice cube tray. In the other end of the tray put room-temperature water that has not been boiled.

Place in the freezer. If you keep an eye on this tray you will find that the boiled water freezes before the unboiled. In fact, previously boiled tepid water will freeze at about the same time as very cold water. This phenomenon is a simple matter of physics.

Boiling forces some of the air bubbles out of the water. Since air bubbles reduce the thermal conductivity of water, they slow down the freezing process. Thus, water that has been boiled will freeze faster than water that has not been boiled, provided that both are at the same temperature when placed in the freezer. Incidentally you will get crystal clear ice cubes by freezing boiled water!

What causes those beautiful strings of bubbles to rise in a glass of beer?

There is nothing like a nice foamy head on a glass of cold beer. Most people don't appreciate, however, what is happening in their favorite brew to produce those lovely bubbles in the head.

There's a great deal of physics in a glass of beer. The head is formed by the release of countless gas bubbles. Beer bubbles are born from minute clusters of CO_2 molecules that gather on microscopic cracks and pits in the beer mug or on tiny bits of floating matter in the beer. When a glass of beer is poured, tiny pockets of air are trapped in these pits in the glass. The trapped air bubbles attract CO_2 molecules, which grow into bubbles. At the spots on the glass where large numbers of gas molecules have accumulated, long strings of bubbles are created and stream upward. As they rise to the surface, the bubbles attract more gas, grow larger, and rise faster (the same process explains the rising of bubbles when you boil water).

If you shake salt into your beer and create that exciting explosion of bubbles, it is not a chemical reaction of salt and beer that's taking place. Salt grains, on a microscopic level, are very pitted and cracked and offer CO_2 molecules excellent places to accumulate. Any similar grainy substance will produce the same effect, even sand. Most people, however, would not want to dump sand into their beer.

In order to get a nice head on the beer, it must be poured

into the glass in such a way to swirl the beer about. The swirling motion of the beer causes minute changes in pressure within it, which causes the gas to expand into bubbles, making the hoped-for head. If your beer starts to foam over the top of the glass, stick your finger into the head, and it will stop rising. This is because the oils on your skin reduce the surface tension in the foam, causing the bubbles to collapse.

So next time you have a beer at the local pub, spend a few minutes watching that endless line of bubbles spring into life in your glass of ale, while contemplating more weighty matters, such as where you parked your car!

Chop Suey

(Odds & Ends)

How are eggs sized?

Eggs are sized according to their weight. The following table lists the USDA terms for egg sizes and the minimum weight per dozen for each.

USDA Label	Weight per Dozen
Jumbo	30 oz.
Extra Large	27 oz.
Large	24 oz.
Medium	21 oz.
Small	18 oz.
Peewee	15 oz.

Medium is the smallest size usually found in the supermarket.

How is egg quality determined?

The USDA grades retail eggs as Grade AA, Grade A, or Grade B. Egg quality is judged by holding the egg up to a light (candling) to examine the size and position of the air space, mobility and visibility of the yolk, and the condition of the white. Grade AA eggs were packed within ten days of purchase, Grade A within 30 days.

Grade A is the most common type found in supermarkets. Grade A eggs will have a firm shell, an air space no bigger than one quarter inch in depth, and a well-centered, slightly mobile yolk. The white in a Grade A egg must have two distinct parts— a firm, thick layer around the yolk and a watery outer layer. The difference between these layers should be well defined.

In Grade AA eggs, the yolk will be centered in the thick white layer, which will stay firmly mounded around the yolk when the egg is cracked open. In Grade A eggs, the yolk is not quite as centered, and the thick white layer will spread more away from the yolk after the egg is cracked. In Grade B eggs, there is no difference between the white layers, and cracking the egg will cause both to run away from the yolk.

What is the difference between brown and white eggs?

Depending upon what part of the country you live in, you are probably used to either white or brown eggs. Some regions of the United States prefer white, some brown. There is absolutely no difference between the two, aside from shell color. Nutrition, flavor, and quality are identical. Brown and white eggs simply come from different breeds of hens. The main producer of white eggs is the White Leghorn hen. Rhode Island Reds lay brown eggs. The brown pigment is picked up by the shell in the chicken's oviduct. But, as with M&M's, many people believe that one color tastes better than another, even though there is no evidence to support this.

Hens starts to lay eggs at the age of five or six months. They are given continuous light, water, and feed. They are kept in cages with sloped floors, and the eggs roll down into a conveyor belt when laid. An average hen can lay up to 300 eggs per year.

Egg consumption in the United States has been declining over the past twenty-five years. In 1960, the average American ate about 330 eggs a year, compared with 240 in 1990.

Do eggs need to be refrigerated?

There are a few of you out there who think eggs left out in a basket are wonderfully decorative. Unless you plan to use the eggs right away, this is not advisable. Eggs kept at room temperature lose as much freshness in one day as eggs kept in a refrigerator do in one week. Even refrigerated, eggs should be consumed within 30 days of being packed. Why not buy some wax eggs for your basket and avoid food poisoning?

Why are the yolks of hard-boiled eggs sometimes greenish?

The green coloration around the yolk of a hard-boiled egg is the result of overcooking. At high temperatures, a chemical reaction occurs that causes this harmless discoloration. It can be avoided by cooking eggs at a lower heat.

The yolks of uncooked eggs can vary in color, depending on the diet of the hen that layed it. Hens which are fed alfalfa, grass, and yellow corn lay darker yolked eggs than wheat-fed chickens.

Another curious thing you may notice about egg yolks is that they occasionally have little red blood spots. The common myth is that these eggs have been fertilized; however, this is not the case. It usually indicates that a little blood vessel on the surface of the yolk has ruptured. It has no effect on the taste or the quality of the egg.

What is margarine?

In the old days it was called oleo (short for oleomargarine). It was originally created as a butter substitute, but has recently become an important food in its own right.

Margarine is one of those foods that was created out of necessity and the incentive of a large cash reward. It was the French governor Napoleon III who, in 1869, offered a prize for a "cheap butter for the army, navy and needy." A French food technologist, Hyppolyte Mège-Mouries, noticed that cow's milk contained fat, even that from underweight cows. So he reasoned that milk fat was actually body fat. He chopped up cows' udders and suet in warm milk, mixed the combination under pressure, and churned it into a solid fat that resembled butter. The resultant product was pearly in color so Mèga-Mouries called his creation "margarine" after the Greek *margarites*, or "pearly." It won the prize and was manufactured under the name "butterine."

It was later learned that the cow udder was superfluous to the manufacture of butterine. All that was needed was to melt out the softer fat of oxen and shake it up with milk. By 1873, the butterine business was growing fast, much to the chagrin of the dairy industry, which claimed this imitation butter was deceiving the consumer. The U.S. government passed legislation that butterine could not be colored yellow like butter. (Butter has been colored yellow since the fourteenth century.) It was sold in its unattractive pearly state and one had to add a packet of colorant at home to make it resemble the more appealing color of butter.

The packet contained beta-carotene, the same colorant used in the butter of the time. In fact, butter and margarine were the first foods to be approved by Congress to have added color. That same carrot-derived colorant—beta-carotene—is still used in butter, margarine, and cheeses today.

Early margarine was a far cry from real butter, though, and it remained a "poor man's butter" until problems with taste, texture, and vitamin content could be worked out. During World War II, all butter went to the war effort, and the general American population was forced to use margarine. Through the use of different oils—first whale, palm, peanut, and coconut oil, and finally soybean and corn oil—margarines have been greatly improved.

Today, partly because of price and partly because margarine is an unsaturated fat, whereas butter is a saturated fat, margarine sales top those of butter by an almost two to one margin. Even now, however, few could argue that margarine has nearly the taste appeal of dairy butter.

What margarine is named for the state flower of Texas?

If you live in Texas, this one is easy, or at least it should be! There was a shortage of butter in the United States during World War II. In 1942, Standard Brands, Inc., purchased the Standard Margarine Company of Indianapolis and decided to add margarine to its Fleischmann's Butter product line. Needing a catchy name for its new margarine, the company sponsored a contest. The winning entry came from a Standard Brands employee in Texas who thought the name of the state flower—the bluebonnet—would be perfect. The company also thought that the name Bluebonnet was perfect, but apparently not the actual flower itself. It used the name but chose a blond woman wearing a blue bonnet for the margarine's logo. Sorry, Texans!

Why do we eat the foods we eat?

Of the five-hundred-thousand known plant species, man has only cultivated about one hundred. A mere thirty of these provide us with 85 percent of our food and 95 percent of our protein and calories. In fact, 75 percent of our food comes from only eight cereal crops—corn, rice, wheat, oats, barley, sorghum, millet, and rye. By the same token, of the forty-five-hundred mammal species on Earth, only sixteen are used as food.

Why is it that such a sophisticated population is content to subsist on the relatively few plant and animal species that our ancestors were able to cultivate or breed thousands of years ago? Surely there are other species that we could use for new sources of food. You may be interested to learn that scientists are now conducting a worldwide search to find new species for food. Particular attention is being paid to finding species that are nutritious and tasty and that can be easily raised on land that is currently unsuitable for crops or livestock, such as deserts and swamps.

Five American species which have potential as future food crops are:

1. Buffalo gourd (*Cucurbita foetidissimia*), a desert melon, has two food sources. The plant's huge root can weigh up to two hundred pounds and is loaded with starch. The melon's seeds are rich in proteins and polyunsaturated oil.

2. Groundnut (*Apios americana*) is a sweet, starchy tuber that the Pilgrims survived on during their first few winters. It was a popular staple of East Coast Indians. Groundnut supposedly has eight times the protein of potatoes.

3. Hog peanut (*Amphicarpa bracteata*) has large edible seeds high in protein and rich in oil.

4. Tepary bean (*Phaseolus acutifolius*) is found along the Mexican border and can withstand very arid conditions. The Native American Indians of Arizona and New Mexico cultivate it.

5. Prairie potato (*Psoralea esculenta*) was grown by the Plains Indians. It has a protein content three times that of the conventional potato.

Some of the animal species being considered as future *major* commercial food sources include antelope, crocodiles, deer, frogs, snails, toads, crawfish, butterflies, turtles, and water buffalo.

Raising these "odd" species as food sources is one thing. Getting people to accept them is quite another. But you never know. Perhaps one day we will be enjoying dinners of grilled water buffalo, prairie potatoes, and desert melons!

What strange foods do other cultures eat?

If you have ever found escargots or sushi rather unappealing, just read the following:

Ants and *termites* are enjoyed prepared many ways in several underdeveloped countries. In Mexico, honey ants are popular at country weddings. African pygmies are fond of ants, while the people of Malawi, Zanzibar, and Zimbabwe prefer termites (which contain three times the protein of steak). In Zanzibar the termites are ground into a paste with bananas, flour, and sugar to make a kind of pie. The people of India prepare a red ant chutney, made with ground ants, chili, and salt.

Bats are considered a delicacy in many Oriental countries. Some Pacific Islanders bake them with salt, pepper, and onions.

Beetle grubs and *caterpillars* are haute cuisine for the Australian aborigines. The grubs are singed in hot ashes to remove any hairs and then eaten.

Bird's nests are a gourmet item in China. Only the nests of a certain variety of swifts found in the Malay Archipelago are edible. Due to their inaccessibility, they are very expensive. Unlike normal bird's nests, these are not made of twigs and mud, but instead are built out of successive layers of gooey bird saliva.

The male swift is the one who builds the nests, high on cliffs or cave walls. He cements his nest together by excreting a continuous thin strand of soft, spaghettilike saliva. The saliva strands dry solidly together and glue the nest to the rocky cliff. The female then lays her eggs and rears the young.

After being collected, the nest is carefully cleaned several times and kneaded with nut oil. It is then cooked in a duck stock. The nest dissolves into thin gelatinous strands, making a much-prized soup. So, how much are people willing to pay for this delicacy? The fresher white nests that are collected before the female has laid her eggs can fetch up to four thousand dollars!

Earthworms are made into a broth by the Chinese. They are actually very nutritious, containing 72 percent protein and less than 1 percent fat!

Monkeys are eaten by the native peoples of South America. They like the flesh of the spider and howler monkeys best. Monkey brains are also eaten by certain African and Asian peoples.

Spiders are eaten by Asian peasants and primitive peoples in Africa and South America. The Thai bite the abdomen off a living giant orb-weaving spider and eat it raw. It is also eaten cooked. The Thai also eat the blue-legged "bird eater" spider whole, after removing its mandibles and roasting.

Udders of cows are eaten in England and France. They are flattened and braised with bacon fat.

These are just a few of the seemingly strange foods eaten elsewhere in the world. They may seem strange to us, but several of our favorite foods are abhorrent to other cultures. Many peoples find milk and eggs repellent. You know, if you really sat down and thought about where milk and eggs come from, you might not enjoy your breakfast as much next time!

What causes food poisoning?

A lot has been written in the press lately about the dangers of food poisoning, and rightly so! Food poisoning can be a very sneaky thing. You may not even realize when you have it.

Odds are that in the past year you have had a touch of something you thought was the flu or a "bug." If you had a headache, vomiting, and diarrhea, it is quite possible that what you actually had was food poisoning. The flu is a virus and its symptoms are more respiratory in nature. If you had intestinal problems, it was probably not the flu, but food poisoning.

The main culprit in food poisoning is the bacterium *Salmonella enteritidis*. Each year, roughly one third of us will get a case of some kind of noticeable food poisoning and thousands will die from it. You may also get several doses of food poisoning a year that you don't really notice.

Salmonella and other bacteria are found among the soil and feces where food animals are raised. The animals can become infected and not show any symptoms. During processing the bacteria can spread from animal to animal. These bacteria can be found in a host of food products, including raw meats, poultry, fish, shellfish, eggs, and milk.

It may interest you to know that most cases of salmonellosis aren't caused by eating out at the local Jack in the Box but by eating at home. The most common cause of salmonellosis in the United States is turkey, followed by beef and chicken. Turkeys, being large and usually sold frozen, are often undercooked. And beef is commonly eaten rare. This is why these two meats are the most dangerous. In order to kill the bacteria thoroughly, the meat must be cooked through to a temperature of 170° F.

Salmonellosis is quite different from the less dangerous and more common food poisoning caused by the bacterium *Staphylococcus aureus*. Staphylococcus food poisoning symptoms appear shortly after the bad food was eaten, and its toxins cause the body to purge itself violently through vomiting and diarrhea. Fortunately, it usually passes in a few hours. In contrast, salmonellosis symptoms appear from several hours to a few days after the tainted food is consumed and can last several days.

Since bacteria can multiply extremely rapidly, a small amount can spread rather quickly in unrefrigerated foods. It is common for one area of a food to become contaminated before other areas are overrun with bacteria. This is how two people can eat a dip and only one will get sick. It depends on which side of the bowl the bacteria begin to grow.

There are numerous ways to avoid food poisoning, most of which you have doubtless heard of many times lately. They include keeping your refrigerator setting below 40° F; defrosting foods in the fridge or microwave, not on the counter; using of different utensils and plates when handling cooked and uncooked meats; cooking meat to 170° F; and thoroughly cleaning anything that has come in contact with raw meat, as *Salmonella* can linger for months in sponges and dishtowels.

What popular salad dressing was created at the famous Brown Derby restaurant?

No, it wasn't Paul Newman's dressing, although that would have been a good guess, as the Brown Derby was "the" hangout for many Hollywood stars in the 40s and 50s.

Actually, it was Good Seasons that was created in the famous Los Angeles restaurant. The supervising chef, Robert Kreis, a native of Switzerland, was well known for his specialty salad dressings. Californians loved the Brown Derby's salads, and Kreis made the best dressings. A proud chef, Kreis was reluctant to give up his secrets, but willing to sell his dressings.

He packaged the dry ingredients in empty olive bottles on which he marked the levels for the amounts of water, oil, and vinegar to be added. He received so many requests that he started a mail-order business in 1947, featuring four varieties of dressings. He originally called them 4 Seasons Salad Dressing Mixes, but changed the name to Good Seasons in 1952.

What is the second largest food company in the world?

It's an American company—Philip Morris. Through an endless series of acquisitions, it is attempting to rule the world of food. It already has annual sales of over $60 billion and produces more than three thousand products! Here is a partial list of the companies and products its empire controls: Miller, Löwenbräu, Molson, and John

Courage breweries; Post and Nabisco cereals, Maxwell House, Brim, Sanka, General Foods, Maxim, and Yuban coffees; Entenmann's bakeries; Lender's bagels; Tombstone pizza; Velveeta and Polly-O cheeses; Louis Rich and Oscar Mayer meats; Breakstone's, Breyers, Light n' Lively, and Sealtest dairy products; Country Time, Crystal Light, Kool-Aid, and Tang beverages; Shake 'n Bake and Stove Top; Log Cabin Syrup; Jell-O; Cool Whip; Parkay, Chiffon, and Touch of Butter; and countless Kraft products.

If they don't got it, you don't want it, or they'll probably get it soon!

Why are pigs so fond of truffles?

Truffles are one of the most expensive foods in the world, because they are so hard to find and extremely difficult to cultivate. As you probably know, man does not find them on his own; he enlists the help of dogs or pigs. Dogs are well known for their phenomenal sense of smell, but what about pigs?

Truffles are pungent underground fungi that have a symbiotic relationship with the roots of oak and beech trees. They range in size from that of a marble to that of an orange. Most culinary truffles belong to the genus *Tuber*. They vary in color depending on species.

The really good black ones (*Tuber melanosporum*) are found almost exclusively in the Umbria region of Italy and the Périgord region of France. They are dug up from under oak trees during the months of December and January. Black truffles of lesser quality also grow in England, North Africa, Poland, and the United States. The even more pungent and expensive white truffle (*Tuber magnatum*) is found in the Piedmont region of Italy. It can be harvested only during a few weeks in the late fall and early winter, and is hard to find at any price. Without dogs and pigs most would go unfound.

Female pigs have an absolute *passion* for truffles. Literally. Researchers believe that truffles give off a scent that is remarkably similar to sex attractants found in male pig saliva. Other animals may have an outstanding sense of smell, but you just can't beat an amorous pig for job enthusiasm!

What American food company spends the most on advertising?

Just think of the food products that you are most sick of seeing incessantly hawked on TV. They are probably the same ones on the following list of advertising spending by various food brands in 1993:

McDonald's	$414 million
Kellogg Cereals	$380 million
General Mills Cereals	$251 million
Budweiser	$227 million
Miller Beer	$222 million
Coca-Cola and Diet Coke	$173 million

What woman standardized the art of cooking?

How much flour is there in a handful? How much salt in a pinch? What temperature is a medium hot oven? Before Fannie Farmer (1857–1915) came along, the average cook had no idea! Until the turn of the century, cooking was definitely more of an art than a science. There were no widely accepted units of culinary measure. Cookbooks of the time tended to use inexact terms. A recipe might call for a handful of this, a pinch of that, cooked in a hot oven until brown. Needless to say, such loose directions tended to give each cook somewhat different, and often disappointing, results.

In 1896, a radically new cookbook was published that would change the face of cooking forever—*The Boston Cooking School Cook Book.* It was written by a practical-minded woman named Fannie Farmer. She was the eldest of four daughters in a Boston family that ran a boardinghouse. Stricken at the age of 17 by a paralytic stroke, Fannie earned her keep by helping with the cooking in the boarding home. She became so enthusiastic about cooking that her family urged her to attend the Boston Cooking School to learn to teach cooking. She not only graduated, but went on to become the director of the school, and later opened her own cooking school. So disgusted was she with the inconsistencies in cookbooks of her time that she decided to write her own.

Fannie made sure that all the recipes in her cookbook were kitchen-tested and could be accurately reproduced by any cook. She accomplished this by standardizing kitchen measurements. It was her book that first encouraged the use of level measurements—teaspoons, tablespoons, cups, etc. She also promoted the use of oven thermometers, and gave exact time and temperature directions in her recipes. Such seemingly logical recipes were thought to be too radical for their time. Like most authors, Fannie had trouble finding a publisher that could appreciate the importance of her book. Eventually, she convinced Little, Brown & Company to print three-thousand copies, but even it was so skeptical that it made her pay all the printing costs.

Housewives and cooks across the nation saw something that the publishers didn't. By 1959, Little Brown had sold more than three million copies of *The Boston Cooking School Cook Book,* or Fannie Farmer's, as it was commonly known.

The best-selling cookbooks of all time are *The Better Homes & Gardens New Cookbook,* first published in 1930, which has sold more than 26 million copies, and *The Joy of Cooking,* first published in 1931, which has sold 11 million copies. They are both still popular today, selling 500,000 and 150,000 copies respectively each year.

Who is the world's best known baby?

The world's most identifiable baby, if you hadn't already guessed, is the Gerber Baby. Though the baby has been recognized by millions since 1931, no one knew the child's name until 1976.

Gerber Baby Foods were first introduced in 1928, and the company needed a baby's face for its first advertising campaign. Several artists were invited to submit illustrations for the proposed ad. Among the entries was a small unfinished charcoal sketch of a neighbor's child submitted by artist Dorothy Hope Smith. The artist indicated that this entry was a rough sketch and she would complete it if the baby's age and size were suitable. The simplicity and freshness of the sketch was found to be very appealing, and the Gerber Baby was born.

The Gerber Baby has appeared on all Gerber packaging and advertising worldwide ever since. Dorothy Hope Smith always protected the anonymity of the cute child. Many rumors circulated as to who the model actually was, however. One persistent rumor had it that the model was the young Humphrey Bogart!

In 1976, the Gerber Baby came out of the closet. She is Ann Turner Cook of Tampa, Florida, a high school teacher who retired in 1990.

Who founded Weight Watchers?

Weight Watchers was founded by a woman with an uncontrollable desire for chocolate cookies. (No, it wasn't Mrs. Fields!) It was a housewife from Queens, New York, named Jean Nidetch.

One day in September 1961, Jean called a bunch of her friends over to her house and confessed her obsession for cookies. The empathy and understanding that she received from her friends gave her the strength to drop seventy pounds. Jean had tried and failed on several fad diets. When she finally found a good diet at a free clinic sponsored by the New York City Board of Health and managed to lose twenty pounds, she had trouble maintaining her motivation. That's when she grabbed the phone and called all her overweight friends for emotional support. She learned that her friends all had their own obsessions with food.

After that first meeting was so successful, the women formed a weekly support group to lose weight. Word spread, and soon more people were showing up at Jean's house than she could fit. A man named Albert Lippart helped Jean found Weight Watchers. She incorporated in May 1963 and held her first public meeting in a Queens loft. Although the meeting wasn't advertised, over four hundred people showed up. The company rapidly expanded as successful members started their own franchises across the country and around the world.

What made the Weight Watchers program unique was that it was more than just a diet, it was a change in eating habits, aided by support and encouragement from people who cared. The diet that launched Weight Watchers was the one Jean Nidetch received when she attended the Kips Bay Obesity Clinic—Dr. Norman Joliffe's Prudent Diet (a diet for cardiac health).

In 1978, an exercise plan was added to the Weight Watchers program.

Weight Watchers International was purchased by H. J. Heinz Company for $72 million in 1978. It now sells a complete line of reduced-calorie, portion-controlled meals to members and non-members alike.

Over the years, Weight Watchers has had over 25 million members. Today about one million members attend one of the twenty-nine thousand weekly meetings.

What two famous ethnic food brands were started by the same man?

Italian-American Jeno Paulucci has the distinction of having created two famous supermarket brands—Chun King and Jeno's Pizza.

Paulucci's rise to processed food stardom began by selling dehydrated garlic. In 1947, he rented a Quonset hut in Duluth, Minnesota, where he grew and canned, of all things, bean sprouts—that oriental staple. He named his business after Chungking, the wartime capital of China. He dropped the *g* and split it into two words to avoid trademark difficulties. He quickly added other oriental foods—chop suey and chow mein.

In 1967, Paulucci sold Chun King to R. J. Reynolds for $63 million. Not one to sit still, he started Jeno's Pizza the next year. He sold his self-named frozen pizza business to Pillsbury in 1985 for $150 million. He is now working on another frozen Italian food business.

Who is the father of the American franchising industry?

He started out making high-quality ice cream in the basement of his Massachusetts home in 1925 and selling it in a store bearing his name. Soon local merchants began buying supplies from him and paying for the right to use his name. Who was he? Howard Johnson.

How do vinegars differ from one another?

Vinegar has been around for as long as wine has. When a wine, sherry, or apple cider is exposed to air, a common airborne bacteria—acetobacter—will begin to grow in it. Acetobacter will convert the alcohol in the wine or cider into acetic acid, turning it into vinegar. The word vinegar comes from the Latin *vin aigre*, or "sour wine."

Wine makers go to great lengths to keep acetobacter out of their wine. Vinegar makers, on the other hand, intentionally inoculate their wine with the bacteria.

Vinegar is ancient and has many uses. Perhaps its most common use is in salad dressings. It is also used to tenderize meats, to keep egg whites from running during poaching, to keep egg yolks from coagulating when cooked in sauces, to keep pickles bacteria-free, to slow the browning of certain vegetables and fruits, and for innumerable household cleaning chores. It's wonderful stuff! And best of all, it virtually lasts forever.

The most common vinegars on the market are the following:

Apple cider vinegar is, as the name implies, made from apple cider. It has a full-bodied, fruity note and is good when used in fruit salads.

Balsamic vinegar is made from white Trebbiano grape juice that is wood-aged in barrels for several years.

Distilled white vinegar, is made from grain alcohol and is too harsh for salads, but is excellent for pickling.

Wine vinegar is made from either red or white wine. The red is good for marinading meats, the white for fish, salad dressings, and in potato salads.

Malt vinegar results from the fermentation of barley malt or other cereals whose starch has been converted by malt.

Heinz is the leading maker of vinegar.